UNMASKING OUR LEADERS

ALSO BY MICHAEL COCKERELL

Live From Number Ten: The Inside Story of Prime Ministers and Television (1988)

Sources Close to the Prime Minister: Inside the Hidden World of the News Manipulators (1984)
(with Peter Hennessy and David Walker)

UNMASKING OUR LEADERS

CONFESSIONS OF A POLITICAL DOCUMENTARY-MAKER

MICHAEL COCKERELL

Biteback Publishing

First published in Great Britain in 2021 by
Biteback Publishing Ltd, London
Copyright © Michael Cockerell 2021

Michael Cockerell has asserted his right under the Copyright, Designs and Patents Act 1988
to be identified as the author of this work.

ISBN 978-1-78590-685-5

10 9 8 7 6 5 4 3 2 1

A CIP catalogue record for this book is available from the British Library.

Set in Adobe Caslon Pro by Futura

Printed and bound in Great Britain by
CPI Group (UK) Ltd, Croydon CR0 4YY

MIX
Paper from
responsible sources
FSC
www.fsc.org   FSC® C020471

To my wonderful wife, Anna Lloyd, who never misses a trick.

CONTENTS

CHAPTER 1

YOU MAKE THEM APPEAR HUMAN

Some years ago, I thought of a deceptively simple question to ask a would-be Prime Minister: 'Do you have any doubts about your ability to fulfil the role of Prime Minister?' Over the years nine of them replied.

The first was Harold Wilson, the northern-born son of an industrial chemist. At the age of forty-eight, he became the youngest Prime Minister of the twentieth century up till then. 'I have no doubt it is a gruelling job,' said Wilson. 'The Prime Minister is finally responsible for all policy. But he can't know all the detail, and I'd be a fool if I tried. And I'd take good care that somebody in the Cabinet did and he can tell it me when it's needed.'

Ted Heath was the bachelor Prime Minister who was the Tories' first working-class leader. He answered the question about whether he had any doubts with a two-letter word: 'No.'

Labour's Jim Callaghan, who left school at sixteen and is still the only man to have held all four great offices of state – Chancellor, Home Secretary, Foreign Secretary and PM – told me:

'I'm going to be very arrogant. I had no doubts at all about my capacity to be Prime Minister of this country – and I took it on with complete confidence.'

I put the question to Margaret Thatcher on the eve of her becoming Britain's first female Prime Minister: 'Well, I look at some of the other people who've held the job, and I really...' – she paused – 'Of course you have doubts. Of course you have doubts. And you're tremendously aware of the responsibility. But I haven't just come to this out of the blue. In British politics you don't just go from the bottom to the top, you climb your way up the ladder.'

John Major, the son of a circus performer who left school age fifteen and took over from Margaret Thatcher, said: 'I didn't know whether I could do the job. I wasn't expecting it yet. But when you walk through the door of No. 10 Downing Street, re-ality walks in with you.'

Tony Blair, not short of charisma and self-confidence, said: 'The one thing I am quite sure about is that I'd do the job to the best of my ability whilst people wanted me to do it. And I've got a feeling that if you have a strong idea of what you want to do and believe in pushing it through, then you are in inverted commas "a dictator" – if you are not, then you are weak. You know – you pays your money and you takes your choice.'

The Eton- and Oxford-educated David Cameron, who was to become the youngest PM in nearly two centuries, said: 'Look, if I had major doubts I wouldn't have put myself forward to lead my party in the first place. You have to be absolutely ready to take the difficult and big decisions you would have to take as

Prime Minister, including sending troops to war. And I decided I was ready for that.'

The vicar's daughter Theresa May said: 'I don't tour the TV studios. I don't gossip over lunch. I don't drink in Parliament's bars. I don't wear my heart on my sleeve. I just get on with the job in front of me. My pitch is very simple: I'm Theresa May, and I'm the best person to be Prime Minister.'

When I asked Boris Johnson, then Mayor of London, if he had any doubts about his ability to fulfil the role of Prime Minister, he replied: 'I think people who don't have doubts or anxieties about their ability to do things probably have something terrifyingly awry. You know, we all have worries and insecurities. And I think it's a very tough job being Prime Minister. Obviously, if the ball were to come loose from the back of a scrum – which it won't – it would be a great, great thing to have a crack at.'

Working in television for over half a century, I have been lucky enough to make films about all the past twelve Prime Ministers – from the Eton- and Balliol-educated classics scholar Harold Macmillan to Alexander Boris de Pfeffel Johnson, the classics scholar educated at Eton and Balliol. I have also specialised in making candid profiles of many of our other top politicians who never quite made it to the top of the greasy pole – including Barbara Castle, Enoch Powell, Roy Jenkins and Denis Healey, as well as the libidinous Alan Clark.

I remember a conversation I had with the late Professor Bob Mackenzie in my early days at the BBC. The LSE academic who doubled as a TV presenter and interviewer said to me:

'Imagine what it would be like if there were videos of Gladstone and Disraeli.' That set me thinking: we well know what the two grand old men looked like, and we know a great deal of what they did. But what were they really like? What were their voices, their accents, their body language, their loves and hates, what made them tick, how would they have answered reporters' questions? It inspired me to try to make a shelf-ful of films about our Prime Ministers and other leading modern politicians.

I have three criteria in choosing what some people call my victims and I call my subjects. They need to be or have been at the top of politics; they have to know where the bodies are buried and be prepared to talk candidly; and they have to have what Denis Healey famously called 'a hinterland' – an existence beyond politics. They had to be interesting enough to fill an hour of television. This book is the stories of these politicians who come in all shapes and sizes. It will tell who they are or were and what they are or were really like on and off camera. It is also a behind-the-scenes account of making the films about them and the coups and cock-ups that happen. It is a story of a life in political television – and of filming round the world, being imprisoned in Africa and nearly killed in the Middle East.

The book will also tell the tragi-comic inside story of the battles for control over the years between the politicians and the broadcasters, and how the two sides have become increasingly savvy and sophisticated, with each accusing the other of dirty tricks and fake news. And it will reveal how I have managed to lull some of the wariest people in the land into candour.

One of the techniques I have always used is to show the

politicians clips of their earlier lives and film their reactions as they watch themselves. It can be very revealing. Most politicians have strong views about television, but they rarely get the chance to watch it. I go to great lengths to find footage of them that they may well never have seen. It really opens them up. They are fascinated looking at their younger incarnations, surprised at their voices, which nearly always sound rather posher then than they do now. And the clips prompt long-buried memories of the way they once were. Sometimes they laugh, and on occasion, like with the old bruiser Denis Healey, they cry.

I remember Ken Clarke saying to me: 'How do you want me to play this?'

I said: 'I'll show you film that we have dug up of your early days in politics and some more recent, and I want you to react naturally to what you see.'

'You mean you want me to sit here and shout at the television like I do at home?' asked Clarke.

'You've got it in one,' I replied.

The politicians tend to get so engrossed in watching themselves that they almost forget they are being filmed and I am able unobtrusively to chip in with questions. After one profile was broadcast, Labour's fabled spin doctor Peter Mandelson glid (or whatever the past tense of glide is) up to me at a party and said: 'You do the most important thing you can do for a politician.'

'What's that, Peter?' I asked.

'You make them appear human.' He then glid away, just as I was about to say: 'Might be difficult with you, Peter.' But the

Prince of Darkness had dematerialised – leaving only the faint-est whiff of sulphur. His of course was a spin doctor's take on my films. I don't make politicians appear human; I try to bring out their human side, which is often masked in conventional TV interviews featuring two men in suits drowning each other out.

CHAPTER 2

THE ROAD TO LIME GROVE

So how did it all start for me? I always wanted to work in television – if I couldn't be a professional cricketer – and I have been fascinated by politics since I was a boy. My father, who became a professor, had worked in naval intelligence during the war. He learned Japanese and did a spell with the codebreakers at Bletchley Park. My mother was a novelist who also wrote plays – one of which was censored by the Lord Chamberlain for being too risqué. They were faithful Labour voters, and we would often discuss politics as I grew up; there was always lively discussion around the dining table with my three younger siblings and the various creative types who would come to dine.

At Kilburn Grammar School in London, history was the subject I most enjoyed, though I was not keen on religious instruction (RI), as it was then called. But one day the RI teacher, who rejoiced in the name of Aubrey Scrace, came up with a lesson that fascinated me. It was about how the gospels were written. From textual analysis, it was clear three of the disciples had used the same single source, called Q for *Quelle*, the German for source. But no one had ever seen Q – if indeed it existed.

I found the whole subject of how history comes to be written riveting; the contents of the Bible not so much.

I was also inspired by my history teacher, Dr Walter Isaacson. A German–Jewish refugee, he was a Renaissance man who knew everything and made history fascinating. I had set my sights on going to Oxford, and he asked what I planned to read. I said politics, philosophy and economics. 'No,' he said. 'You must do a real discipline – like history. You can read PPE books in your spare time.' I thought that was a rather idealistic notion and managed to get a place at Oxford to read PPE.

I went up to Corpus Christi College after spending the summer at Heidelberg University studying what they called 'Germanistik' – a crash course in German language, history and culture. Apart from the fact I had a German girlfriend, I wanted to find out just fourteen years after the war how the country had allowed itself to fall for the Nazis. I didn't succeed beyond noticing that German is a great language for commands – *Achtung*! *Verboten*! *Sieg Heil*! – yet its people didn't seem to understand the English concept of a queue.

I arrived at Oxford on the day after the 1959 general election. I vividly recall the freshers' fair: the Conservative students' association were exultantly chalking up the results of the Tory landslide as they came in. By contrast, the university Labour club members were a picture of dejection. The first meeting they advertised was to be addressed by an Oxford city Labour councillor called Brian Walden. The subject had been hurriedly changed from 'Priorities for the new Labour government' to 'Labour: psychologically happier in opposition?'

I was delighted to be surrounded by a new world of politics. I joined all three of the party clubs – Conservative, Labour and Liberal – as they each promised enticing political speakers at their meetings. The victorious Prime Minister Harold Macmillan came up and gave a spellbinding speech at the Oxford Union. He talked very movingly of his contemporaries at Balliol who all signed up when the First World War began. Macmillan was wounded three times in the war, once very badly in the Battle of the Somme. And he said that of the twenty-eight of his Balliol contemporaries who went to the front line, only he and one other survived the war. When the war ended, he declined to go back to Balliol to complete his studies, feeling that Oxford would never be the same again. 'I was sent down by the Kaiser' was the way he put it when I saw him at the Union. Little did I know that within a decade I would be married to his granddaughter.

The following week, the star turn was the newly elected Liberal MP, one Jeremy Thorpe. He was a former president of the Union and an oratorical throwback to the Edwardian age – a compelling mix of high politics, wicked wit and merciless mimicry.

My college, Corpus, had a majority of public-school chaps, and we grammar-school boys were regarded as something of an anomaly. I remember particularly an extremely bright public-school product of Winchester called Richard Gott. He told a story of going to dinner the previous year in the college hall: 'And there was a man wearing a garish blue sweater and no jacket. I was shocked,' said Gott. 'I had never consciously met someone from grammar school. Did this fellow not realise or innately understand that wearing such attire in the hall was extraordinarily inappropriate? Apparently not.' Gott went on to have a distinguished career as a journalist and historian specialising in Latin America until he was fingered by *The Spectator* as a Soviet operative. He resigned as literary editor of *The Guardian* after admitting he'd accepted travel expenses from the KGB while denying being 'an agent of influence' – or what Lenin used to call 'a useful idiot'.

At Corpus I edited the college magazine. I also played cricket, played the drums in a jazz band and played the field. My politics tutor, Michael Brock, was a wonderfully enthusiastic contemporary historian. His specialist subject was the Liberal Prime Minister H. H. Asquith and his colourful wife Margot, whom he quoted as saying: 'I hate all journalists – it's a vile profession. Nothing is sacred; even corpses are copy.'

My great hero was the historian A. J. P. Taylor. Although a don at Magdalen, he gave weekly lectures that were open to all students. He would saunter up to the podium and speak fascinatingly without a note for exactly an hour. AJPT was a contrarian, always challenging the orthodox version. His lectures were so popular that they had to be held in the biggest indoor space in Oxford, the examination schools. They would start at 9 a.m. sharp, on the assumption that many students would be non compos mentis and unable to rise at that early hour.

When I was in my last year at university, my economics tutor asked: 'What do you plan to do when you go down?' At the time I was a fan of James Dean, the moody Hollywood star of

Rebel Without a Cause who had been killed in a car crash six years earlier. I told my tutor I was not planning to do anything, because I would be dead by the time I was twenty-four (as Dean was). 'Cockerell, you disappoint me,' he said. 'I hoped you would have some interesting wasting disease.' The tutor, Christopher Foster, went on to receive a knighthood as an adviser to successive governments.

When I came down, I wrote to every TV and radio station, every newspaper and magazine, applying for a job. All of them said no. I kept all the letters, remembering the story of the young Disraeli who had been laughed off the stage in his Commons debut. 'I will sit down now,' said Dizzy, 'but one day you will hear me.' Pretentious? *Qui, moi?*

The BBC even invented a new channel, and they had big newspaper ads saying, if you have been rejected by the BBC, please apply to BBC 2 as we are looking for people who don't fit the usual mould. Clearly, I thought, that's aimed at me; but once again I didn't even get an interview. It looked as if the Beeb and I were not destined for each other.

At first I thought I could make my money on the horses. But I soon understood why horses don't bet on people. After months out of work, I at last found a job as an editorial assistant at a magazine for Social Democratic parties across the world – like the British and Australian Labour Parties or the German SDP. My task was to produce a fortnightly digest of what the parties and their leaders were doing and saying.

From an office above a greengrocer's in St John's Wood High Street near Lord's Cricket Ground, I would go through masses of newspapers that were sent daily from all over the world. I was looking for articles and speeches, translating some of them myself from French and German publications and sending other likely-looking pieces in languages I didn't know to local translators who lived among the sea of European émigrés in that part of London. I would sometimes get into hot water for including pieces questioning the British Labour Party's policy on immigration and whether Harold Wilson's sanctions on Rhodesia were tough enough after its unilateral declaration of independence. At annual conferences, I met party leaders like Harold Wilson, Willy Brandt, François Mitterrand and Olof Palme.

I was learning a great deal about how political leaders around the world operated, and I became fascinated by the politics of newly independent African countries. In 1966, I managed to get a three-month trial contract to work as a radio producer with the BBC's African service. It broadcast on shortwave from Bush House in London to Africa. My boss was an inspirational figure called Dorothy Grenfell Williams. She was a wonderfully innovative programme-maker who believed life was meant to be fun. Though she insisted we all had to be scrupulously impartial, to be boring was a cardinal sin.

Dorothy was always looking for mischief and was a contrast in almost every way to the head of the African service. He was an old colonial type of South African origin called Eliot Watrous. Described as a reactionary by his sons, his first job at the colonial office was to write anti-communist propaganda for broadcast to Malaya. He saw me as a dangerous Trot because of my previous job and my long hair, and he said I should be kept off the air because my voice didn't sound right. Happily, Dorothy thought differently. I was made a producer as she set up a new daily radio programme called *Good Morning Africa*, which mixed news reporting, features and pop music. It was a world away from the stuffy, old-fashioned programmes for expats, like *Calling Sierra Leone* – and it was an immediate success.

I was greatly enjoying myself at Bush House, working with people from all over the world broadcasting in some fifty languages. It was like a mini-United Nations, with a top-class subsidised canteen which produced a range of exotic foods each day. So tempting was it that an impoverished young lawyer would often come to lunch from the nearby law courts in the Strand. He was called Derry Irvine and was later to become Tony Blair's impossibly grand Lord High Everything Else.

But in 1968, I decided to give television one more try and was given a three-month attachment to BBC TV current affairs at the fabled Lime Grove Studios. Lime Grove was where factual television in Britain really began. It was a converted old film studio in West London's Shepherd's Bush, which the BBC had bought from J. Arthur Rank in 1949. On arrival there, I discovered a ramshackle building that resembled an East German detention centre, with a labyrinth of corridors and a series of black-painted exterior iron staircases. Lime Grove was where *Panorama* and many other great TV current affairs programmes were born. It was also where successive Prime Ministers sought to come to terms with the cameras – with varying degrees of success and pain. The studios had also witnessed many a bloody battle between politicians and broadcasters. Though I couldn't know it at the time, some future battles would involve programmes I was to make.

Lime Grove seemed to me the ideal vantage point for witnessing at first hand what our political leaders were really like and moving towards my ambition to become a TV political reporter.

CHAPTER 3

OLD DOGS, NEW TRICKS

Our political leaders spend their careers spinning their images and polishing their achievements; I've spent my professional life stripping off the gloss. The way television has developed is central to my work. The small screen has transformed the art of political communication, and every modern Prime Minister has loved, hated or feared television – some have done all three.

I have made programmes about how our political leaders and their spin doctors have sought to use the media to their advantage – from Boris Johnson all the way back to his great hero Winston Churchill. The grand old man was the subject of Johnson's last book, which pointedly showed how Churchill the journalist-turned-politician modelled his career on that of our current Prime Minister (or vice versa).

Winston Churchill returned to No. 10 in 1951, ousting Labour's Clement Attlee, Britain's first post-war Prime Minister. Neither man had any time for television. Attlee took the view that it would have been better if TV had never been invented:

it was, he said, nothing more than an idiot's lantern that would turn politicians into entertainers. For his part, Churchill said: 'Television is a tuppenny ha'penny Punch and Judy show. Making speeches is difficult enough; it would be intolerable if one also had to consider how one would appear, what one would look like all over the land.'

For his first two years back in Downing Street, the PM reacted to the TV cameras in the manner of a seventeenth-century aristocrat who did not want the vulgar mob to stare at him. He would either walk straight past the cameras or put his hand over the lens if they came too close. Churchill was never interviewed on television. His first broadcasting officer was one John Profumo. Supposedly in charge of radio, Profumo later told me he visited the US during the 1952 presidential election and came back dazzled by what he had seen. It was, he wrote to the party chairman on his return, 'absolutely essential to get all our people on all the programmes we can: my view is that television is the real thing'.

Churchill was unconvinced. And he was at first strongly opposed to the televising of the new Queen Elizabeth's coronation. But the monarch herself and her husband were in favour. The huge success of the coronation broadcast with its record-high audience helped persuade the PM he could no longer ignore television; it was not going to go away.

In 1954, the Tories' newly appointed television adviser, Winifred Crum Ewing, persuaded Churchill to have a TV screen test in 10 Downing Street. She and the camera team were instructed to keep the whole proceedings absolutely confidential. And for over thirty years they succeeded in keeping the secret, until my producer, Sally Doganis, and I made a programme called *TV and No. 10*. Sally went to see the elderly Mrs Crum Ewing in hospital and was delighted to learn she had a copy of the screen test under her bed at home. She gave the keys to her house to Sally, who unearthed two large cans of film labelled 'Churchill'.

When we managed to find a machine that would play the near-obsolete format, we feared the worst while hoping for the best. Churchill, wearing a black jacket and spotted bow tie, sat at his desk with a microphone rigged above him. He growled: 'I have come here not to talk to you and certainly not to spread the tale all over the place, but just to enable me to see what are the conditions under which this thing they call Tee Vee is going to make its way in the world.'

Churchill's contempt comes over strongly: he makes 'this thing they call Tee Vee' sound like a communicable sexual disease. 'I am sorry to have to descend to this level,' the PM continued, 'but we all have to keep pace with modern improvements, and therefore I have consented to come and have this exhibition made. Which is for one person only to judge what is to be done with this. And I am that person.' Here Churchill spreads his arms out wide: 'There is no other in this business.'

He then read out an extract from one of his speeches and ended by reciting a poem which he had learned forty years earlier from *Punch*:

Beside the water in St James's Park,
I stretched myself to rest by this old tree,
But can't for all the cackle squeak and squawk,
Of these 'ere ducks and such like blooming poultry,
These fowls have nowt to do but fill themselves with buns,
Thrown to them by blooming nuns.

Sally and I were thrilled by the unseen screen test. Mrs Crum Ewing told us she had laid on a special showing of the film for the Prime Minister at his country home. Churchill hated it, saying, 'I should never have appeared on television.' It may be he was taken aback by his octogenarian looks. In fact, he comes over very powerfully in the film. His bulldog face matches the shape of the television screen, his voice is resonant and his eyes sparkle. But the Prime Minister ordered Mrs Crum Ewing to destroy the offending screen test. To her credit, Mrs Crum Ewing felt the film was a historic document and defied the PM's orders.

Television was not for him, said Churchill, who stuck to his belief that it had no part to play in the coverage of politics. Surprisingly, his view was shared at Alexandra Palace, where BBC television news started. There was no political editor, but E. R. (Teddy) Thompson was 'parliamentary correspondent' – the BBC hierarchy thought the word 'political' was itself too political, and it wanted to be above politics.

How things have changed. These days, the Prime Minister and leading politicians are all over the bulletins, and BBC Westminster at Millbank, where I worked for many years, is a huge processing plant for political news. But seventy years ago, both No. 10 and the television broadcasters were feeling their way in the gloom.

Churchill was succeeded by Sir Anthony Eden, whose problem was not so much that he thought he was terrific on TV (though he did) but that he saw television as essentially a kind of megaphone for the government. He sought to use TV to promote his controversial Suez invasion. But his press secretary, William Clark, told me that Eden claimed 'those communists at the BBC' were trying to bring him down and they would purposely shine the studio lights in his eyes during a broadcast, so Eden couldn't read his script. The PM had a blazing row with the BBC and ordered Clark to find ways of taking over the Corporation. It didn't happen.

After less than two years as Prime Minister, Eden was forced to resign and make way for an older man. Harold Macmillan had first appeared on television in 1953, making a Conservative party-political broadcast as Housing Minister. It took the form of a completely rehearsed interview of Macmillan with his cod questioner, the Tory MP Bill Deedes. They spent eight hours rehearsing in the Lime Grove Studio until they were word-perfect. Before the broadcast went out live, Deedes told me: 'The producer said we should have a rest, so we went downstairs to the basement in Lime Grove, and we were put into a couple of bunks, just to sleep under a blanket for half an hour. And Macmillan muttered in the dark, "This reminds me very much of the trenches. It's like the night before you go over the top."'

Quite an analogy from a war-wounded veteran of the Somme.

When Macmillan saw a telerecording of the broadcast, he told a BBC producer: 'I don't think I look very good on that thing, and I don't want to have any more to do with it.' But once in No. 10, everything changed.

Macmillan told me that on the night he became Prime Minister, he took his Chief Whip, Ted Heath, out for a celebratory dinner at The Turf, an exclusive gentlemen's club in St James's. 'Unhappily the news was obtained by some source,' said Macmillan, 'and as we came out our way was barred by the usual paraphernalia of press and television, to which I had not yet become accustomed. I thought my guest and I were entitled to a bottle of champagne and some game pie. But the food, the drink and above all the place were seized upon with avidity as the symbols of a new reactionary regime.'

It was a graphic reminder that from now on the PM would always be on parade and would have to come to terms with a media that he neither liked nor trusted.

'Coming into a television studio is like entering a twentieth-century torture chamber,' said Macmillan. 'Television has introduced a new dimension into politics and some of us don't quite know what to make of it. But we old dogs have to learn new tricks.' He told me that when he first saw himself on television: 'I presented the appearance of a corpse looking out of a window.' And he talked about the difficulties he had when he first went into the TV studio to make a broadcast direct to camera: 'People of my age were brought up on the hustings, where something comes back to you from the audience all the time. Now with television it is like playing lawn tennis and there isn't anybody to hit the ball back from the other side of the net – nothing comes back. It took me a long time to learn. I think I got a bit better at it. I remember being told there will be 12 million people watching tonight. And I said to myself no, no, two or three people – you are talking to two people. It's a conversation, not a speech.'

Much of his early experience of appearing on camera was conducted at Heathrow Airport against a background of multi-patterned curtains. It had become the major gateway through which politicians from the PM downwards came and went. 'Television and jet aeroplanes have made the life of a modern Prime Minister almost impossible,' Macmillan half-jokingly complained in one speech. 'Because it is in airports that tele-vision chooses to lurk. You go by sea, you go by road, you go by rail – nobody bothers you very much. But if you go by air, there it is – that hot pitiless probing eye. After fourteen hours of travel, you get off the aeroplane wanting only a shave and a bath – oh no, you are cornered. The lights in your eyes, the camera whiz-zing. You put up your hand to shade your eyes and the next day there you are in the *Daily Clarion* looking weary, old, worried under a caption that implies you are past it.'

Before Macmillan, no one had heard of a prime ministerial 'image'. He was the first to try to project one – with the help of prototype spin doctors. He had become Prime Minister with trousers that disgraced his tailor, an unkempt moustache and his teeth in disarray. Within months he was wearing a spruce new suit, the moustache had been trimmed and the apologetic toothy smile had gone. The end-product was an assiduously cultivated

TV image – of a world statesman, effortlessly in control and reading Trollope in the evenings.

The great cartoonist Vicky hoped to ridicule Macmillan by depicting him as Supermac flying through the air. In fact, the cartoons played into his image of what was called 'unflappability' – though that was far from the reality. Macmillan was a highly emotional man who would suffer agonies of nerves and was sometimes physically sick before big speeches or TV performances. But he was a good enough actor to hide impairments in public.

Macmillan was the first incumbent of No. 10 to emerge as a TV persona. His skilful use of the small screen during the 1959 election helped win him a landslide. But he was also the first Prime Minister to discover the fragility of a television image. After losing a series of by-elections and fearing a plot against him, Macmillan panicked and sacked a third of his Cabinet, including his Chancellor, in the Night of the Long Knives. He morphed from Supermac to Mac the Knife. And things only got worse with spy scandals and the Profumo affair. Under the satirical glare of new television programme *That Was the Week That Was* and the relentless *Private Eye*, he came to appear like an outmoded Edwardian throwback – fuddy-duddy and out of touch. And he was up against a formidable new opponent, the new Labour leader Harold Wilson, who was determined to present himself as the polar opposite to Macmillan.

CHAPTER 4

THE WILES OF WILSON

The new Labour leader Harold Wilson sought to present himself as everything that Harold Macmillan was not. Wilson was the northern grammar-school boy who had made it to Oxford on his own merits. Macmillan was Eton-educated and married to a duke's daughter. Wilson suggested that his own family had been so poor that he had to walk barefoot to school. Macmillan responded: 'If he was barefoot as a boy, it was because even then he was too big for his boots.' In fact, Wilson was the son of a chemist and a teacher – and always had shoes.

He had become a Cabinet minister under Attlee at the age of thirty-one and grew a moustache just to look older. He had a great talent for equivocation and manoeuvring, which he used to gain the leadership and hold the party together. 'Mr Wilson has a nimble mind,' said Macmillan. 'Sometimes a revolutionary driving the tumbril – sometimes affecting the part of moderate statesmanship.'

Wilson said that Tories like Macmillan and his even more aristocratic successor Lord Home – who renounced his peerage to become Prime Minister as plain Sir Alec Douglas-Home

– felt they were born to rule. And, so Wilson told me, they had little or no understanding of the contemporary world and the lives of ordinary people. Instead, he said: 'Labour will create a society in which brains will take precedence over blue blood.'

Wilson sought to play up a modern, classless man-of-the-people image – with a well-publicised love of HP sauce and a carefully preserved Yorkshire accent. He kept the expensive cigars he smoked in private away from the cameras. And he sought to personify the meritocratic future he envisaged for the country, saying: 'You need men with fire in their bellies and humanity in their hearts to create a dynamic, expanding, confident and above all purposive new Britain.'

In the 1964 general election, Wilson just scraped home, managing to turn the Tories' 100-seat majority into a Labour lead of just five. Asked how he felt on becoming Prime Minister, he replied: 'Quite frankly, I feel like a drink.'

The new PM aimed to use two American Presidents as his role models. Like President Franklin Roosevelt, he planned to have 'fireside chats', delivering fortnightly reports to the public direct to camera. His second presidential template was John Fitzgerald Kennedy. Aged forty-eight, Wilson was the youngest PM of the century, up till then, and he sought to project himself as the British JFK. He acquired video recordings of President Kennedy's White House press conferences and studied them closely, seeking to replicate JFK's charismatic style. 'What we want', said Wilson on television, 'is what President Kennedy had after years of stagnation in America: 100 days of dynamic action.'

His political secretary, Marcia Williams (later Baroness Falkender), became his image-maker-in-chief. She virtually never gave interviews, but she told me: 'We realised as you were broadcasting into people's homes you couldn't be some stiff, remote figure; you had to be a relaxed figure that people could identify with. To stop Harold gesturing to camera with his fist clenched, which looked rather threatening, we gave him a pipe to smoke during TV interviews. And he would put his left hand on his cheek which showed up his wedding ring. It was Harold the family man, and a subtle contrast with Ted Heath when he became Tory leader, who was of course a bachelor.'

'Television had one great advantage for the Labour Party,' Wilson told me: 'Most of the press were against us, and if the right-wing press were tempted to say about me, "This is a terrible man, he looks like an ogre, his voice is terrible," then you go on TV and people say, "Oh look, he's an ordinary chap like the rest of us."'

But Wilson was far from an ordinary chap: he was a complex self-creation.

The long-serving Labour MP Gerald Kaufman, who was Wilson's parliamentary press officer in Downing Street from 1965 to 1970, told me: 'Harold is the only man I know who deliberately acquired a sense of humour. I remember when I first knew him in 1948, I was chairman of the Oxford University Labour Club. And I have to say it, he was an extraordinarily boring speaker. And then suddenly he decided to have a sense of humour: he turned himself into a politician who could make very amusing sharp, witty cracks. He just worked on it, and he did the same with television. Harold was the first Prime Minister to realise that on television you don't have to speak in sentences with a subject, verb and object. He took great care to use language that was clear, direct and uncomplicated.'

From the moment he walked into No. 10, Wilson was determined to do everything he could to ensure that when he called a snap election, he would significantly enlarge his minuscule Commons majority. Week by week he would announce a new plan, initiative or mission. 'Harold is just moving from emergency to emergency, picking up bright ideas as he goes along,' a leading member of his kitchen Cabinet, the Housing Minister Dick Crossman, noted in his diary. 'He jumps from position to position, always brilliantly energetic and opportunist, always moving in zig-zags.'

His plan for fortnightly fireside chats was turned down by the broadcasters. Instead, for his first eighteen months in office, Wilson was ever eager to be interviewed on BBC and ITV current affairs programmes. 'Harold didn't go to the TV studios to answer the questions,' Gerald Kaufman told me. 'The questions were an irrelevance. He went there to say something. He decided the message he wanted to communicate. And then regardless of the questions that were put to him, he said what he meant to say.'

But to Wilson's chagrin, TV interviewers were becoming much tougher than the traditionally kid-gloved BBC men. Leading the pack was Robin Day, a former barrister who wore a bow tie and what one comedian called cruel glasses. The forensic Day would not let Wilson get away with not answering the question. Having started with a marvellous honeymoon in the media, by 1966 the Prime Minister was becoming convinced that the broadcasters were joining the press in being biased against him. The BBC's Director-General Hugh Carleton Greene told me: 'After thirteen years in opposition, Labour leaders had become very close to the BBC. Harold Wilson thought he had money in the bank with us, but when he came to cash his cheque, it bounced.'

The PM called a snap general election for March 1966. Eighteen months earlier, as opposition leader Wilson had made great play of challenging the then Prime Minister, Sir Alec Douglas-Home, to a live head-to-head TV election debate. But Sir Alec said: 'I'm not particularly attracted by confrontations of personality. If we are not careful, you'll get a sort of *Top of the Pops* contest. And you would then get the best actor as leader of the country, and the actor would be prompted by a scriptwriter.' He turned down flat the invitation to appear in a debate.

But the Conservatives now had a new leader – a grammar-school boy from an unprivileged background like Wilson. Ted Heath was chosen partly because Tory MPs believed he would be a match for Wilson on TV. There was no love lost between the two men. Heath told me: 'I am sick to death with people who talk about political life in terms of image and imagery. I was against gimmicks. I was against all the cosy pipe smoking and evading every issue. Mr Wilson always seemed to be concerned with some improvisory device to tide him over and in that he was supreme at getting the press on his side.'

In the 1966 election, it was Heath who challenged Wilson to

a live TV debate. The PM seemed to accept the challenge publicly, but behind the scenes it was rather different. 'We felt that
a confrontation on TV would have given Heath an advantage,'
Marcia Williams told me. 'Heath was trying to make his leadership stick. Harold was by then a very well-known figure. It
would have given Heath a lot of exposure as a potential Prime
Minister in a setting that he wanted. Harold's office would have
rubbed off on Heath. We decided that Harold was not going to
appear on equal terms with him.'

The problem was that tactically Wilson wanted neither to
appear with Heath nor for it to look publicly as if he were refusing to do so. With a piece of characteristically fancy foot-
work, Wilson managed to stymie the whole project by accusing
the BBC, which had enthusiastically promoted the idea of the
debate, of supporting the Tories.

Instead, Wilson wanted to conduct a low-key campaign. The
image would be of a Prime Minister and his government resolutely tackling the problems they had been bequeathed with
calm confidence and efficiency. In two of Labour's five election
broadcasts, the Prime Minister spoke reassuringly to the camera
from behind an imposing desk. Wilson later told the Irish
Prime Minister Seán Lemass about the image he had wanted to
project. 'Harold Wilson said that a political leader should try to
look, particularly on television, like a family doctor,' Lemass told
me. 'He should come over as a family doctor who inspires trust
by his appearance as well as by his soothing words – and whose
advice is welcome.'

It worked. Dr Wilson won by a majority of nearly 100. But as often happens with landslides, things quickly went belly-up. Dick Crossman claimed that within four months of his famous victory, Wilson had 'gone from catastrophe to catastrophe and suffered the most dramatic decline of any modern Prime Minister'. The economy was on the slide, the trade unions were out of control and the markets believed the pound would crash. From the moment he had stepped into No. 10, Wilson had pledged to protect the value of sterling. He was only too well aware that the previous Labour governments had failed to do so. But in November 1967, Wilson reluctantly gave up the unequal struggle and announced he was devaluing the pound by 14 per cent. He appeared on television for a special broadcast to the nation.

But Wilson went too far. He sought to play down the significance of devaluation and even suggest it was part of his own cunning plan. In the most notorious passage of the broadcast, he said: 'From now on the pound is worth 14 per cent less in terms of other currencies. This does not mean that the pound here in Britain in your pocket or purse or bank has been devalued.' In his self-proclaimed role of economics tutor to the populace, the PM was trying to tell people that if they went into the banks or shops the next day, they would still get twenty shillings for every pound they had. But it looked as though he was effectively trying to deny that devaluation had happened. The broadcast was met with rage across the country.

As Wilson's closest adviser, Marcia Williams stood loyally by him. She told me: 'It would have been unnerving for the people to see their Prime Minister appearing full of woe and foreboding, rather than reassuring them and giving them reason to hope. The leader had to rally the troops.'

The fact was that devaluation represented a crushing political defeat for Wilson. He was well aware that he had broken his private axiom; that King Canute would have done better if the tide was going out. By attempting to present devaluation as a panacea and implying that he had really favoured it all along, the PM had shot a large hole in his own foot. All oppositions seek to prove that governments cannot be trusted and the Tories had spent nearly five years seeking to demolish Wilson's home-spun credibility on television. Now, his own broadcast had done it for them.

It became open season on the Prime Minister. On a topical BBC comedy programme there was a bitter joke: 'You know how you can always tell someone is lying – there are always unconscious bits of body language that give him away every time he tells a whopper. It might be a nervous tic near his eye or his hand may go up to his face or a vein on his neck may stand out. But what's the tell-tale body language when Harold Wilson is lying? [Pause] When you see his lips move.'

The PM threatened to sue, and the BBC sent him a letter of apology.

Wilson was widely seen as having devalued himself, and his carefully crafted image as a trusted family doctor had fragmented. After devaluation, Marcia Williams told me: 'We had three years of public meetings where Harold had been heckled badly, eggs had been thrown as well as tomatoes and flour. He used to come home looking absolutely awful. So we had these bad images on television and we were determined to counter them.'

When Wilson called the 1970 general election, he appeared on BBC TV's *Election Forum*, which had solicited questions from viewers. Robin Day began the programme saying: 'This question represents an angry theme running through many of these cards. In view of your past record of lies and broken promises, do you really expect the electorate to place any reliance on your word?' Wilson calmly turned the question round to say that he hoped to have the opportunity of nailing the lies that had been told about him for the past six years. But while he sounded cool, he looked hot and bothered.

The next day the *Daily Telegraph* headlined the Prime Minister's perspiration. His press secretary Joe Haines suspected BBC dirty tricks. He told me: 'The studio was intolerably hot that day and almost as soon as Harold went on the sweat was running down his face. It looked on television as if he was wriggling under intensely hostile questioning. And it was made much worse when the floor manager of the BBC apologised and said that when Mr Heath had been in the previous day, it had been so cold that she had to send out for a cardigan. Hence conspiracy theory.'

In contrast to Wilson, the Tories' slogan for their leader was 'Ted Heath: A Man to Trust'. When the votes were counted, Wilson's landslide majority was wiped out and the Tories returned to power with a narrow lead.

CHAPTER 5

ON THE ROAD

The year 1970 was quite a packed one for me. I was direct-
ing films at home and abroad for the nightly programme *24
Hours* on BBC 1. When filming, I nearly became a casualty of
war in Africa and then in the Middle East. I also made films
about the British general election and played cricket for the
MCC. And it was the year I married a BBC colleague, Anne
Faber, who was Macmillan's granddaughter, and we had our first
child.

At the start of the year, I was sent to Nigeria, Africa's largest
country by population, where the two-and-a-half-year civil war
was coming to an end. Even by the standards of such conflicts,
the war was an especially brutal affair. It had been triggered by
oil-rich eastern Nigeria seceding and declaring itself the independent Republic of Biafra. The federal government, with its
massively superior firepower, invaded the rebel state and fighting
continued for more than two years – with the rebels accusing
the invaders of deploying starvation and genocide as weapons
of war. As the conflict was in its last throes, the world's press
descended on Lagos.

Working as a film director, I was there with the renowned reporter Tom Mangold. We knew it was going to be a hard slog, partly because the Nigerian government hated the BBC for what it called biased reporting and what we called refusing to swallow the increasingly shrill propaganda claims and counter-claims of both sides. When we arrived, the federal government had imposed a ban on journalists travelling out of Lagos to what was left of the self-proclaimed Biafran Republic.

There was a surreal moment when the Nigerian Red Cross called a press conference for hundreds of journalists and camera crews. The organisation's head took to the platform and an-nounced: 'The Nigerian Red Cross has called this conference to say that the Nigerian Red Cross has nothing to say to the press at this time.' He then left the room, refusing to take questions. The cream of the media were reduced to interviewing each other.

We were getting nowhere, and I approached the chief press of-ficer of the Ministry of Information, Sam Epelle. He wore dark glasses and a menacing mien. I said: 'I am from the BBC, and I wonder if you could help me. We are finding it very difficult to film here or to get any government ministers to speak to us.'

He replied: 'It will do the BBC good to eat some of its own poison for a change,' and he walked off.

Despite that we did manage to make a film about life in post-war Lagos. And we had a coup when we exclusively secured film of the commanding officers of each side signing a peace treaty together – in secret. Their dialogue was matchless. The govern-ment man said to his opposite number: 'Hello, old boy. Haven't seen you since Sandhurst. How are things going?'

His Biafran counterpart was equally plummy: 'It's been a bit of an up and down ride but mustn't grumble.' We sent the film back to London, where it led the BBC News.

But the big question was: what had happened to the leader of secession – the self-proclaimed first President of Biafra, the charismatic General Emeka Ojukwu. Through his TV interviews, he had become quite a well-known and sympathetic figure in Britain. We had a tip-off that General Ojukwu had fled the country and been given sanctuary by the nearby former French colony Ivory Coast, which was one of only five countries that had recognised Biafra.

We flew to the capital, Abidjan, and went to see the Biafran ambassador, who denied all knowledge of Ojukwu's whereabouts. Tom and I then split up and arranged to meet later. I went to film at a camp for refugees from war-torn Biafra. They were less than pleased by our presence and came out *en masse* and grabbed us. The police arrived, we were arrested, taken to jail and accused of being Nigerian spies. There, we had to hand over all our belongings including the TV camera and were made to strip to our underpants. We were put into a tiny cell which contained a pail for ablutions and a hapless Ivorian, also in his pants, apparently being held for beating his wife.

A tough-looking police officer then came in and demanded '*Où est le quatrième*' – where is the fourth one of you? It meant that they must have been following us before we split up. I said I would take them to the café where I was due to be meeting Tom. But Tom wasn't there. So, we went to our hotel, and as we were in the lobby I saw a white man in a business suit. I separated myself from my police escort and asked the man if he would let the British ambassador know that four journalists from the BBC had been arrested. He turned out to be South African and said in a thick Afrikaans accent: 'I am having nothing to do with this,' and walked off. I then saw another besuited white man and asked him too if he would inform the British Embassy of our arrest. He said: 'I am from the embassy.' At that stage my police escort had had enough, and ignoring the British diplomat, they manhandled me out of the hotel and back into their car. I remember thinking as I was being driven back to the prison through some of the roughest parts of the town that this was the kind of place where I might easily be beaten up and dumped – or worse.

But we reached the prison, and I was put back in the cell in my underpants. Shortly afterwards Tom was brought in to join us. They said to him: '*Déshabillez-vous*' – get undressed. He went up greatly in my estimation when he summoned up his hazy French and said: '*Non, je refuse absolument de me déshabiller.*' They repeated the instruction in a much more threatening tone. Again Tom refused, saying: '*Pourquoi me déshabiller? C'est ici un pays civilisé*' – why should I undress? This is a civilised country. The copper responded: '*Incivilisé.*' It was one of the most chilling monosyllables I had ever heard. Tom stripped off.

So, there we all were in the cell: Tom, me, the cameraman and the sound recordist all stripped to our underpants. Tom broke the silence when he looked round the cell and said, 'That's the last time I come on a Clarkson's package holiday.' We all laughed to keep our spirits up – gallows humour in the manner of plucky

British prisoners of war. The guards came to the barred window of the jail and told us to shut up – or else.

After a few more hours in the cell, we suddenly heard a very English voice echoing down the corridor: 'Is the BBC team here? Can you answer me if you are?' We yelled ourselves hoarse. The voice turned out to be that of the resident MI6 officer in the British Embassy. He was allowed to take charge of us and said that the embassy had reached a deal that we be released from jail and kicked out of the country as personae non gratae.

Later, over celebration drinks at the embassy, Our Man in Abidjan told me it was very lucky that I had bumped into one of his colleagues in the hotel lobby. Otherwise, he said, there would have been nothing to stop the Ivory Coast government denying all knowledge of us and keeping us incommunicado in jail for months. And then, he said, we would be produced and put on a show trial as spies and/or white mercenaries – both of which malfeasances carried very heavy penalties. Instead, we flew out of Abidjan on the first plane to Paris, where the BBC had laid on a private plane to take us home.

A few months later, I was filming another civil war with another battle-hardened reporter, the late David Lomax. We were in Amman, the capital of Jordan, where the army was on the brink of war with Palestinian guerrilla groups based in the country. In what became known as Black September, one radical group had hijacked three Western airline jets with over 350 passengers aboard and landed them in the Jordanian desert. After decanting the passengers, the hijackers dramatically blew up the three planes in front of the international press.

We managed to film one group of the guerrilla fighters, known as fedayeen, training in a secret encampment using live ammunition. And we interviewed their leader, who said their main aim was to get rid of who he called the 'Fascist leader of Jordan', King Hussein.

In the previous months, the King had escaped three assassination attempts by the fedayeen. He felt that Yasser Arafat's Palestinian Liberation Organization (PLO), which had moved its headquarters to Jordan following the loss of the West Bank to Israel, was acting as a state within a state. Some 70 per cent of Jordan's population was Palestinian, 2 million of them in refugee camps. And, as we discovered when we filmed, in much of Amman the fedayeen ruled the streets and were a law unto themselves.

King Hussein was coming under huge pressure from his army to act against the guerrilla groups or face a military coup. We learned that when Hussein went to inspect a crack tank squadron, he saw that instead of flying Jordanian pennants they were flying black brassieres. The King asked what was meant by that – and the reply was: 'If you treat us like women, we will behave like women.'

While the rest of the 250-strong international press corps were staying at a modern skyscraper hotel above the city, we were billeted at a back-street hotel below – close to fedayeen strongholds. On 17 September, King Hussein ordered tanks into Amman, and the army launched a full-scale attack on Palestinian guerrillas across the country. The airport and the country's borders were sealed, and all telecommunication lines were closed down.

I was woken at dawn by the sound of heavy shelling and gun-fire. With the explosions and collapsing buildings worryingly close, we tried to find somewhere to shelter in the hotel. We discovered it didn't have a basement, but there was a large communal bathroom in the middle of the ground floor protected by two sets of walls. Also on the search for shelter were six other hotel guests: two Americans from the TWA airline who had arrived to fly their hijacked plane home only to see it blown up; a Bolivian housing expert; a French male nurse; and two Russian documentary makers who had come to make a film about Petra, the famous Rose Red City half as old as time. As a mini-UN, we shared out the sleeping spaces on the floor of the bathroom: David's was between the bidet and the loo; mine between the loo and the bath. We brought down pillows from our rooms.

This was where we would try to sleep for the next week with the power and water cut off. Each day the army poured mortars, shells and heavy artillery into the fedayeen strongholds close to the hotel. One of the worst moments was when we realised that fifteen fedayeen had taken over the next-door house armed with Kalashnikovs. Every burst of fire from them would attract shells from the army up the hill above – and it seemed only a matter of time before there would be a direct hit on our hotel.

I remember trying to keep the spirits up of my bathroom companions by acting insouciant. 'I'll say this about you, Michael,' said the shrewd David Lomax, 'you are just as scared as the rest of us.' He wasn't wrong. I remember thinking as I lay in my allotted bathroom space that it would be an inglorious way to die – as the incidental casualty of other people's combat. Without any contact with the outside world, we were encouraged to hear on our transistor radio that the British ambassador to Jordan hoped we were safe. At that moment, a huge shell came crashing into the hotel. Happily, it didn't reach the bathroom.

Some days later, we suddenly heard the sound of a tracked vehicle coming down the hill. It turned out to be the Jordanian Army, and they stopped outside the hotel to pick us up. David and I went upstairs quickly to pack some clothes and a portable typewriter – and the others waiting for us in the tank felt they were sitting ducks and shouted at us when we clambered in. As we trundled up the hill to the Intercontinental Hotel where all the other journalists were staying, we saw a scene of devastation with scarcely a building left intact.

The two Russians had declined to come with us. A day later we learned that one of them had put his head out of the window of his room and been shot dead by a fedayeen. As I commiserated with his colleague, I asked why they hadn't come in the tank with us. He replied: 'I wanted to come, but Boris refused to leave his TV camera kit behind.' But did it belong to him? I asked. He said: 'No – it was the property of Moscow Central Documentary Films.'

We had a much clearer view of the continuing fighting from the sixth floor of the Intercontinental. We could see whole houses disappearing as Jordanian Army shells smashed into the residential district opposite. There were piles of debris and twisted metal wherever we looked, and columns of thick oily smoke belched out from various targets all over the suburbs.

What was worse were the plumes of white smoke from shell fire rising from the Palestinian refugee camps where thousands of people were living in tin shacks.

Among the journalists at the Intercontinental was the celebrated war photographer Don McCullin, whom I knew. Like the rest of us, he had been confined to the hotel by the army. One evening he said to me: 'Come upstairs and watch the fireworks.' We went up to the roof of the hotel and his fireworks consisted of tracers followed by shells and rockets and journalists shouting 'outgoing'. And occasionally 'incoming'. At one moment a missile flew straight at us. It smashed into the back wall leaving McCullin and me spreadeagled on the roof where we had dived for cover. I noticed that Don thought it was all great fun. I thanked him for the fireworks party and left.

After the army and the PLO signed a ceasefire, we eventually made it to the airport, where a Red Cross plane was to fly us out to Beirut. There was an airport sign which said: 'Thank you, come again!' We cheered.

When I arrived at Beirut, I was at last able to talk to my wife, who was six months pregnant with our first child. I said I hoped she hadn't been too worried. She replied that she had tried to keep her spirits up but the worst moment was when her mother said to her: 'Oh God, I can't bear it. It's like the First World War – widowed before you've had the child.' Very comforting.

David Lomax managed to make it back to London in time for that night's transmission and was in the *24 Hours* studio with one of the first eye-witness accounts of the Black September civil war. None of the journalists who had been incarcerated in the Intercontinental Hotel had managed to escape its confines and do any first-hand reporting. Instead, they had agreed that a different one of them each day would write a pooled despatch in the hope the Telex machine would start to work. It made for a good cartoon in the *London Evening Standard*, which depicted many idle journalists in the hotel and an editorial figure with an eyeshade carrying a piece of paper and saying: 'Here's a pooled despatch – you are all fired.' Happily, the BBC gave us a hardship bonus instead.

And on Christmas Eve 1970, our first child was safely born. It had been quite a year.

CHAPTER 6

INSIDE THE NATIONAL FRONT

In the early 1970s, I had become a BBC TV reporter and made a film about the National Front – at the time the fastest growing political party in Britain. That was partly because General Idi Amin, the capricious strongman President of Uganda, was acting as recruiting sergeant for the Front; Amin's sudden expulsion of Uganda's Asian population caused 30,000 refugees to come to Britain and led to big National Front protest marches and a rapid increase in its membership. The Front gave us access to film in the hope of cleaning up its image. One of its great problems was that many of its members – including its leaders – had distinctly murky pasts.

The Front's first chairman was a veteran far-righter called A. K. Chesterton – cousin of the renowned G. K. Chesterton. A. K. had been a founder member of Oswald Mosley's pre-war blackshirt British Union of Fascists. He resigned as National Front chairman saying: 'I had more than enough after four years of stamping upon nonsense such as plots to set fire to synagogues.'

Two former leaders of the British Nazi Party had taken over the leadership of the Front. One was the party organiser, Martin

Webster, who had said about his previous party: 'We are setting up a well-oiled Nazi machine in the country.' And about the National Front he claimed: 'We aim to kick our way into the headlines.' The new chairman of the Front was John Tyndall – who had been an avowed Nazi and spent several spells in jail for assault and stirring up racial hatred. But he had decided the National Front needed a fresh image as a party of respectable British nationalists. He himself had now taken on an ersatz version of the upper-class accent and gestures of a latter-day Oswald Mosley.

Mosley himself was now staying in some style as a would-be grand old man in the Ritz Hotel in Piccadilly. When my producer Colin Martin and I went to see him there, he addressed us as if we were a public meeting. In an interview with me, he dismissed any linkage between himself and the National Front leaders, declaring in a booming voice: 'If people are at one moment hopping around in Nazi uniform – that is, dwarves masquerading in the uniform of dead giants – and if they then switch over to a John Bull poster in order to get votes on the immigration question, that is something completely ridiculous.'

As part of the report, we filmed at a packed National Front rally in Central Hall, Westminster. 'Why did we fight the last war to see the best of our people replaced by what?' demanded one speaker. Some of the audience responded 'w*gs'; others were split between 'traitors' and 'syphilis'.

When I interviewed Tyndall, I quoted back to him a line from his speech in which he had said: 'Let us rejoice that fate has called us out from the dull grey masses to lead lives of great challenge and great purpose.' I went on: 'It does sound from that as if you see your own supporters as the chosen people.'

His unsmiling eyes narrowed, and he said with a touch of menace: 'Aren't the Jews the chosen people?'

At that moment the film ran out and we loaded up a new roll and I put the question again. This time Tyndall answered soothingly: 'Oh, it may seem like that to you, but I assure you that's not the way it is.' We played both answers in the finished film. When he wrote about the programme in the NF magazine *Spearhead*, Tyndall said: 'I felt it useless to argue with the interviewer – a distinctly foreign-looking type, despite his English sounding name of Cockerell. Dealing with these people was like dealing with slime. You think you have it in your hands – only to see it slip through your fingers and form again before your eyes.'

A. K. Chesterton had his own take on our film. He wrote in *Candour*, his monthly British newsletter: 'Not content with befouling the air with this vile and tendentious programme, Michael Cockerell said I wrote an adoring biography of Sir Oswald Mosley. It may be that I overestimated the qualities of that nevertheless great man. But it was not an "adoring" biography. Cockerell seems fond of the word and it may be that in the world wherein he dwells men adore other men. In my world they do not.'

You would need a heart of stone not to laugh.

When we filmed at Front rallies and marches, we noted that two leading Tory MPs were always subjects of their attention. One was a hate figure; the other a hero. 'Heath is a traitor!' the marchers and their placards would proclaim, while many others

would chant: 'Enoch was right!' Ted Heath and Enoch Powell
had once been close colleagues but had fallen out big time and
become sworn enemies. Heath, who had been elected Conservative Prime Minister in 1970, had sacked Powell from his shadow
Cabinet two years earlier following his notorious anti-immigrant
'Rivers of Blood' speech. He had also gained the hatred of the
National Front for taking Britain into the European Union. I
filmed and interviewed the two Tories over the years and was
later to make films about their lives. They were both mystical
men: ideal subjects for political psychotherapists – and for our
cameras.

CHAPTER 7

A VERY SINGULAR MAN

Of all the leading politicians I have made films about over the years, the trickiest to deal with was Ted Heath. He was a man of many moods. Sometimes when you made the pilgrimage to film him at his breathtakingly beautiful house that resembled a mini-chateau in the grounds of Salisbury Cathedral, he would be jovial and ebullient; at other times he would be in a total grump and monosyllabic in his answers. His customary mode of greeting was to make you feel *not* at home, to try to destabilise you before you had even started. As we sat down for one interview, he said: 'Have you got your usual list of boring questions?' Yes, exactly the same, I replied.

'Oh well, we'd better get it over with.' I thought the interview went reasonably well, and when it was finished I asked if he thought the questions had been as boring as usual. 'Oh yes,' he replied, 'but infinitely more irrelevant.' I told his private secretary about this – 'That's good: if he's rude to you it means he likes you.'

On another occasion Heath said: 'I was thinking about you as I was coming here and I want to ask, do you have any training at all for this?'

I replied jokingly: 'No, none at all. I don't do any reading about you, either books or newspapers. I don't talk to people who know you, nor do I listen to old radio or TV interviews you have done.' (The exact opposite of what I always do.)

He replied: 'Oh, that would account for it.'

When my producer Matthew Barrett and I were making a film about his life, Heath told me that he decided he was going to be Prime Minister when he was at the local grammar school in the Kent seaside town of Broadstairs. 'But I didn't tell the other boys as they might have been jealous,' he said.

Taking Heath back to Oxford to film him in Balliol – he had won an organ scholarship to the college – put him into one of his genial moods. In the grand dining hall, we talked as we inspected the imposing portraits of old Balliol men who had become Prime Ministers – Asquith, Macmillan and Heath himself. Boris Johnson had yet to come.

I asked Heath if he thought Balliol imparted some quality that helped in becoming Prime Minister. 'Oh yes, complete mental control – intellectual control,' said Heath.

'You mean what Asquith called "the tranquil consciousness of effortless superiority"?' I said.

'Yes, absolutely,' he replied. 'It's the first thing, they teach that from the moment you get here.' And he felt that for the rest of his life? 'Yes, that's what caused so much trouble.' And he gave his shoulder-heaving laugh.

Heath was an exact contemporary at his college of two 'best Prime Ministers we never had': Denis Healey and Roy Jenkins, both former Labour Chancellors. Healey told me that at Balliol,

Teddy Heath, as he was then known, was shocked to learn that a fellow student planned to spend the weekend with his girlfriend at a hotel outside Oxford. Heath asked Healey: 'You don't think they are going to sleep together, do you?'

The more worldly Healey replied: 'I haven't asked, but I imagine so, yes.'

'Good heavens,' responded Heath, 'I can't imagine anyone in the Conservative association doing that.' When I told Heath what Healey had said, he replied deadpan: 'And were they both Conservatives?'

We took Heath back to Nuremberg, where he had gone as an undergraduate in 1937 to assess for himself the menace of Nazism. Heath told me that as he sat next to the gangway, Hitler brushed his shoulder as he strode up to address the rally. What he witnessed there and later as an artillery officer during the Second World War inspired in him the idea that would dominate his whole political life. 'I saw in German cities practically everything was destroyed. And I was convinced then that what my generation had to do was to create a unity in Europe which would mean that this would never happen again.'

While Heath would talk fluently about the political influences on him, he was notoriously guarded about his private life. The one exception came when we arranged to film him in Broadstairs, where he was born and grew up. I met him when he stepped out of his car and instead of his usual insult for a greeting, he beamed at me and said: 'Smell that air – wonderful isn't it – the best in the world.' He was relaxed and amicable over our lunch in the best hotel; he ate smoked salmon and fresh asparagus with hollandaise sauce. But he refused a drink: 'Never before a big interview,' he said. When we began recording, for the first time he opened by a fraction the doors onto his feelings.

He had never before talked publicly about his girlfriend from Broadstairs. She was Kay Raven, the daughter of the local doctor who went out with Heath before the war and for six years waited patiently for his return from the front. Heath did take up with her again after the war and his friends expected the couple to marry. But he never got round to proposing. Why was that? I asked. 'She decided she would marry someone else, but I don't discuss these things,' said Heath.

'Did you get over it?'

'Yes.'

'It was said you kept her photograph by your bed.'

'Yes.'

'Did you?'

'Yes,' and Heath looked away, as if he was close to tears.

He also talked so movingly about the death of his beloved mother that I felt we had crossed a barrier and when we next met he would be more forthcoming. The opposite happened. It was as if he had decided to give me just a single glimpse – but never again. Discussing Heath later with his great friend the former Cabinet Secretary Robert Armstrong, I said how difficult I had found it to get him to open up about his personal life. Lord Armstrong replied: 'You got more out of him than I have managed in fifty years of friendship.'

Heath became a Conservative MP in the 1950 general election

along with Enoch Powell, and they joined the newly formed One Nation group of Tory modernisers. Appointed a junior whip, Heath developed a reputation as a skilled party manager and would spend most of the next decade operating behind the scenes. I asked if he enjoyed the business of organisation. 'Oh immensely, yes. Because I loathe incompetence and inefficiency and bungling and waste and all those things.' Within four years the organisation man was made Chief Whip.

He was seen as formidably efficient – skilled at shepherding Tory MPs through the right division lobby via a mixture of persuasion, promise and threat. He faced his biggest challenge to party unity with the 1956 Suez Crisis. Heath's mentor, Prime Minister Anthony Eden, sent British troops to seize back the Suez Canal from the Egyptian military strongman Colonel Nasser, who had nationalised it. There was speculation that Eden had secretly collaborated with the French and the Israelis to stage the invasion. Heath told me a remarkable story about what had happened to the secret Cabinet papers about the invasion.

He said that Eden had a meeting with the government's top civil servant, the Cabinet Secretary, Sir Norman Brook. Heath continued: 'Norman Brook came out of the meeting and said, the Prime Minister has told me to burn the lot.' Of the secret Cabinet papers on Suez? 'Yes.' And, I asked, is that what the Cabinet Secretary went off and did? 'Yes.' And what did you feel about that? 'Well, the Cabinet Secretary was carrying out the PM's orders about Cabinet documents.' He was only obeying orders, I said. 'Yes,' said Heath.

But, I persisted, what did you feel about a Cabinet Secretary going off and destroying secret documents, which if they had been made public would prove the Prime Minister had lied to the House. 'The Cabinet Secretary was doing his job.' But what sort of view is this of the morality of a Prime Minister who lies to the House and then tells the Cabinet Secretary to destroy the documents? What was your view about that? 'Well, my view is that I haven't destroyed any Cabinet documents.'

Even forty years after Suez, Heath's sense of loyalty meant that he could not bring himself to utter a word of condemnation of the Prime Minister he still saw as his patron. Anthony Eden had died twenty years before our interview, although Eden's wife was still alive, and it may be that Heath did not want to offend her.

The Tory Chief Whip is the keeper of the party's secrets and makes it his business to know about the sexual and financial indiscretions of his MPs. In February 1958, a scandal blew up involving Colonel Ian Harvey MP, one of Heath's Oxford contemporaries and a junior minister. Homosexuality was still a criminal offence, and Harvey was found having sex in the bushes with a guardsman in St James's Park. Winston Churchill, who was then still an MP, laughed it off: 'On the coldest night of the year? It makes you proud to be British.'

Harvey stood down from Parliament and later wrote a book, *To Fall Like Lucifer*. One of the researchers whom Heath employed to help write his autobiography noticed Harvey's book on Heath's bookshelf. The researcher opened it and found it had a handwritten dedication from Colonel Harvey: 'To Ted – who knows what it's like.' But when the researcher went to look at the book the next day, it was gone, and it was never seen again. The researcher didn't have the confidence to ask Heath about the inscription.

In 1965, after the Tories had had three Old Etonian Prime Ministers in a row, Heath stood for the party leadership against the former Chancellor Reggie Maudling and Enoch Powell, the former Health Secretary. It was the first time Tory MPs could vote for their leader. Previously, the leader would emerge via what one Tory grandee described as 'the customary processes of consultation conducted by the magic circle of Old Etonians'. Heath won and Powell came third – but as he put it: 'I left my calling card.' Heath had been elected because Tory MPs thought a grammar-school boy of humble origins would be a match for the Labour Prime Minister Harold Wilson, who was running rings around them. But when Wilson called the snap general election, Heath was buried by a Labour landslide.

Heath was soon under pressure for lack of leadership. In contrast to Wilson, whom he scorned as a confidence trickster, Heath was an image-maker's nightmare. He despised the whole process, disliked television and generally felt that there were more important things in life than being interviewed on camera. But as things went from bad to worse Heath agreed to appear on a *Panorama* programme about the Tories' troubles. The programme's presenter, Robin Day, began his interview with: 'Mr Heath, how low does your popularity have to sink among your own supporters before you consider yourself a liability to the party you lead?'

Heath answered: 'Well, popularity isn't everything.' Robin's had been one of the great 'have you stopped beating your wife' questions – although famously of course Ted Heath didn't have a wife. And the polls suggested that Heath's bachelor status told against him.

A Tory backbencher, Sir Tufton Beamish (the role model for *Private Eye*'s fictional knight of the shires Sir Bufton Tufton), had helped organise Heath's leadership campaign and now came up with a cunning plan. He would try to find Heath a wife. He knew that Heath had a shared love of music with the great concert pianist Moura Lympany – and that the two were close friends. Sir Tufton arranged to meet Dame Moura.

We flew to Monte Carlo to talk to the grande dame. She told me: 'Tufton came to see me and said "Moura, Ted must get married. Will you marry him?" I replied if Ted asked me to marry him, I would have considered it a great honour.' And would you have said yes? 'Ah, well, if I hadn't been in love with someone else.'

We showed the clip to Heath, whose face lit up when he saw Moura on the screen. 'I liked her and apparently she liked me. We had a common interest in music, good food and wine.' I asked Heath if he had known about Beamish's démarche. 'No, Tufton never discussed it with me'. So does that come as a surprise to you? 'Nothing surprises me these days,' said Heath. And did you think of asking Moura Lympany to marry you? 'I never discuss these matters at all.'

'Ted is a little bit defensive on women of course, for obvious reasons,' said his lifelong friend Brigadier Ken Hunt, who had been at school with him. 'First of all people say he's queer, or that he's sweet on Moura Lympany, that sort of thing. And actually he's wedded to his politics and that's it. There is no place for anybody else.' And Dame Moura said: 'The most intimate thing Ted has ever done over the years was to put his arm round my shoulder.'

To the astonishment of pundits and politicians alike, the Tories won the 1970 general election. And as Prime Minister, Heath's prickly personality came to count against him with the public. 'A string of publicity advisers tried to change my image,' he told me, 'but they soon found there was nothing they could do about it – and gave up in despair.'

Heath cut a lonely figure in No. 10. One of his closest acolytes, Cabinet minister Peter Walker, told the journalist Max Hastings that he never left a meeting in No. 10 without a sense of sympathy, even pity, for Heath. 'If I make a speech,' said Walker, 'my wife Tessa is always there to mutter, "Wonderful speech, darling; such a pity your fly buttons were undone." Ted has absolutely no one in his life to say those things.'

I asked Heath if he felt he had missed out by never having married. 'No – a lot of people say I have gained, because instead of having to spend time with one's family or not spending time and being divorced, I've just been free to use my time in the world of politics.'

Heath had moved his own grand piano into No. 10. His political secretary, Douglas Hurd, said that Heath had the disadvantage of not having a wife to discuss matters with at the end of the day, 'and going upstairs and playing the piano is not really quite an adequate compensation for that'. Heath saw things differently. He told me: 'Music is a complete contrast to one's daily work and what it does is to absorb the mental and emotional feelings. And you can then produce them yourself in whatever way you want – whether it's on the piano or any other instrument.' I asked Heath, do you think that music has been a substitute in your life for love? 'No, not at all; you can have love in a variety of ways and music is one of them.'

His most controversial achievement was to take Britain into the European Community. Previous attempts at entry had been blocked by the French. Heath decided to woo them in their native tongue; his pronounced English accent was the worst heard from a British Prime Minister since Churchill, who made no attempt at all to sound French. We played Heath a clip of his speech, and I asked what he thought of his accent. He replied: 'Well, I think it's very good. But nobody here in Britain thinks so. The French on the other hand are always very kind and say, *c'est magnifique*. And over here they say what an awful noise he was making.'

But he struck up a personal relationship with President Pompidou, who lifted his predecessor General de Gaulle's veto on British entry. The lifelong Europhile Ted Heath said the day he signed the Accession Treaty was the proudest of his life, and that night he went to his piano and played part of Bach's *The Well-Tempered Clavier* to celebrate. A small group of Tory anti-European MPs led by Enoch Powell were not so happy.

Heath was facing a rough time on the home front. He ran

into a range of economic and trade union problems and was forced into a series of policy U-turns. We filmed as I quoted to Heath a passage from Douglas Hurd's diary: 'The government is wandering round the battlefield looking for someone to surrender to and being massacred all the time.'

Heath responded: 'That was silly, very silly. I mean the very language of it was silly. How can a responsible person, especially someone who's a political secretary to the Prime Minister, produce stuff like that in his diary?'

One member of Heath's Cabinet totally agreed with Hurd: Margaret Thatcher. She said nothing at the time, but she later wrote in her memoirs about Heath's numerous policy U-turns: 'Although we had totally changed course, we had kept the same helmsman. And even as we headed for rock-strewn waters, he remained supremely confident of his navigational skills.'

I put the quote to Heath, and he said: 'Well, somebody must have written that for her – she couldn't do it herself.'

As inflation soared and oil prices quadrupled, the miners went on strike. Britain was subjected to various expedients to save electricity, such as the three-day working week, and there were ministerial exhortations to clean your teeth in the dark. Although as Prime Minister Heath normally preferred to hold grandiose press conferences in the aloof style of President de Gaulle, when he came under siege in late 1973, he turned to television. He sought to use straight-to-camera broadcasts to try to rally the public behind the government. But he had made no previous effort to establish a rapport with the viewers.

One of his great friends, former BBC Director-General Ian

Trethowan, said to me: 'When it mattered most to Ted, he failed to get his private charm across on television.' When I put that to Heath, he looked at me with his baleful light blue eyes and replied: 'I don't think a miners' strike is the time to come on television and ooze charm, do you?' Heath called a snap general election asking the question – who rules Britain? It invited, and received, the response: 'Not you, matey.' Harold Wilson returned to No. 10 as leader of a minority government.

Ted Heath was a man capable of denying point-blank things that were a matter of public record. He would claim that he never committed a single policy U-turn as Prime Minister, even though his last years in office bristled with them. Nor was he prepared to admit that he had made mistakes in his career. When I put this to him, he said: 'There seems to be an obsession with interviewers on mistakes. I don't know what to do about it. I might introduce a school course or something. How to say good things about people.'

One of the people Heath himself could never say a good word about was his bête noire, Enoch Powell. After Heath had sacked Powell from the shadow Cabinet in 1968 after his notorious 'Rivers of Blood' speech, the two men who were once friends never spoke again. Yet they had a number of traits in common – not least in their private lives.

CHAPTER 8

ODD MAN OUT

Enoch Powell admitted that for much of his life he had a compelling ambition to become Prime Minister. But he saw himself as a loner. 'I never played the game – the political game of snakes and ladders,' he told me. 'So I was like the man on the playing field who wasn't playing the game. I was the odd man out.' That was the three-word title of the film I made about him, produced by Bill Treharne Jones.

An only child, Powell was born in a thunderstorm in Birmingham in 1912. His life was to be punctuated by regular explosions – a number of which he detonated himself. Precociously bright, he was not like other children, and he told me he was known at his grammar school as 'scowly Powelly' for his dedicated work ethic. At seventeen, he won a classics scholarship to Cambridge. There, he would get up at five in the morning and study all day with his door locked.

'I knew nothing else but to work,' he said. 'I had no social life and was surprised to discover women at Cambridge. I wondered what they were doing there, because the analytical faculty is not developed in women.' Yet at Cambridge he wrote erotic love poetry which revealed the intensity of feeling beneath the ascetic facade. In one poem, Powell talks of seeing the one he loved unexpectedly. He wrote: 'I felt a flow of white hot lava seething up the old volcano shaft.'

When I asked Powell to whom the poem was written, he said: 'It wasn't written to anybody; it was a work of the imagination.' In fact, after his death copies of letters Powell had written to his mother revealed his feelings were for a fellow male student.

Powell became the master of several ancient and modern languages and a professor of classics at the age of twenty-five. Two years later, in 1939, fearing the Nazis would win the war, he signed up for the army as a private. On *Desert Island Discs*, where half his choices were from Wagner operas, Powell said: 'I wish I had died in the war' and told of his lifelong feelings of survivor's guilt.

Powell was posted into the Intelligence Corps, where he met and was to become lifetime friends with the flamboyant Hardy Amies, later the Queen's dressmaker. I interviewed Amies, who said: 'We saw Enoch as a bit of a nutcase. He didn't join in the boisterous boozing. He was forever lying on his bunk and reading the New Testament – in ancient Greek.' When I asked Powell why he thought he got on so well with Amies, he replied: 'If I say his gaiety, that must not be misunderstood. Let's say his *joie de vivre*.'

Powell was sent to work as an intelligence officer with the Eighth Army in North Africa. His task was to get inside the mind of the German Army Commander General Rommel, by deploying his professional skills as a textual critic. The secret signals being sent by General Rommel's Afrika Korps were all being intercepted by the British. And though Rommel was known as the Desert Fox, Professor Powell came to understand more about the general's plans than anyone else in the British Army. After our victory at Alamein, Powell was to become, along with Fitzroy Maclean, one of only two privates throughout the war to reach the rank of brigadier.

He was posted to India and spent his first night sleeping at Delhi railway station. 'When I woke up,' he told me, 'I discovered I'd fallen in love with India. The smells, the sights – everything. There is a natural attraction between India and England – a shared dream, inexplicable, a weird thing.' He conceived the romantic notion that he might one day become viceroy – even though the facts on the ground said Imperial India was doomed.

On his return to England after the war, Powell took up fox hunting and fell passionately in love with a fellow huntswoman called Barbara Kennedy. He had never before taken a woman out. On their first date, they went by bus to the music hall in Wolverhampton. She told him that if he wanted to take her out again, he had better get a car. But Powell chose to write her poetry instead. We filmed as he read aloud from the poem he wrote about the end of their relationship:

> You ceased. The wind that through the sward
> With steady-breathing passion swept,
> From flower and grass and heather blent
> 'Amen' to that strange sacrament;
> And silent, as it seemed, we wept.

With tears in his eyes, Powell told me: 'You mustn't put me in a situation where I am so overcome with emotion – old emotion summoned by poetry written under the spell of that emotion.' Forty-seven years on, Barbara Kennedy was less smitten. She said: 'Enoch was desperately shy – very handsome with piercing, penetrating eyes. But it was more emotional than physical. He wasn't the sort to crawl all over you. Ours wasn't a sexual relationship.'

When Barbara announced her engagement to a Shropshire businessman, Powell arrived at the Kennedy family house and protested that she had agreed to marry him. 'I don't ever recall him proposing,' said Barbara. 'But I didn't understand a word he was saying; he was so erudite.'

Powell said of the relationship: 'It failed. I was not satisfactory.' And what happened then? 'I took up with the lady who became my wife – and lived happily ever after, I believe one adds,' he said with a sort of smile.

Pamela Wilson, who was Powell's secretary, was married to him for nearly fifty years until his death. She told me: 'When Enoch proposed to me – on bended knee, no less – he said, "I can't promise you anything but a life of grinding poverty and a life totally on the back benches."'

Powell had been elected MP for Wolverhampton in the 1950 general election along with Ted Heath. They were both moderate One Nation pro-Europeans. Soon after becoming an MP, Powell was asked to present an edition of BBC Radio's *The Week in Westminster*. In a confidential assessment, his producer wrote: 'An outstanding, brilliant account, showing a penetrating and original shrewdness of observation. Brisk, rather harsh Midlands voice – not the least bit cosy. Professes never to listen to the wireless, yet knows how to write a script and how to address a microphone.'

After a spell as a junior Housing Minister, Powell was made a Treasury Minister in Macmillan's government. He had become a prototype monetarist, and in 1958 he resigned from the Treasury along with the Chancellor in protest at what they saw as the government failure to control public spending.

But four years later, Powell, who had built up a reputation as a great parliamentary orator, was in the Cabinet as Health Secretary. And he had a devoted admirer on the Tory back benches: the young Margaret Thatcher, who had become an MP in 1959. 'Enoch was the best parliamentarian I ever knew,' Mrs Thatcher told me. 'He would argue from first principles with remorseless logic. And he spoke with his whole body.'

Powell himself told me that he would always make an important speech on a full bladder: 'You should be tense before a big speech. Nerves are part of the act. You shouldn't be at ease – and if you need to drain your bladder in order to relax, you should refrain if possible.'

In 1965, with the Tories in opposition, Powell stood for the party leadership but was easily beaten by Ted Heath. To show there were no hard feelings, Powell invited his new leader to dinner at his home. There, Heath met the family hamster, the special pet of Powell's daughter, Jennifer. She said: 'At this dinner party, Ted Heath did not like having my hamster running all over him, but the hamster liked Heath and sat on his lap and washed its little face. That's the greatest compliment a hamster can pay to a human being to demonstrate how relaxed and comfortable they are. And Ted Heath was the only guest who was paid that particular compliment. We subsequently realised that was a momentary lapse of judgement by the hamster, but we didn't hold it against him.'

Relations between the two men quickly soured, as Powell saw a way of widening his popular appeal. He espoused provocatively unorthodox views and built up his own agenda to the right of his leader. Heath came to dislike and distrust Powell but felt he could not sack him from the shadow Cabinet as his own political position was so insecure.

The crunch came in 1968. Powell tipped off the editor of his local paper: 'I'm going to make a speech that is going to go up "fizz" like a rocket; but whereas all rockets fall to the earth, this one is going to stay up.' 'Rivers of Blood' turned out to be the most explosive speech by a senior British politician since the war.

Central to the speech was that Powell was an English nationalist who had an almost mystical belief in the nation. The England of '68 was another country: TV newsreaders and reporters were almost without exception white-skinned, as were the England football and cricket teams. On the taboo subject of race, Powell was alarmed at what he saw as the dangers of Asian and black immigration to the nation. Having decided to quote directly from letters his constituents had sent him about their experiences with immigrants, Powell did not pull his punches. He talked about 'grinning wide-eyed piccaninnies posting excrement through letter boxes of their white neighbours'. He claimed it was literally mad to let in so many immigrants and their dependents: 'It is like putting a match to gunpowder.' And he forecast civil war in Britain between white and black people.

Though Powell never actually used the phrase 'Rivers of Blood', he said that like the Roman prophet he seemed to see the Tiber foaming with much blood. And he added: 'In this country in fifteen or twenty years' time the black man will have the whip hand over the white man. I can already hear the chorus of execration: how dare I say such a horrible thing? How dare I stir up trouble and inflame feelings? My answer is that I do not have the right not to do so.'

The speech generated a tsunami of rage and recrimination against Powell among MPs and the media – but an even more powerful counter-flow of support for him. The London dockers and meat porters marched on Parliament chanting 'We want Enoch Powell,' some factories went on strike in his favour and polls showed 75 per cent support for the speech.

Powell had deliberately neglected to forewarn his party leader about the speech. Heath only learned of its incendiary nature from the television news. Having consulted his shadow Cabinet, Heath rang Powell and told him he was sacked from the shadow Cabinet because 'the speech was racialist in tone and liable to exacerbate racial tensions'.

'Heath ran away,' Powell told me. 'He was alarmed, he was frightened out of his wits.' By what you had said? 'By the outcry – and scenting danger, he ran for cover.'

Powell received over 100,000 letters, mostly of support. And there was a sharp rise in hate crimes against immigrants. We filmed Powell watching an interview with Paul Boateng, who would later be a Labour minister and is the British-born son of Ghanaian parents. Boateng said: 'I was eighteen and at school at the time, and I was one of those wide-eyed grinning piccaninnies that Powell talked about. For the first time in the country of my birth – the country to which I am proud to say I belong – I was shouted at, spat at and abused in the streets on the day after that speech.'

Powell told me he believed Boateng's account, and I then asked: 'Can you understand how your speech was inflammatory and could be used by racialists against black people in Britain?'

Powell replied: 'What's wrong with racism? Racism is the basis of nationality.'

'Are you saying that Boateng can't be black and British?' I asked.

'It's not impossible, but it's difficult,' said Powell. 'Nations are on the whole united by identity with one another – and that's normally due to similarities which we regard as racial similarities.' I asked him how his speech tallied with his earlier expressed love for India. Powell replied: 'India is India; England is England. And an Englishman can have a love for India without wishing to see India on the streets of Birmingham.' The Prime Minister, Harold Wilson, attacked the virus of Powellism, which he claimed was taking over the Tory Party. Powell responded: 'Yes, I am a virus: I am the virus that kills socialists.'

His sacking from the shadow Cabinet greatly increased Powell's value in the media market. Although he would never reveal

his earnings in the Register of Members' Interests, he apparently made more from his press articles, broadcasts and speeches
than he did as an MP. Negotiating with him for a TV interview would now involve a discussion of precisely what one was
buying. 'How long do you want this interview to last?' he would
say to me.

'Three or four minutes,' I once replied.

'But which? If you want three, then I shall speak for three
minutes; and if four, then I shall speak for four.' He took out
his stopwatch to ensure that he would give not a second more
than agreed. 'And if you want more,' he said, 'you will pay for it
commensurately.'

In the 1970 general election, to Heath's embarrassment,
Powell stood again as the official Conservative candidate in
Wolverhampton. Heath, who was expected to lose the election,
studiously avoided any reference to Powell. But the left-wing
Labour Cabinet minister Tony Benn said in a campaign speech:
'The flag of racialism which has been hoisted in Wolverhampton is beginning to look like the one that fluttered twenty-five
years ago over Dachau and Belsen. Enoch Powell has emerged
as the real leader of the Conservative Party. He is a far stronger
character than Mr. Heath. He speaks his mind; Heath does not.
The final proof of Powell's power is that Heath dare not attack
him publicly, even when he says things that disgust decent
Conservatives.'

When the election results came through, Heath had won a
shock victory. There was a swing to the Conservatives that was
much larger in Powell's Wolverhampton constituency and the

surrounding West Midlands; it may well have tipped the balance in a close election. But Powell was depressed because Heath was now Prime Minister. 'That was my chance gone,' said Powell.

But he now became a bigger thorn in Heath's flesh – particularly on Europe. Powell, who had become an arch anti-European, was determined to prevent Heath taking Britain into the Common Market. In a speech in the Commons, Powell declaimed that the battle over Europe 'is a life-and-death struggle for Britain's independence and authority. A struggle as surely about the future of Britain's nationhood as were the combats which raged in the skies over southern England in the autumn of 1940. The gladiators are few, their weapons are but words. And yet the fight is every man's.'

Although Powell voted over 100 times against the legislation to take Britain in, he and his followers failed to block the Accession Bill. But when Heath called an early election in 1974, Powell detonated his latest bombshell. He resigned as Tory MP for Wolverhampton and called on the public to vote Labour, which favoured a referendum on Britain's membership.

'My first loyalty is to the people of this country,' Powell told me, 'and I felt they were being deprived behind their backs of something they valued – their self-government through Parliament.' At a packed eve-of-poll meeting of the Get Britain Out campaign, Powell faced a shout from the audience of 'Judas' for betraying the Tory Party. He flashed back: 'Judas was paid – I am making a sacrifice.'

Heath lost the election by the narrowest of margins, with Labour returning to power in a hung parliament. And once again it seemed that Powell's intervention had a decisive effect, as the anti-Tory swing was more marked in the key marginal West Midlands seats than anywhere else in the rest of the country.

The morning after the election, Powell in his dressing gown picked up his morning paper, which read: 'Heath's gamble fails'. 'I retired to the bathroom and sang the "Te Deum",' Powell told me. 'It seemed as if my work was accomplished. I had had my revenge on the man who destroyed the self-government of the United Kingdom.' So you had helped bring him to power and now you helped bring him down? 'I put him in and I took him out is a cruder way of putting it,' he said with a half laugh.

Powell famously said that all political careers end in failure. When I interviewed him three years before his death in 1998, I asked him if his own career had followed that pattern. 'Political failure. Yes,' replied Powell. 'Mine has ended in failure from one point of view: without a seat, without office and without apparent achievement. But I have achieved a good deal. And I hear my voice coming through in what is said about Europe, about the nation, about immigration. It was heard and is still echoing.'

And three lines of his later poetry, he said, summed up his view:

> If my ship sails from sight,
> It doesn't mean my journey ends,
> It simply means the river bends.

Powell also revealed the romantic side that lurked beneath his remorselessly logical exterior. He said that each year on their wedding anniversary, he wrote a poem for his wife and gave her a red rose. But he showed that even in romance, he had not lost his eye for the market: 'I tell Pamela jokingly that the poems are her pension. I say you can publish these when I am dead. But I shall not be here to receive the royalties.'

CHAPTER 9

WOMEN TROUBLE

When I filmed with Harold Wilson during the February 1974 election, I asked how long he would stay in No. 10 if he won. He replied, 'The problem is still whether I am too young for the job – remember that Gladstone formed his last ministry when he was ninety – so you could still have another thirty years of me in No. 10.'

Wilson returned to power as the head of a minority government. He had begun to develop footballing metaphors in television interviews to enhance his folksy image. He told me that in his first term, so few of his colleagues had ministerial experience he had to do everything himself. 'I had to take corner kicks and penalties, administer to the wounded and bring on the lemons at half-time and score all the goals myself. Now I will be the deep-lying centre-half, concentrating on defence, initiating attacks, distributing the ball for my star forwards. They'll score the goals and, by heavens, they *are* scoring goals.'

But, in fact – although it was not known at the time – in 1974, while he was Prime Minister, Wilson suffered from a similar racing heart complaint to the one that would affect Tony Blair thirty years later. It hit Wilson during an official visit to see the French President. His personal doctor ordered him to take a complete rest.

'I told the press, who believed me when I said that Harold had the flu,' his press secretary, Joe Haines, admitted to me. 'We had an economic crisis and we had a majority of three. If I had said, "He's got a heart problem," then the Cabinet would have been queueing up to take over from him, and the stock exchange would have fallen through the floor. So I didn't have the slightest compunction about not telling the truth.'

One of Wilson's big problems on his return to office was the bitter feuding and jealousy among the three most influential advisers in his kitchen Cabinet. On one side was his long-term political secretary Marcia Williams, whom he was soon to ennoble as Lady Falkender. On the other side were his two more recent recruits – his press secretary Joe Haines and the LSE academic Bernard Donoughue. 'Marcia had a considerable hold over Harold,' Donoughue told me. 'He was frightened of her. He became difficult, almost unpleasant, only when she was attacking him. This made him edgy, with black rings round his eyes, and he reached for the brandy bottle. I was there once with him in the No. 10 study. The phone rang and he obviously knew it was her. He leapt to his feet and ran across the room to the bathroom in the corner. And as he went in, he said, "Tell her I'm not here." My concern was that it diminished his capacity to function fully as a Prime Minister.'

Joe Haines fought a permanent battle with Lady Falkender in No. 10, believing she offered bad advice and that her influence was wholly destructive. She in turn thought much the same of the two men and later told me: 'There was a great deal of intrigue and it was unpleasant and nasty. I felt most offended because it implied that no woman could in fact hold a high position in Downing Street.'

The irony for Haines and Donoughue was that the Prime Minister, the master schemer who was forever scenting plots against himself, seemed to revel in the rivalries within his own court – damaging to him though they often were.

Wilson's personal doctor, Joe Stone, was always on call in No. 10. And Haines told me an extraordinary story: 'Dr Stone came into my room one day saying he was worried about the stress that Marcia Falkender was causing Harold. And he said something has to be done about it. I said: "Joe, I've tried it. He won't get rid of her – there's no way." Then Joe Stone said: "I could dispose of her. I'm her doctor. And I would write the death certificate."'

Donoughue corroborated the story when he told me: 'I remember Joe Stone said to me: "It's the national interest that Marcia be put down."'

But Haines said: 'Bernard and I both said no. Just imagine: "Press secretary kills Prime Minister's secretary". Or "Press secretary in conspiracy to kill Marcia Falkender". "Murder in No. 10". I could write the headlines now. So we said no.' The spin doctor seemed more worried about getting bad press than the morality of a medical doctor trashing the Hippocratic Oath.

Meanwhile, across the political divide the PM's long-term adversary, Ted Heath, who had lost three of the four general elections he had fought against Wilson, was under siege in his own party. The bachelor Tory leader was facing an unprecedented challenge for his crown from an MP of the opposite sex: Mrs Margaret Hilda Thatcher.

I first filmed her in 1975, when she launched her challenge to Ted Heath for the Tory leadership. I wanted to make a documentary about the contest, and my producer John Penycate and I sought access to the two campaigns. Though Heath's people agreed, Mrs Thatcher's team refused. On an appropriately foggy night, we drove to a secluded house in Oxfordshire to see her campaign manager, a former intelligence officer who had escaped as a prisoner of war from Colditz, the infamous Nazi prison-castle. Colonel Airey Neave had become a right-wing Tory MP and relished his secretive and conspiratorial reputation.

He told us that his campaign strategy did not include any co-operation with us. We said that would be a pity because Heath's people were playing ball and we would be forced to rely on library footage of Mrs Thatcher for balance. We said we had been through the archive and there was very little of her – with two exceptions. One was when she was the controversial Education Secretary who had stopped free milk for school children. There was film of many demonstrations against her, with the protesters chanting: 'Margaret Thatcher, milk snatcher!' along with clips of her struggling to defend the policy.

The other main footage was of Mrs Thatcher as she endorsed food hoarding during economic crises. Pictured in front of her two larders, she gave an interview encouraging people to stock up on tinned foods: 'Ham, tongue, salmon, mackerel, sardines and baked beans, as well as tinned fruits because of the sugar shortage.' Attacked for encouraging panic buying, Mrs Thatcher said she thought everyone was doing it, adding: 'Buying in bulk is not creating a shortage; it's being prudent.' Neave looked pensive and the following day we got a call saying that we could have access to film Mrs Thatcher and she would give us an interview.

When Mrs Thatcher had finally decided to run against Heath, her husband Denis said: 'You would be out of your mind. Heath will murder you.' Undaunted, she went to Heath's room in the Commons to tell him of her decision to stand. 'If you must – you'll lose,' was Heath's response. Mrs Thatcher said: 'That remark gave a certain zest to my competitive spirit.'

Heath claimed that Mrs Thatcher wanted to turn the Tories into a 'middle-class preservation society' and his people dismissed her as the Finchley housewife. When I interviewed Heath for our programme, I asked: 'Do you see any irony in the fact that you are a bachelor and your main opponent is a woman?'

'No,' he replied. 'I see no irony in that at all.' At the end of the interview, Heath's aides asked us to film the interview again, as he would produce better answers the next time. We agreed, but only on the condition that we could use the first interview or the second – or parts of both. When I put the question to Heath again, he said: 'Women play a great part in the Conservative Party both in Parliament and in the country. They are invaluable.'

When I interviewed Mrs Thatcher for the programme, I asked whether as a middle-class woman from the south, she was the right person to win back lost Tory votes in the industrial north. 'But it wasn't I who lost those votes,' she replied. 'It was Mr Heath. And he is a middle-class Conservative gentleman from the south of England.' Touché.

When the interview was finished, Mrs Thatcher said to me: 'Why is it that all you young men always ask me what I look like?'

I replied: 'I wasn't asking about what you look like. It was a question of how people in the north might perceive you. It may seem to people who work in a factory or a mill that you don't share or even understand their daily concerns.'

'Yes, all you young men ask me what I look like. I'm forty-eight so I suppose it's flattering that you concentrate on my appearance.' (She was in fact forty-nine.)

'I wasn't asking what you look like; I was asking about your political image.'

'Yes,' she said. 'You always ask me about what I look like. Why do you do that?'

I got quite heated: 'Mrs Thatcher,' I said, 'you know I was not asking you about what you look like.'

She leant forward and patted me on the knee. 'There, there,' she said, 'don't get upset. Remember, I was the one being asked the nasty questions, not you.' The camera crew laughed noisily: there is nothing they like more than seeing the front man discountenanced by the interviewee.

The Tories' first woman leader and her closest supporters celebrated a famous victory with champagne at Airey Neave's Westminster house. Heath felt every cork was aimed at him.

He told me later: 'I didn't think their campaign was conducted in the way of colleagues. When we had the original leadership campaign in 1965, we didn't carry on with great TV and radio campaigns and press campaigns behind the scenes. The three of us who stood against each other would never have had celebrations with champagne. You could say I was simple and taken unaware. But I'm afraid I had standards.'

According to Thatcher's official biographer, Charles Moore, Heath was somewhat less decorous when he told Bernard Weatherill, then Deputy Chief Whip and later Speaker of the House, that the Tory Party consists of three groups: 'Shits, bloody shits and fucking shits.'

When I interviewed Mrs Thatcher on the night she grabbed the Tory crown in February 1975, she seemed as fragile as porcelain. 'It is like a dream', she said, 'to follow in the footsteps of the great Winston, of Harold Macmillan and of Ted Heath. I almost wept when they told me I had won – in fact, I did weep.' She bit her lip and her eyes glistened. According to Charles Moore, she spoke with 'an intense, almost sensual expression'.

Mrs Thatcher's first big challenge as leader was whether she would protect the legacy of Heath's proudest achievement as PM: taking Britain into the European Community. Within four months of her election there was to be a referendum, called by the Labour Prime Minister Harold Wilson, on whether we should remain a member. With Labour split down the middle on the issue, Mrs Thatcher had to decide how to position the Tory Party. The referendum would turn into a shapeshifting, cross-party event – which created the most unlikely liaisons.

CHAPTER 10

TIPTOEING INTO A BROTHEL

Faced with an increasingly Eurosceptic Labour Party, Harold Wilson had called a Yes/No referendum on Britain's place in Europe as a way of holding his party together – rather as David Cameron was to do forty years later. The choice was whether or not to remain in the European Union, which we had joined two years earlier. 'Yes' to stay in; 'No' to get out. The big beasts in Wilson's Cabinet were deeply split. The Home Secretary, the claret-loving Europhile Roy Jenkins, led the majority of Yes ministers; the teetotal Tony Benn, the controversial left-wing Industry Secretary, led the significantly smaller group of dissenters.

The No ministers, who included Barbara Castle at Health and Michael Foot at Employment, were out of the blocks straight away on the day Wilson announced the referendum date. At a joint press conference, Benn said they were campaigning for 'Britain's independence day', the exact phrase Boris Johnson was to use four decades on.

To start with in the 1975 referendum, two thirds of the public wanted us out, but by end the figures were exactly reversed. So how did this remarkable transformation come about? I made a number of films during the referendum campaign which told a tragi-comic tale of high politics and low cunning that yoked together the strangest of bedfellows. Behind the scenes, supporters of the Yes vote had been at work preparing for the referendum campaign since Harold Wilson's surprise general election victory in February 1974. The penthouse of the Dorchester Hotel in Mayfair was their top-secret headquarters.

'We had to have somewhere to meet that was private and confidential,' the millionaire businessman Alistair McAlpine, who became treasurer of the Yes campaign, told me. 'My family owned the Dorchester and so I had some sway with the management.'

Pro-Market politicians from the left and right, who were normally dedicated political opponents, along with sympathetic industrialists would be discreetly summoned. 'Somebody would telephone you and say could you come to breakfast on Tuesday at the Dorchester?' remembered Bill Rodgers, then a Labour minister. 'You never quite knew who was going to turn up,' said McAlpine. 'It was a melange of people who wouldn't have wanted to sit down together in a public restaurant.'

Douglas Hurd, Ted Heath's former political secretary who had become a Tory MP, told me: 'At the Dorchester breakfasts were a mix of people from all parties who were united by a common idea – to keep Britain in Europe.'

'They were very good breakfasts,' said McAlpine. 'Kidneys, sausages, bacon, scrambled egg, kippers, all that kind of thing, laid out on a big buffet. The point of the buffet was we didn't have any waiters in the room, so no one could hear what we were plotting – it was all good plotting stuff. It had to be confidential as we were planning the strategy about who we were going to influence and how we were going to fight the campaign.'

'It was a world away from draughty Labour Party committee rooms, soft biscuits and the milky brown concoctions that passed for tea,' said Rodgers. 'If this was the way politics was going to be, it was a very attractive way of doing things. And it was this personal contact which made the difference, and we built the Yes organisation.'

'Of course we didn't know each other very well to start with,' says Hurd. 'And there was a slightly daring feel about working together with people who were normally your political enemies. It was rather like tiptoeing into a brothel; you felt that you were doing something which might or might not be pleasant but was certainly rather risqué.'

For some time the opinion polls had been showing the anti-Marketeers in the lead, but as the campaign started it was clear that there was nothing like a balance of power and resources between the two opposing sides. The 'Keep Britain in Europe' campaign was well staffed, well funded, well organised and consisted of like-minded people from the centre ground of the three main parties. The Nos came largely from the left wing of the Labour Party, the right wing of the Tories, the Welsh, Scottish and Ulster Nationalists and the far fringes beyond – from the National Front to the Communist Party. A number of these groupings were sworn enemies of each other and refused to share a platform together.

The No campaign's umbrella organisation was run on a shoe-string and began life operating out of two small rooms in an attic off the Strand. Its organiser was Marie-Louise Marten, the 22-year-old daughter of Neil Marten, a veteran Tory anti-Market MP. She told me: 'I got rather thrown in the deep end and told in no uncertain terms to go and set up and equip the whole office and be really quick about it. It was quite daunting. I had a terribly small budget and I remember scuttling off to a second-hand furniture place on the Commercial Road in the East End and buying everything for as little as I could possibly spend.'

The well-heeled Yes campaign had no such problems. Alistair McAlpine told me: 'I was able to help them get what they needed. I said to them I've found 10,000 square feet you can have for six weeks – for nothing. I've found fifty desks and I've got a guy who can give us thirty typewriters.'

After its months of meticulous planning, the Yes campaign emerged publicly at the Dorchester. Sharing the launch plat-form with the Labour Home Secretary Roy Jenkins were the Tory deputy leader Willie Whitelaw and Jo Grimond, the former Liberal leader. Jenkins told me afterwards: 'To see pol-iticians of different parties sitting and working together was a pleasant shock for the public. Also we looked like good solid men who had been well fed by the resources of the common agricultural policy.'

When I filmed at the Yes campaign HQ, I saw graphic evi-dence of the disparity in funding between the two campaigns. In an office crowded with young enthusiasts, the Sloaney figure of Caroline de Courcey Ireland told me how she was organising plane-loads of pro-European speakers from all parties across the country to be flown over for briefings in Brussels by top-level Eurocrats. 'We chartered a series of 100-seater jet planes from British Caledonian airlines – and all those nice little girls in their kilts. We took nearly 1,000 people in all.'

And where, I later asked her, had the money come from? 'From the European Commission: it was a sort of special dispensation. I don't know how they fixed it, because one didn't ask too much. I just said: "Thank you very much" and got on with organising it.'

That fact was not known at the time. But it was known that big business in Britain was overwhelmingly pro-European. 'When the campaign started, money rolled in,' McAlpine told me. 'The banks and the big industrial companies put in very large sums of money.' And what about the idea that you could be seen as fat cats who wanted to stay in Europe, I asked him. 'We were the fat cats. But we were the intelligent cats. The cats who knew about the economy. We were the cats who were warning the public that if they took us out of the Common Market, they'd be out of work: the economy would collapse.'

The fact that leading anti-Marketeers included such figures as Enoch Powell, Tony Benn and Dr Ian Paisley played into the hands of the pro-Europeans. 'What did those individuals have in common?' said Douglas Hurd. 'They were all in a literal sense "eccentric" – outside the centre of things.'

McAlpine was less oblique: 'The whole thrust of our campaign was to depict the anti-Marketeers as unreliable people, dangerous people who would lead you down the wrong path. It wasn't so much that it was sensible to stay in but that anybody who proposed that we came out was off their rocker or virtually Marxist.'

I put this to Tony Benn, saying that opinion polls at the time all gave a negative rating to the leading No campaigners like himself and Powell, while the Yes men all had a positive rating. 'Media coverage,' he responded. 'If you haven't got a single newspaper supporting you, you don't expect good coverage. It's quite straightforward – nothing strange about it.'

Benn had a point. As the campaign got into its stride it became clear that, almost without exception, the press favoured Britain staying in, including the *Daily Mail*, the *Daily Telegraph* and Rupert Murdoch's *The Sun*. The only notable anti-Market papers were the communist *Morning Star* along with *The Spectator* and the *Dundee Courier*.

With the press stacked against them, the No campaign put a great premium on television. As in a general election, the two sides had their own series of broadcasts. Again, the disparity was obvious. The Yes broadcasts used the new techniques of filming their star speakers on location with hand-held cameras. They wanted to counter their elitist image. 'We would film people protesting directly to our speakers,' said Justin Cartwright – later to become a celebrated novelist – who worked on the Yes broadcasts. 'But of course we would trump them in the cutting room by giving our speakers the final say.'

The broadcasts, which went out simultaneously across the three existing TV channels, would attract audiences of up to

20 million people. Shirley Williams, a Europhile Cabinet minister, said: 'The sheer liveliness and the tremendously close relationship – almost a physical touching of the politicians by the people crowding round them – is an image you never see any more.'

In contrast, the Nos were restricted to studio broadcasts presented by two political journalists – Paul Johnson and Patrick Cosgrave – reading sternly from an autocue. Johnson told me that the No campaign excluded Benn from their broadcasts, fearing he would alienate undecided voters. But as the opinion polls steadily turned against the Nos, Benn decided to up the ante. He used his authority as Industry Minister to make a headline-grabbing claim: 'Half a million jobs lost in Britain and a huge increase in food prices as a direct result of our entry into the Common Market.'

These claims earned a magisterial rebuke from his Cabinet colleague Roy Jenkins. 'I'm afraid I find it increasingly difficult to take Mr Benn seriously as an Economic Minister. The technique is just to think of a number and double it, and if challenged you just react by thinking up some new claim of what you've read.'

The press gleefully took up Benn-baiting, with the *Daily Mirror* labelling him 'The Minister of Fear' and other papers depicting him as 'dangerous', 'devious', 'fanatical' and 'lunatic'. When I asked Benn for his reaction to being so personally targeted, he said: 'All the party leaders, all the money and all the newspaper proprietors were determined to get a "Yes" vote and destroy anyone who took a contrary view. Full stop.'

Harold Wilson had made the unprecedented decision to suspend collective Cabinet responsibility and allow his ministers to campaign publicly against each other. I made a film about what was called the battle for the soul of the Labour Party that was going on within the referendum campaign. (Only forty years on I was to make a comparable film about the battle for the soul of the Tory Party – insofar as it had one – between David Cameron and Boris Johnson in the 2016 referendum.) When I asked Roy Jenkins in 1976 what effect he thought Wilson's decision would have on the unity of the Labour Party and the Cabinet, he replied in his characteristic drawl: 'I do hope this whole wefewendum campaign can be conducted without any wancour on either side.' The sound recordist had to stifle a fit of giggles.

Tony Benn was not best pleased by my soul of the Labour Party film. In a speech to a packed meeting of fervent anti-Marketeers, he said: 'Did you see that film by Michael Cockerell on the BBC last night? There it was dripping with distortion from every frame.' Prolonged cheers. I felt obscurely proud. Since there are twenty-four frames to every second of film, it would have been a Sisyphean task to hand-paint distortion into every one of them.

Benn had watched my film go out at his home in Notting Hill with other No campaigners. One of them told me that when the film ended Benn pulled a miniature Dictaphone from his top pocket and dictated to it: 'Memo to my private office, remind me never, repeat never, to talk to Michael Cockerell again.' Happily for me, he was on the telephone the following week asking if I could get him a recording of a programme that had nothing to do with the referendum – which I did. And we were to have many spiky interviews over the following years.

Meanwhile, the Conservative Party was overwhelmingly pro-Market, with 90 per cent of its MPs in favour of a Yes vote. Their new leader, Margaret Thatcher, had at first seemed so unwilling to come out publicly on the issue that Harold Wilson labelled her 'the reluctant debutant'. Although the wounds of the Tory leadership contest between herself and Ted Heath were still raw, the new and old leaders agreed to share a vote Yes platform together.

'Naturally it is with some temerity that the pupil speaks before the master,' said Mrs Thatcher as Heath looked up at her on the podium. The view of Europe she then articulated could be summed up in three words – 'Yes, yes, yes.' And she said in a TV interview afterwards: 'I think it's absolutely vital that people should turn out in this referendum and vote for us to stay in Europe, so that the question is settled once and for all.' On the eve of the referendum vote, Mrs Thatcher wore a specially knitted jumper which featured the flags of the then nine EU nations. And she said she wanted 'a splendid and decisive Yes vote which would prevent future wars in Europe'.

In his last speech of the campaign, Roy Jenkins said: 'For Britain to withdraw from Europe would be to retire into an old people's home for fading nations. I do not think it would be a very comfortable old people's home,' he added sharply. 'I do not like the look of some of the wardens.'

When the votes were counted forty-five years ago, it was clear the well-oiled Yes machine had succeeded in dramatically transforming public opinion – the Remainers won by an unassailable 67–33 per cent majority. Jenkins hailed a day of satisfaction and jubilation.

Years later, I asked Tony Benn how he saw the 1975 referendum now. 'You have to make your case, and sometimes you win, sometimes you lose. But in the sense that Margaret Thatcher came round to my view, Rupert Murdoch came round to my view, it wasn't unsuccessful, was it?'

The Prime Minister, Harold Wilson, had played an uncharacteristically low-profile role in the campaign, limiting himself to a couple of speeches. And the following spring he astonished the political world by suddenly announcing his resignation. He had been party leader for thirteen years – nearly eight of them as PM. He had grown tired in the job, and the viewers had grown tired of him. It is what television schedulers call 'the wear-out factor'. He quit No. 10, telling me in an interview: 'My trouble is I keep seeing the same old problems coming round over and over again – and all I can think of are the same old answers.' As it turned out in the Labour leadership election that followed, Harold Wilson – like Anthony Eden before him – had retired to make way for an older man.

Reporting for BBC TV in the February 1974 general election.

Me on the grass aged fourteen in Labour's Fabian Society cricket team. Back row third from left, Bill Rodgers, and to his left, Roy Jenkins. At end of row, the scorer, Gerald Kaufman.

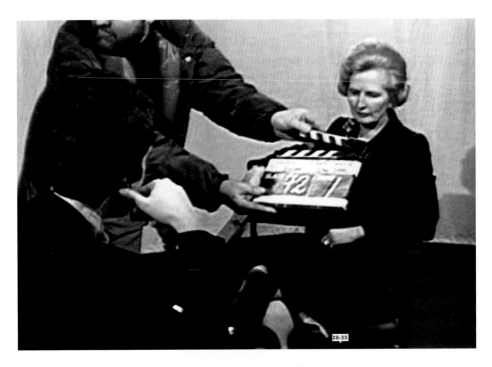

Interviewing Margaret Thatcher in 1975, on the night she wins the Tory leadership.

On Mrs Thatcher's battle bus with her husband Denis in the 1979 general election. I'm top left.

Me in the *Panorama* cutting room in Lime Grove with long-serving film editor Ian Callaway.

Outside Conservative Central Office in the 1983 general election with Mrs Thatcher's dapper image-maker, Gordon Reece. © Judah Passow

I have just asked the German Chancellor Helmut Schmidt whether he thinks the new Prime Minister will be 'a soft touch' over Europe.

After ten years in power, Mrs Thatcher tells me in No. 10 she is not immortal.

CHAPTER 11

NOT SO SUNNY JIM

At the age of sixty-four, Jim Callaghan was four years older than Harold Wilson, whom he succeeded into No. 10. By 1976, I had become *Panorama*'s main political reporter and made a fast turnaround film about Callaghan and later a full-length TV biography. Callaghan was the first and to date only Prime Minister to have held all three of the other great offices of state: Chancellor, Home Secretary and Foreign Secretary. Though he traded on a genial public image as 'Uncle Jim', this was flavoured with a dash of menace.

I remember my first confrontation with Callaghan four years before he became PM. He was shadow Foreign Secretary and the question of a referendum over Europe was splitting the Labour Party. I telephoned to invite him on to a late-night TV political programme. He promised to get back to me and thirty minutes later rang to decline, saying he would prefer to be in bed at that time. I said I quite understood and would book someone else. 'No,' said Callaghan. 'You can have my deputy.' I said that was kind but just as he had a perfect right to decline an invitation, I had the right to choose the person I wanted to appear. His tone became intimidating: 'You don't seem to understand, Mr Cockerell – I have arranged it with my deputy and spent some time briefing him on the subject.'

I still demurred and said I had someone else in mind who, unlike his deputy, had actually already been a Cabinet minister. He turned up the heat: 'If you value your career in the BBC and you want to go further, Mr Cockerell, I suggest you have my deputy on your programme. Remember, I know some very influential people.'

I was taken aback. This man had by then been both Chancellor and Home Secretary and was a leading contender to No. 10, so it was not without trepidation that I declined the offer – and I never heard any more. Who knows? I might have become Director-General had I agreed. But Callaghan didn't seem to bear a grudge. Years later, when I was making the film about his life, I asked him about what I called his bullying. He chuckled: 'I never like to bully people who can't answer back. I only believe in bullying people like you, who are my equals and can stand up for themselves.' But I was not remotely your equal, I protested; I was a very junior producer, and you were a very senior political figure. 'Yes,' he replied, 'but you went to university, didn't you? And I never did.'

Bernard Donoughue, who had stayed in No. 10 as a close adviser to the new PM, told me of Callaghan's non-attendance at university: 'This mattered only because Jim felt it did. And he thought that was why his parliamentary colleagues did not rate him at his true worth.'

Unlike most other Labour leaders, Callaghan had come not from the professional middle classes but from a poor working-class background. His father, a naval petty officer, had died of wounds he had received in the First World War when Callaghan was nine. He and his mother, who had no money, lived in a series of Portsmouth boarding houses. 'Sometimes all I had to eat was bread and dripping and a cup of cocoa made with water,' Callaghan told me. He left school at seventeen to become a clerk in the Inland Revenue and then worked for the tax collectors' trade union. It was the start of a lifelong devotion to the trade union movement. He had also become a staunch Labour supporter after the party's first government in 1924 introduced widows' pensions, which provided his mother with an income.

During the Second World War, when Callaghan became a naval lieutenant, he decided to go into politics. In 1945, he stood for Labour in Cardiff South. He was up against the Tory Colonel Sir Arthur Evans, who had held the seat for twenty years. Callaghan told me: 'Arthur Evans had a lady friend from Penarth who used to come and sit on the platform with him at his election meetings. He was married and our lads would go and stand at the back of the hall and when he got up to speak, they would burst into song: "Hello, hello, who's your lady friend? Who's the little girlie by your side?" Poor Arthur Evans – he didn't have a chance.'

Callaghan won comfortably in the Labour landslide and was to hold his Cardiff seat for the next four decades. As an MP, he built up a power base in his party through his close contacts with union leaders and became known as 'the keeper of the cloth cap'. He was also an early political star of radio and TV, with the press praising his 'chin-thrusting fluency'.

In the Commons, Callaghan developed skills as a party manager, and though still quite young he began to be seen as a wise old bird. The Labour MP Brian Walden said: 'Jim let it be known that he wasn't a man for new-fangled, complicated theories. Nothing la-di-da about him, plain common sense was his forte. Son-of-the-soil type. And Jim had no vices. Devoted to his wife and family, he didn't chase women and he didn't get drunk. Obviously a stable, dependable, judicious type, with his finger on the nation's pulse.'

So who better to take over the reins at No. 10 when Wilson suddenly resigned in April 1976? To his satisfaction, Jim Callaghan beat five Oxford-educated rivals – Roy Jenkins, Denis Healey, Tony Benn, Michael Foot and Anthony Crosland – in the MPs' ballot for the Labour leadership and became Prime Minister. Wilson had bequeathed him a government without a majority in Parliament and an economy in dire straits. It required all Callaghan's formidable political skills just to cling on to office.

'The first two people I saw when I became Prime Minister once I'd appointed the new Cabinet', Callaghan told me, 'were the governor of the Bank of England and Jack Jones, the general secretary of the Transport and General Workers' Union. And what I heard made my hair stand on end.' Callaghan discovered his legacy was a country that seemed to be heading fast towards bankruptcy, with inflation at 30 per cent and sterling in crisis yet again. He applied to the International Monetary Fund (IMF) for a huge loan. But the IMF's demand for swingeing cuts in public spending in return threatened to bring down the government, with both the Cabinet and the party bitterly split. The left, led by Tony Benn, favoured a siege economy and telling the IMF to get lost; other ministers across the spectrum, including the Chancellor Denis Healey on the right, all had their own pet schemes for some kind of negotiated settlement with the fund.

Callaghan, an avid student of Labour history, told me he feared becoming another Ramsay MacDonald. In Labour mythology, MacDonald, the party's first Prime Minister, had gone down as a traitor: his head having been turned by society hostesses like Lady Londonderry, in 1931 he sold out his party to the bankers. 'I'm a child of 1931,' Callaghan told me. 'I was just coming to manhood at that time, and I saw how MacDonald's government broke up. And during the IMF crisis I thought it would be too difficult to get an agreement; I thought we might even have a 1931 situation. I was determined to avoid it.'

To hold his Cabinet together, Callaghan held an unprecedented number of Cabinet meetings – eight in twelve days – where he gave each of his ministers the chance to put forward their own plans and be questioned by their fellows. In the end, they reached a compromise – and not a single minister resigned. It was seen as a triumph of Cabinet management.

In fact, Callaghan had already come to believe in the necessity for deep public spending cuts. He told me: 'I used the IMF as a convenient screen. Some people would put it the other way and say we were just creatures in the hands of the IMF. In fact, as far as I was concerned the IMF was a very useful creature for me to get through the cuts in public expenditure that we needed.'

The IMF agreed to lower slightly its demand for cuts, and things started to look up for the economy after the loan was agreed. But the following spring canny Callaghan suffered an uncharacteristic self-inflicted wound. He came up with the shock appointment of the financial journalist and TV presenter Peter Jay to the top diplomatic post of British ambassador in Washington, where Jimmy Carter had just become President. Jay had worked in the Treasury but was not a diplomat; he was, however, married to the Prime Minister's daughter Margaret. The press made a meal of it with headlines like 'The son-in-law also rises' amid colourful charges of blatant nepotism.

An ill-judged lobby briefing from Callaghan's press secretary, Tom McCaffrey, only made matters worse. He suggested that the forty-year-old Jay would be a breath of fresh air compared to Peter Ramsbotham, the rather older man he was replacing. McCaffrey implied Ramsbotham was an out-of-touch, superior Old Etonian career diplomat. The two London evening papers came up with the same headline: 'Snob envoy had to go'.

Callaghan told me that the idea of sending Jay to Washington had come from the 38-year-old Dr David Owen, the man whom he had made the youngest Foreign Secretary since Anthony Eden in 1935. Owen had asked for Jay to become ambassador as he was the ideal man to get on with the newly elected President Carter and his youthful Georgian advisers. 'I at once reacted negatively,' said Callaghan. 'Everyone knew Peter's great ability, but he was my son-in-law and I could imagine how malicious tongues would wag.' The PM told Owen to go away and think again.

Callaghan dismissed the matter from his mind, but some six weeks later Owen came back saying he had looked everywhere and was sure that Jay was the man for the job. The PM recalled that when he became Labour's Chancellor in 1964, Peter Jay had been a high-flyer at the Treasury. But Jay had felt compelled to resign just as he was in line to receive one of the best postings in the institution. Callaghan told me he thought it would be unfair to deprive Jay of a second plum job 'just because he was my son-in-law, when David Owen clearly wanted him on his merits. So I agreed.'

Peter and Margaret Jay became a power couple in Washington despite what Callaghan described as a 'constant trickle of criticism of Jay's appointment, some of it motivated by envy'. Jay agreed to let us film his first months in the embassy. He told me of the revealing conversation he'd had with his father-in-law before he had flown to DC: 'The Prime Minister put it to me as we walked the white cliffs overlooking the English Channel that he saw his role as being like that of Moses: to lead the people away from the fleshpots of Egypt and into the desert and in the direction of the promised land.' Ambassador Jay seemed surprised when I told him what a gift I thought this imagery would be for the cartoonists, the media and the opposition in Britain.

Jay told me that he had appointed his wife as a 'co-ambassador' to take over some of the heavy burden of his work. While we were filming, the co-ambassadors invited us to have tea on the terrace of their luxurious Lutyens residence – with its impressive grounds, swimming pool and tennis court. Jay asked me and my mischievously creative producer, Clive Syddall, about how we were making our film. He said: 'I can't understand it – you seem to be going round the embassy and if you find something or someone that interests you, you just film it. But when I worked as presenter of *Weekend World*, I would write the whole script in advance and we would send a producer and cameraman to get pictures to cover my words.'

At that moment, Margaret Jay chipped in and said: 'And that's why the films on your programme were always so fucking boring, Peter.' We all laughed – the ambassador rather less than the rest of us, as he and his ITV colleague John Birt saw themselves as TV gurus. And I thought maybe this is not, as billed, the happiest marriage in Christendom.

While we were filming at the embassy, the opposition leader, Mrs Thatcher, came on a visit to Washington. At the press conference afterwards, she praised the ambassador, who had preceded her and Jim Callaghan as a convert to monetarism. I asked the Tory leader: 'Since you seem to get on so well, if you become Prime Minister will you keep Peter Jay on as Our Man in Washington?' There was a collective sharp intake of breath, and Mrs T smiled sweetly and said: 'Oh, Peter and I are great friends. I've been an economic disciple of his for years.' So is that a yes? I asked. 'When I become Prime Minister, I will keep my options open. It's a good socialist and Conservative phrase, *n'est-ce pas?*' Mrs Thatcher replied, turning diplomatically to Jay.

Back in Britain, Jim Callaghan was now facing major challenges from the very people he had spent his career defending and promoting: the trade unions. After the IMF settlement, their leaders had agreed with the government to keep wage demands down to 5 per cent. But the agreement had ended, and Callaghan wanted to persuade the union leaders to sign up to a new 5 per cent deal.

Callaghan's economics private secretary, Tim Lankester, told me the moment he realised the policy was doomed was at a meeting in the Cabinet Room between Callaghan and the leaders of the most powerful trade unions in the country. 'At one point,' said Lankester, 'Moss Evans, the leader of the Transport and General Workers' Union, banged the table with his fist and announced: "Jim, it's your job to get inflation down to 2 per cent; it's mine to get an 18 per cent rise for my members." I was the only civil servant present and I was sitting next to Callaghan. He looked at me and rolled his eyes as if to say: "We might as well give up."'

It was the start of the 'Winter of Discontent', a series of highly damaging strikes by public-sector unions. They were a head-on challenge to Callaghan's key selling point. As 'the keeper of the cloth cap', he was meant to be the man who could handle the unions, whereas, it was claimed, if Mrs Thatcher became Prime Minister, there would be industrial chaos.

Yet now there was chaos under Callaghan – with the dead left unburied, ambulances unmanned and the uncollected rubbish piling up in the streets to the delight of the rats. And Callaghan made it worse. As Britain froze under snow and sleet, he flew to an international summit meeting in Guadeloupe, where he was photographed swimming in the Caribbean close to a bikinied blonde (whom he had not, in fact, ever seen before). Then at a televised airport press conference on his return to England, the PM played down the effects of the strikes, telling journalists: 'Do you know I actually had a swim? I know you think that's the most important thing that happened, but you mustn't allow jealousy to get in the way.'

So what did he think, asked a reporter from *The Sun*, about the 'mounting chaos' in the country? 'Perhaps you are taking a rather parochial view,' responded Callaghan. 'I don't think that other people in the world would share the view there is mounting chaos.' Callaghan's political adviser, Tom McNally, told me he stood just behind, watching his boss's performance with a growing sense of gloom: 'Jim Callaghan was coming over as a guy back from sunny climes who wasn't even sure that the streets weren't being de-iced in Oldham or people buried in Liverpool.'

The Sun's famous headline next day was 'Crisis – what crisis?' Not words that Callaghan had actually used, but McNally, whom Callaghan called his 'mine detector', felt it was a fair paraphrase: 'That was the impression Jim gave. His mind was still full of summitry – international disarmament and the whole future of mankind – while Fleet Street had been trying to get a picture of him with a topless swimmer. The whole thing was a total disaster. Some commentators said we never recovered from it.'

Callaghan had built his career on his closeness to the trade unions. But now, when he needed them most, they turned on him. Or, as Brian Walden put it: 'Jim had spent his life polishing and sharpening the dagger that was about to be shoved into his back.'

When I asked Callaghan whether he felt betrayed by the trade union leaders he had spent a political lifetime supporting, he told me: 'I wouldn't use the word betrayed. I think that most of the trade union leaders certainly felt as deeply as I did about it. But they didn't have the capacity to lead. There was an air of madness which overtook people at that time, together with political inspiration by the militants and Trotskyites – no doubt about that – leading the rank-and-file followers.

'Some of the things that went on were quite disgraceful,' continued Callaghan. 'There was the refusal to bury the dead. There were the hospital workers who, immediately they put in a claim, turned off the heating boilers in the hospital. I was disgusted with the trade unionists who did that sort of thing. Mind you, they weren't real trade unionists. I mean, the kind of trade union atmosphere in which I was brought up would never have allowed that kind of thing to happen.'

Roy Jenkins had served with Callaghan in the Commons for three decades, including eight years in Labour Cabinets, and was one of the five Oxford-educated contenders Callaghan had beaten in the race to become Prime Minister. Jenkins always liked to identify qualities that would take a man to the very top, and he said to me of Callaghan: 'There is no other case I can think of in history where a man combined such a powerful personality with so little intellect.'

But when I put to Callaghan Jenkins's characterisation of him, Sunny Jim had the last laugh: 'I don't know how clever I was. A lot of people think I'm not clever at all, although I think I was probably cleverer than they thought I was. And it's true I haven't got a huge intellect. But then again, I became Prime Minister – and they didn't.'

As he was fighting the 1979 general election, which I was covering, the PM said: 'There are times, perhaps once every thirty years, when there is a sea change in British politics. I suspect there is now such a change – and it is for Mrs Thatcher.'

CHAPTER 12

MAGGIE, MAGGIE, MAGGIE

When she fought the 1979 general election campaign against Jim Callaghan, Margaret Thatcher was determined to counter Labour's charges that she was dogmatic and uncaring. In an interview with me during the campaign, she assumed a kittenish persona. I put it to her that there sometimes seemed to be two Mrs Thatchers: one toured supermarkets and factory floors, exhibiting endless fascination about the minutiae of people's lives and jobs; the other was the platform politician, full of passionate conviction.

'How many Mrs Thatchers are there?' I asked. She smiled and replied confidingly: 'Oh, there are three at least. There is the intellectual one, the intuitive one, and there's the one at home.' Her voice was so low and breathy, her manner so intimate – even coquettish – that the late Robin Day, watching in the studio when the filmed interview went out, joked: 'The untold story of the election campaign: Margaret Thatcher is having an affair with Michael Cockerell.'

Although she was to rise totally against the odds to become one of the country's most formidable prime ministerial performers, in her early days as opposition leader it was not like that at all. According to *The Times*, she came over on TV 'with all the charisma of a privet hedge'. But from the outset Mrs Thatcher was concerned not to become a casualty of the cameras. She knew that her predecessor Ted Heath's unappealing TV manner had helped to bring him down. And at first the new Tory leader would react to the sight of a TV crew almost in the manner of a superstitious tribesman faced with a white man's camera – it was as if she thought it might somehow take her soul away.

She appointed as her media adviser a diminutive *bon viveur* called Gordon Reece. He was a former TV producer and advertising man who looked rather like Ronnie Corbett. 'Gordon runs on champagne,' said one of his close colleagues. He also smoked huge Havana cigars. Mrs T later knighted him for services to her professional image.

Under his guidance, she underwent a complete makeover. At the time, she played down Reece's contribution. When I asked Mrs Thatcher during the 1979 general election campaign how important Reece was to her, she responded wide-eyed: 'Gordon Reece? Do you know I think he comes to me for advice not the other way round. And it's always been that way.'

Thatcher was being economical with the *actualité*. After she left office, she was more candid: 'Gordon was absolutely terrific. He said my hair and my clothes had to be changed and we would have to do something about my voice. It was quite an education, because I hadn't thought about these things before. He was a real professional.' And she quoted advice Reece had given her about what she should wear for TV: 'Avoid lots of jewellery near the face. Edges look good on television. Watch out for background colours which clash with your outfit.'

But Reece's focus group findings told him that while many voters welcomed the strength of her free-market convictions, on television she often came over as shrill, domineering and un-caring. Specifically, Mrs Thatcher's voice put people off – it was perceived as too high-pitched.

Reece arranged for a voice coach from the National Theatre to teach her techniques to lower her pitch. One was to practise humming; the other was to keep repeating the sound 'ngakok-ka'. And Reece would bring a microphone to rehearsals before her radio and television appearances so she could practise being just the right distance from it. He told Mrs Thatcher to get as close as she could to it as it would make her voice sound 'more sexy, confidential and reasonable'. I asked Mrs Thatcher about her new voice and she said: 'When you ask me a question, I say to myself "think low".' I wasn't sure whether or not that was a comment on my interview technique.

Reece also taught her to stop worrying and love the boom microphone. He told her that recorded snippets of her conver-sation when she met the public would make her sound more down-to-earth and in touch with voters. In later years she could never see a microphone without offering some seemingly spon-taneous comments to people she met – whether it was another political leader or someone in a factory or hospital – knowing that TV people cannot resist 'natural sound'.

But there were some things Mrs Thatcher would never say

on camera. When we filmed her visiting the British Embassy in Washington, the ambassador Peter Jay asked: 'What would you like to drink?' She made no reply but out of sight of the camera wrote a brief note to the ambassador. I retrieved it afterwards and it read: 'Whisky and soda'. The PM in waiting was certainly not going to be filmed asking for one, still less drinking it.

Reece also arranged for Mrs Thatcher to appear on TV programmes that were outside the standard round of news and current affairs. In 1977, as opposition leader she agreed to appear on *Jim'll Fix It*, starring the late and unlamented Jimmy Savile and a group of children who had asked him to fix for them to meet Mrs Thatcher. On air, one little girl announced that her ambition was also to become Prime Minister. 'Wonderful, two generations,' enthused the Tory leader. 'My dear, we must keep in touch and get the next fifty years sorted out together.

'When I was small,' Mrs Thatcher continued, 'I didn't think there ever could be a woman Prime Minister. But, Jimmy, we hope you're going to fix it for me.'

'I already have done so privately,' Savile responded, 'but I didn't want everyone to know.'

When, at the time, Tory critics claimed that Mrs Thatcher's appearance on the programme was demeaning, Gordon Reece responded: 'Rubbish. I simply encourage her to appear everywhere she can to the best advantage. It's the most ludicrous intellectual snobbery to say that a politician shouldn't appear on general interest programmes because the viewers are supposed to be on a lower level of humanity than the people who watch

Panorama. They have votes too and if she talked down to them they would soon rumble her.'

Savile himself was to become one of Mrs Thatcher's regular Christmas guests at Chequers. And she gave him a knighthood for his services to charity – even though her Cabinet Secretary Robert Amstrong had warned her against it: 'I don't like the smell or feel of it.' Her appearance on *Jim'll Fix It* along with all Savile's other shows – including two more with Mrs Thatcher – have been consigned to the BBC's 'dark vault', never to be seen publicly again.

By the time I filmed behind the scenes during her 1979 general election campaign, Mrs Thatcher had become very media savvy. Reece had introduced the photo opportunity, beloved of American presidential hopefuls, into British elections. Until 1979, no previous aspirant to No. 10 had given an election campaign press conference clutching a two-day-old calf in a meadow. When I asked her about it at the time, she replied: 'The press said they did not want a picture of me with a load of, er, bullocks. There was this tiny calf. The photographers have their job to do, and I am very conscious of that.' Her husband Denis, watching his wife, muttered: 'If she's not careful, we'll have a dead calf on our hands, which won't go down too well, I imagine.'

I went on to ask the Tory leader whether she had any doubts about her ability to fulfil the role of Prime Minister. 'Well,' she said, 'I look at some of the other people who've held the job, and I really... Of course you have doubts. Of course you have doubts. And you're tremendously aware of the responsibility.

But I haven't just come to this out of the blue. In British politics you don't just go from the bottom to the top, you climb your way up the ladder.'

For someone who was to become such an imperious Prime Minister, it was a fascinating admission which was in stark contrast to her Iron Lady rhetoric.

But what about those men, many of them in her own party, who couldn't accept the idea of a female Prime Minister? 'I know that one or two men are prejudiced,' she replied. 'But after all their prejudice is *so, so* ridiculous; that doesn't deal with it. No argument will deal with prejudice. But some people are prejudiced. I say to some of them sometimes: "You know it's a good thing you didn't live in the time of Queen Elizabeth I, isn't it?" After all, I wonder if we should have grown to such a fantastic nation if we hadn't had people like her. And of course look at Golda Meir in Israel, a woman Prime Minister during Israel's most difficult years. And she was *marvellous*. I can put all these arguments. But I know you can never deal with a prejudice by argument.

'I just hope that they will take me, as I am, for what I can do. Not as man or woman, but as a personality, who has an absolute passion for getting things right for Britain. I can't *bear* Britain in decline. I just can't. We who either defeated or rescued half Europe, who kept half Europe free, when otherwise it would be in chains. And look at us now. I just hope they'll look at that and say: "Does it matter whether it's a man or a woman? Isn't it just best to get it right?"'

I then asked Mrs Thatcher, why did you say that you will not be given another chance if you lose this general election? 'Oh,' she replied, 'there's only one chance for women. 'Tis the law of life.'

But she of course won the 1979 election with a comfortable majority of forty-three. The first female Prime Minister in the Western world came to power with no direct experience of foreign affairs. She brought with her a fierce hatred of communism, which led the Soviet newspaper *Red Star* to label her the Iron Lady. When she was first told about it, she said: 'Oh, that's awful.' But her spinmeister Gordon Reece felt it was the exact mix of strength and femininity that he was looking for, and he advised her to turn it to her advantage. From then on, in speeches she would say: 'The Russians said that I am an Iron Lady: Britain needs an Iron Lady.' The line always brought a lusty 'hear, hear' from her husband and enthusiastic applause from the faithful.

From her formative years during the Second World War, she had become immensely patriotic and developed a profound distrust of Germany. It was ironic therefore that within days of becoming Prime Minister her first official foreign visitor was Helmut Schmidt, the Social Democratic Chancellor of West Germany. He had months earlier accepted the invitation to come to Britain, thinking he would be meeting his fellow socialist Jim Callaghan.

'Why is he coming?' the new Tory Prime Minister complained to the Cabinet Secretary, Sir John Hunt. 'I didn't ask for it.' In her speech at a dinner in Downing Street on Schmidt's arrival, Mrs Thatcher warned that she would not be 'a soft touch' in

European matters. The following day, the two leaders emerged for a joint press conference – Mrs Thatcher's first media appearance since winning the election. I was sitting in the front row, and when she called me, I said: 'A question for the Federal Chancellor. Without wishing to appear indelicate, do you think Mrs Thatcher will be a soft touch?'

'I told you you'd get some difficult questions,' Mrs T said sotto voce to Schmidt.

'No, I don't think so,' he answered. 'And I guess she wouldn't consider the Germans to be a soft touch either.'

'Well done,' said the PM. 'There, does that satisfy you?' she asked me.

I persisted with the Chancellor. 'I just wondered if you thought you would achieve the same sort of personal relationship with Mrs Thatcher as you had with Jim Callaghan, whom you used to refer to as "my friend Jim" on occasions like this.'

Schmidt started to answer but Mrs Thatcher talked over him and said to me: 'Ah, but you are very, very aware that the policies that the Chancellor follows in Germany are not unlike the policies we have…'

Schmidt interjected: 'Don't go too far, Prime Minister.'

Riding the audience amusement, Mrs Thatcher continued: 'I mean we both believe in free enterprise. We both believe in incentives. And if we could emulate his tax system, I'm sure everyone here would stand up and cheer.'

Schmidt responded: 'Don't go too far, Prime Minister. And do not spoil my relations with my own party please.' Cue laughter both on the platform and in the packed hall at the revelation that Germans have a sense of humour.

Mrs Thatcher was to get on rather less well with the French President Valéry Giscard d'Estaing – even though he was a fellow conservative. He exuded a sense of Gallic superiority and claimed descent from King Louis XIV. I had made a film when Giscard first stood for the presidency. He was up against the socialist François Mitterrand and the Gaullist Jacques Chaban-Delmas. On the campaign trail, I asked Giscard about the fact there were two candidates of the right and noted that some people saw little difference between them. I said the current joke was that they might as well be called Valéry Chaban-d'Estaing and Jacques Giscard-Delmas. The real Giscard responded grandly (and this needs to be said in a posh French accent): 'I think that jokes, if they illuminate politics, may be funny. But this is neither funny nor illuminating.' The line was delivered with such hauteur that my producer, John Penycate, said afterwards he wished the floor would open and swallow him up.

Mrs Thatcher had something of the same experience with Giscard when she went to see him at the Élysée Palace on her first trip abroad as PM. The President laid on a luncheon for the UK's first female Prime Minister. Mrs Thatcher waited for her dinner to arrive and was surprised when Giscard was served before her. The President later said it was a question of protocol because he, unlike her, was a head of state and had to have precedence as he was 'in the line of sovereigns'. Mrs Thatcher had not been told in advance of the rule. 'Her lips tightened as she noticed,' said the British ambassador to France, Bryan Cartledge. 'Giscard was insufferable to her.' Mrs Thatcher felt insulted and said afterwards: 'Giscard was so [very long pause] *noble*.' Giscard later told Charles Moore, Mrs Thatcher's official biographer, what he had thought of the British Prime Minister: 'When our children were young, my family, being rather snobbish, employed an English nanny. She was very correct, very tidy and with a very neat hairdo. She was efficient, religious, always opening the windows especially when the children were ill – rather tiresome. Mrs Thatcher is exactly the same – *exactly* the same!'

For her part, Mrs Thatcher recounted what Giscard said to her when he came to Downing Street: 'I recall watching him in the dining room gazing at two portraits – one of Nelson and one of Wellington. Giscard remarked on the irony. I replied it was no more ironic than when I was in the Élysée having to look at portraits of Napoleon. In retrospect I can see this is not quite a parallel: Napoleon lost.'

For Mrs Thatcher's years in power, I was making films on national and international politics for *Panorama*. She was less than delighted with some of my efforts – none more so than the film I made about the Falklands War, which caused a major bust-up between the Prime Minister and the BBC.

CHAPTER 13

HAWKS AND DOVES

The Falklands War was to define Margaret Thatcher as the indomitable Iron Lady and help her win a huge landslide victory in the 1983 general election. My Falklands film, which was to cause such a storm, went out on *Panorama* the previous year, before our troops had landed and while the conflict in the South Atlantic was still unresolved.

When the news had come through in April 1982 that Argentina had invaded the Falklands, many people did not quite recognise how big a story it would become. According to Mrs Thatcher's daughter, Carol – who wrote a biography of her father – Denis Thatcher said: 'I remember looking at the *Times Atlas of the World* to find out where the bloody hell the Falklands were.' The Prime Minister herself knew she had to act strongly and speedily, otherwise, as she later put it, 'I wouldn't have been Prime Minister by the end of the day.'

The invasion of British territory by the Argentine junta had immediately aroused very strong emotions in Britain. As she set off the next day for an emergency debate – the first time the House had met on a Saturday since Suez – the Prime Minister was booed by some in the large crowd assembled at Downing Street. There were shouts: 'What are you waiting for?' 'Nuke them!' 'Go on Maggie. Get them back!'

The government had a two-pronged approach: Mrs Thatcher would speak softly but carry a big stick. Britain would aim at a negotiated settlement – but would use force if necessary. With remarkable speed, a large military task force was put together to sail 8,000 miles to the South Atlantic. At the same time, top diplomats from across the world sought to come up with a peace plan. The editor of *Panorama*, George Carey, asked me to make a film which would examine ways military conflict might be avoided.

According to the polls that was the position supported by some 30 per cent of the country. And the BBC's veteran political editor John Cole calculated that around a fifth of Tory MPs had reservations about government policy – which they would not voice publicly.

I talked to a number of Conservative MPs and ex-Cabinet ministers. Off the record many of them were sceptical and voluble about the whole venture. But almost all of them wanted to keep their doubts private. Just three Tory MPs agreed to talk on camera. One was Anthony Meyer, an Old Etonian baronet who as a Scots Guards officer had been wounded in the Normandy landings. The second was the MP for Canterbury, David Crouch, who had served in the war as a major in the Royal Artillery. The third dissenting Tory MP, the former government whip Robert Hicks, we dropped for reasons of time.

As we were making the film, with the task force steaming

south the divisions between the pro-war Hawks and the pro-peace Doves both in the Conservative Party and in the country were intensifying. Alan Clark, the Tory MP who was also a military historian, told us: 'The Hawks have more or less cornered the mass circulation dailies – the *Sun*, *Star*, *Express*, *Mail* and *Telegraph* – and have whipped up public fervour to a state unequalled since the Jameson Raid that began the Boer War. The Doves counter this by careful leaks and briefings from ministers and officials who had private doubts to the much smaller "quality press".'

By the time our programme was due to go out, the BBC was fast becoming the target for Hawkish Tory MPs. First in the firing line was the authoritative and amiable *Newsnight* presenter Peter Snow, who used the phrase 'British troops' rather than 'our troops', as well as saying 'if the British are to be believed' about Ministry of Defence briefings. On 9 May, the Tory MP Robert Adley claimed the BBC was becoming 'General Galtieri's fifth column in Britain'. The following night's *Panorama* seemed to many of his Tory colleagues to confirm Adley's view.

Our programme was called *Can We Avoid War?* It began with the presenter stressing that it would examine the minority view of those who had misgivings about a potential military solution. It then moved to New York and an interview with the Argentine representative to the UN about a potential negotiated settlement, which was subsequently seen by some as giving comfort to the enemy. It was followed by an interview with an English woman married to an Argentine and shots of her children singing Argentine songs.

Next came my film, which was clearly labelled a report on the minority view in Parliament. It included sections of my interviews with the two Tory MPs, David Crouch and Anthony Meyer, as well as interviews with two anti-war Labour MPs and extracts from speeches and interviews with Mrs Thatcher. Crouch said: 'I think the House was very impressed with the way the task force was marshalled so quickly, but whether we really appreciated the military detail of what was about to happen – I'm sure we didn't.' And he said about the Falklanders: 'They've all played their part as very, very loyal Britishers, we can't ignore that; but at the same time it just isn't reasonable to say that 1,800 people should determine our foreign and defence policy.'

Crouch accepted that we were standing on the great principles of defending our people, our territory and freedom itself. But he added: 'If the war goes on, it becomes escalated and bloody. I think that would be disastrous. We would lose so much support for our rightful aims and I believe that we may be judged to be standing on our dignity for a colonialist ideal.'

Anthony Meyer said he had supported the sending of the task force 'as the Argentine aggression was a very wicked thing to do and we were not going to accept what had happened without reacting very firmly'. He went on to say that he hoped the presence of the task force would get the necessary concessions without bloodshed. But, he said, if we were now planning 'to use force to kill a lot of people to ensure the Union Jack flies again in Port Stanley – I don't think that is justifiable.'

When I put it to Meyer that he was being defeatist, he replied:

'Well, once you get into a war situation anybody who says, "For God's sake, let's stop it" is labelled as defeatist. My experience in the 1939–45 war was no worse than anybody else, except that all my friends were killed. I saw the effect it had on their families and it left me with a horror of war which goes very, very deep. If our national survival is at stake, we have to fight. I'm not a disarmer or a unilateralist. If we are faced with the Russian threat, of course we fight. But anything short of that, I don't believe that killing can ever be the answer.'

I reported that a number of other Conservative MPs privately shared the doubts of Meyer and Crouch. The programme ended with a lengthy live studio interview. Cecil Parkinson, a member of the War Cabinet, put the government's case. He was also Conservative Party chairman and watched my film in the studio as it went out, but he did not comment on it in his interview.

Parkinson was relaxed and jovial in the hospitality room afterwards, but when he got back to the Commons that evening, he rang the *Panorama* editor and said: 'There's a bit of a stink going on down here at the Commons.' As the programme was going out, the BBC switchboard received some 300 calls, mainly from angry viewers complaining about the two Tory MPs. And some viewers suggested that those responsible for the programme should be taken out the next day and shot.

Dressed to go out to dinner, according to her press secretary Bernard Ingham, Mrs Thatcher watched the programme 'transfixed', seated on the edge of her armchair in the flat at No. 10. The next morning, the *Sun* headline read 'Storm at *Panorama*'s despicable Argie bias', while the *Daily Express* had a cartoon labelled 'Traitorama'. The right-wing Conservative MP Sir Bernard Braine, known as Braine of Britain, attacked the programme as 'enemy propaganda amounting to a sort of treachery'.

At the lobby briefing that morning, Bernard Ingham told political reporters of Mrs Thatcher's anger and that they should be sure to watch PMQs that afternoon. They were not disappointed. The former Conservative minister Sally Oppenheim (who I later discovered had long held a grudge against me, as she wrongly believed we had once deliberately filmed her from an unflattering angle) had polished her question: 'Will the Prime Minister take time off in the course of her busy day to watch a recording of last night's *Panorama*? Is she aware that for the most part it was an odious and subversive travesty in which Michael Cockerell and other BBC reporters dishonoured the right of freedom of speech in this country?'

The Prime Minister replied: 'I share the deep concern that has been expressed on many sides particularly about the content of yesterday's *Panorama* programme. I know how strongly many people feel that the case for our country is not being put with sufficient vigour in certain BBC programmes. The chairman of the BBC has assured us in vigorous terms that the BBC is not neutral on this point. And I hope his words will be heeded by the many who have responsibilities for standing up for our task force, our boys, our people and the cause of democracy.'

The chairman of the BBC was George Howard, the eponymous owner of Castle Howard, where ITV had filmed *Brideshead Revisited*. A colourful aristocrat with a penchant for wearing kaftans, Howard had also fought in the Second World

War, with the family regiment the Green Howards, and been wounded in Burma. He decided along with the newly appointed Director-General of the BBC, Alasdair Milne, that they should go to Westminster to try to assuage Tory feelings. They agreed to talk to a meeting of the Conservative backbench media committee, which they were told would be attended by at most twenty-five members. In fact, feelings were running so high that 125 MPs crowded into Committee Room 13.

It was a very hot and sticky night, and soon the bulky figure of Howard was sweating and mopping his brow. He began by saying he understood the depth of feeling among members, but he didn't believe the *Panorama* programme was a mistake and he would make no apology for it. At this the serried ranks of Tory MPs with one voice chorused: 'Shame, shame!' As Milne later told me, 'We were clearly in for it, and George's occasional tendency to perform like a great Whig grandee addressing his retainers was not helping.'

The two BBC men were met not with questions but accusations, as the meeting became ever more bitter and hostile. Milne later said: 'The first time I spoke they barked, "Can't hear you," so I said I'd speak up. It was like being in the Star Chamber.' One MP accused Anthony Meyer of treachery, said Milne, 'and then they got really angry. They started waving their order papers and growling like dogs.'

Howard raised hackles further when he claimed the BBC was trying to live up to its Second World War standards. This was too much for Winston Churchill MP, the grandson of the wartime Prime Minister, who declared: 'At least during the war the BBC did not see fit to give equal time to Dr Goebbels's propaganda machine.' Churchill went on to demand the sacking of the *Panorama* team, or at the very least the resignation of Howard and Milne.

As the two were getting up to leave, a young Tory MP approached Howard and hissed: 'You, sir, are a traitor!' The BBC chairman, who had a distinguished war record, jabbed a finger back at the MP and retorted: 'Stuff you!'

As MPs stalked out, Hector Munro, a former minister, observed: 'It was the ugliest meeting I have ever attended in all my twenty years as an MP.' And other MPs competed unattributably with colourful metaphors: 'The honourable members went for the BBC's throats'; 'George Howard was absolutely crucified'; 'He was roasted alive'; 'There was blood and entrails all over the place.'

After the meeting, the chairman and DG went for a discreet drink in the Commons room of the Home Secretary, Willie Whitelaw, who was a fellow landowner and very old friend of Howard. He was also a product of Winchester College, like Alasdair Milne. Over a much appreciated whisky, Whitelaw told the BBC bosses that the meeting had to have happened. It was 'a ritual bloodletting to allow the MPs to get it off their chests' – and, Whitelaw added, to save the BBC from a worse fate of a potential government takeover.

On the *Today* programme the following morning, George Howard said: 'When you recollect that 30 per cent of the population is not in favour of the government's policy, this ought from time to time to be looked at.' He also pointed out that the previous week's edition of *Panorama* had consisted of a single hour-long interview with the Prime Minister.

For Alasdair Milne, there was a strong feeling of *déjà vu*. Twenty-five years earlier, he had produced Anthony Eden's first Suez broadcast. And as controversy grew about Britain's invasion of Suez, he had seen the government attack the BBC and threaten to take over the Corporation. Milne said: 'I had always thought once the Falklands conflict began that the government would turn on the media – and particularly the BBC. It had come a little earlier than I thought, but with a ferocity I did not expect. Although with memories of Suez still vivid in my mind, perhaps I should have known better.'

Following the programme, I received a number of letters – some pro but many anti. The one that intrigued me most was written with a fountain pen, in an elegant hand on smart writing paper and postmarked SW1. It said: 'You snide bastard. We are sick and tired of you sitting in your cushy jobs and not having the decency to remember your duty as an Englishman. If you handled a programme like *Panorama* in Argentina the way you did, you would have disappeared off the face of the Earth. We want and expect patriotism and loyalty from our reporters in emergencies like this. You'd better watch it. We will be watching you, just as, thank God, Special Branch is.'

The letter was unsigned.

In the following Sunday's *Observer*, Julian Barnes saw things rather differently. He wrote: '*Panorama* examined the chance of a diplomatic solution, the voices of parliamentary dissent and Argentine reaction to the task force. Given the war hysteria in other parts of the media, this was a gratifyingly measured, original and unsensational programme in the best traditions of the BBC.'

My feeling was that our cardinal sin had been to interview two MPs from Mrs Thatcher's own party who had the temerity to voice their misgivings publicly about government policy. Though the programme had repeatedly made it clear the MPs were very much in the minority, it seemed to me that when 'Our Boys' go into harm's way, the first casualty is often the BBC – as Tony Blair's war in Iraq would once again demonstrate.

One Tory MP who might have been expected to join the chorus of outright condemnation of *Panorama* was the right-winger and military historian Alan Clark. Instead, he wrote in the *Washington Post* about the controversial programme: 'What the Conservative Party will not accept or forgive was the Corporation's attempt, under the pretence of objectivity, to get in and stir up the divisions of which most Conservatives are at the present time uncomfortably aware.' Alan Clark was to become the subject of one of the most jaw-dropping political profiles I ever made.

CHAPTER 14

LOVE TORY

Alan Clark was a throwback to an earlier type of politician. A mega-rich Etonian, he had inherited a castle full of old masters and impressionist paintings from his father Kenneth, the cultural panjandrum who became known as Lord Clark of Civilisation. Alan Clark was wealthy enough to live on what he called the income on his income and fostered the impression that he didn't give a damn what anyone thought of him. In fact, he was a creature of moods, often depressed, who would scour the media for mentions of his name. And he wrote the most revealing, outrageous and painfully funny political diaries of the twentieth century.

I discovered that throughout Clark's time at Westminster, the woman who mattered most to him (apart from his wife and his mistress of the month) was Margaret Thatcher. She reminded him of his own mother. 'My mother was a terrific lip-curler,' said Clark. 'I remember her saying to me when I was thirty, anyone who isn't married at that age has to be a pansy. That was just monstrous. She knew very well I wasn't a pansy. She was often very cruel. I didn't have any standard to compare her with until I sat round a Cabinet table with Mrs Thatcher – and then I saw a woman being as cruel to men as my mother was. That was quite a useful grounding, in a way; these are the women you want to prove yourself to.'

Against the advice of some of her senior Cabinet colleagues and officials, Mrs Thatcher kept Clark in her government for most of her time in office. 'I was in the loop,' he told me. As Minister for Trade and then as Minister for Defence, Clark used to attend Cabinet committees, and he had access and influence at the top. 'Margaret would always let me see her and she always listened. And if I rang her at Chequers or at No. 10, she would always take the call – and take it immediately. She allowed me what are called "liberties", in that I would say things sometimes that made everybody else in the room gasp and say, "Gosh, now he's really torn it – the conceited little shit. He's going to catch it this time" – but she did rather enjoy that.'

Clark was a notorious sexual swordsman. In the TV profile I made of him, which we called *Love Tory*, he talked about his serial infidelities, including one with three women – a mother and her two virgin daughters – whom he called the 'coven' and for which, he said, he deserved to be horse-whipped.

He agreed to us filming him watching clips that we had garnered of his earlier life – the technique that I'd often used before which tends to open people up. The first film we showed him was a newsreel – which he had never seen – of his wedding. It had been taken because his father was so famous. It was 1958.

Alan was thirty and was marrying Jane Beuttler, a colonel's daughter, who was just over half his age.

He was immediately captivated as he watched his slim bride emerge from her limousine: 'Oh, Jane looks absolutely lovely. I'm amazed at my luck in getting such a beautiful girl to marry me. Her dress is cut with a deliberately very, very narrow waist – because everybody assumed that we were getting married because she was pregnant, age sixteen. And we thought we'll jolly well show them otherwise.'

Clark continued: 'God, that's me! I do look a complete prat – what a dreadful man. And what a great waste of a beautiful girl. Jane has hardly changed at all in her appearance, her face. But mine is corroded by misdeeds and self-indulgence of every kind.'

Jane Clark had not intended to appear in the programme at all. But on the day we were due to film long interviews with her husband at Saltwood, the Norman castle in Kent where they lived, there was no sign of him. I said to Jane, 'Where's Alan?'

She replied, 'Oh, he stayed the night in London. *Seeing his publisher*,' saying it in a nod-and-wink voice – we know what that means.

'When's he going to be back?'

'Well, he said he might be here by lunchtime.'

So I said: 'Can we possibly film you?'

'No, no,' she said. 'It's Alan's show. I don't want to be in it.'

'Can we film anything you might be doing around the castle before he comes?'

'I suppose I couldn't stop you.'

We took shots of the castle. Eventually, Jane emerged carrying an old cocoa tin full of grain to sprinkle on the lawns to feed their peacocks. She could see us filming her, and the producer David Pearson and I started chatting to Jane in the hope that she would agree to talk about her husband. I asked her about the peacocks. 'Oh, they're upper-class vandals,' Jane replied. 'Alan has a whole collection of vintage cars which he keeps highly polished and sometimes the peacocks see the reflection of their tail feathers in the car and they think it's a rival and they take off and fly at the car. So all our cars get covered in blood and feathers. Whenever anyone asks about it, I just make a joke about it and say we've driven through a charity cycle race.'

I could see that she had a nice black sense of humour, so I suggested to her that her husband had certain peacock-like qualities – and that was the moment. Here was a woman who had met Clark when she was fourteen and he was twenty-eight. He used to arrive in his open-top Maserati to take her out from her convent school. For the following three decades, no one seemed to have asked what she thought of her husband. And she started talking about him, leaning against a well and looking into the middle distance.

She revealed that on their honeymoon in Positano, a former girlfriend of his had turned up. 'She was called Christina and she was quite nice actually,' said Jane. 'All the rest of his girlfriends have been pretty good rubbish since then. But I liked her. We could have had a Buñuel situation on the honeymoon and just done away with him.' Were you tempted? I asked. 'I have been plenty since. He was when we married and he still is a S-H-one-T.'

Jane added: 'Al sometimes says to me, "Would you like to be married to an old buffer?" And I say, "No, but I just wish you wouldn't have so many girlfriends." And he says, "You should be more French – French politicians have girlfriends and mistresses." So I say: "I am *not* French."' She continued: 'I could quite cheerfully throttle him sometimes, but I throw things instead. I did actually throw an axe at him once. As it whizzed through the air, I hoped it would cleave his skull in two. But it missed and I was quite glad my aim was very bad – because I do still love him.'

I had felt like a priest in the confessional. And when Clark eventually sauntered into Saltwood five hours late and without an apology, he said: 'I hear you have been talking to Jane. That's good.' But he had no idea what she had said.

When I asked Clark how he thought his wife had put up with his behaviour over the years, he replied: 'I suppose it's easier if you know the person loves you.' He dedicated his published diaries to his wife: 'To my beloved Jane, around whose cool and affectionate personality there raged this maelstrom of egocentricity and self-indulgence.'

We filmed Clark watching a clip of himself sitting on the front bench in the Commons, looking Mrs Thatcher up and down as she spoke at Prime Minister's Questions. 'She had very pretty ankles and little feet and pretty wrists,' Clark commented. And he told how awestruck he was when he saw her sweeping through Parliament all dressed up for her first TV interview as Prime Minister: 'Goodness, she was so beautiful, made up to the nines of course for the TV programme, but still quite bewitching. Just as Eva Perón must have been. I couldn't take my eyes off her and after a bit she, quite properly, would not look me in the face.'

He admitted that being in her presence aroused him. 'Of course it did. The radiation of vitality was such that you felt electrified, but you also felt uncertain – you didn't know what was going to happen next. I never felt that with any other government minister. I didn't give a damn what they wanted. But with her, I wished to please her, and not just for my own advancement but because she was such a remarkable individual.'

Mrs Thatcher's most trusted adviser, Charles Powell, said of Clark: 'He is the Lucifer of the Thatcher government – a brilliant, dark, quixotic and bawdy presence.' But Alan Clark was more than just a right-wing Tory cad. He had an original, creative, political mind – and his views were often unpredictable. For instance, he loved the Russians yet hated the Americans. He was a passionate campaigner against cruelty to animals and banned hunting on his estates. And as a young military historian, he wrote a book about the First World War which excoriated the bone-headed, upper-class British generals who sent countless brave young soldiers to their deaths – 'the lions led by donkeys'.

As a minister, Clark would greatly enjoy enraging both his political masters and his civil servants by stating the case for something in the most extreme terms. This was the only way, he felt, to force his colleagues to think outside the boxes of convention. He told me that he felt his schooling at Eton, which he had hated, was the perfect apprenticeship for life at the top of the Tory Party: 'Yes, Eton was very brutal and you learned very early on about deceit and cruelty. These are essential components of politics. The enjoyment of the pain of others, the sound of the tumbrils, a few people in trouble or going to be sacked or in scrapes or a bad performance or losing their ratings. I think everybody enjoys that.'

Clark had more than his fair share of ministerial scrapes and gaffes. He talked about migrant workers coming to Britain from 'Bongo Bongo Land'; he appeared at the despatch box in charge of a ministerial statement while drunk and he attacked his own government's policy on the BBC's *Question Time*. Yet Mrs Thatcher still kept him under her wing.

I asked Clark if he would ever flirt with The Lady, as he called her in his diaries: 'I think everybody tried to flirt with her if they could. She liked that. I think she took it as her due that you should flirt with her. She was fickle and quite – and I use the word purely in a technical sense – promiscuous in her affections. Unquestionably she used to build up personal relationships – of a non-carnal kind, I assume – with a succession of handsome or interesting men.'

But Clark was becoming unhappy that his ministerial career was not progressing fast enough. 'More and more I'm convinced that the most precious commodity is time,' he said. We filmed him watching a clip of his father, Lord Clark, who said: 'I have from my earliest years been obsessed by the passage of time. I am the original White Rabbit of *Alice in Wonderland*: "Oh dear! Oh dear! I shall be too late!" Several of my lady friends have told me they've never known anyone look so often at his watch – not ideal for a ladies' man one would have supposed.'

Alan Clark was fascinated by the clip, which he hadn't seen before, and said: 'That's absolutely my father at his best – relaxed and funny. It shows that at least one trait is genetically transmitted.' Which is that? I asked. 'The obsession with the passage of time.' And the son, who admitted he did not weep easily, was moved to tears by seeing and hearing his father from beyond the grave.

His own persistent philandering proved too much for his long-suffering wife, and she moved out of Saltwood Castle for a time. 'I wanted to teach Alan a lesson,' said Jane. 'He is impossible – absolutely dreadful half the time and I could cheerfully kill him. But I still think he's lovely.' And we filmed her saying to me in front of Clark: 'All his girlfriends are like bluebottles; it's just this latest one was harder to swat.'

'That will go down big,' responded Clark with an elaborate sigh.

Clark was also having problems with his political mistress. What he most wanted from Margaret Thatcher was a seat in her Cabinet. He told me he believed in 1990 that he was on course to becoming Defence Secretary in the promised reshuffle. But then came the Cabinet coup against her and she was gone.

That was our last piece of filming for *Love Tory*, and I wondered what Alan and Jane Clark would make of the finished programme. As we were going to preview it to the press, David Pearson and I agreed to show it to Clark before transmission – but only if he accepted that he had no editorial rights and could make no changes.

He agreed and came along with Jane to watch it in our Soho cutting room. No one made any comments during the viewing, and we waited tensely for his reaction. But at the end he just sat there in silence – for eight minutes, which I surreptitiously timed. It felt like an age. None of us talked – we all instinctively knew he had to be the first person to speak. His first words were pure bathos. 'Could I have a pen and paper please? I have so many thoughts running through my head, I just need to put them in order.'

Clark wrote busily for another two minutes. I thought to myself: 'Oh gosh, a letter to My Learned Friends.' At last he said: 'Jane was the star of that, it wasn't me; she's never said any of that to me. It was like watching yourself naked on the screen for fifty minutes.'

Some months later, Clark told me that he had been stopped in the street by what he called 'a dear old lady' who said she had seen the programme. 'Ah,' he had said. 'Jane was the star, I was just the chief supporting actor.' The dear old lady had replied: 'Chief supporting bastard you mean.'

He also told me later over the phone that he'd had two other love affairs which had never been made public. 'But', he added, 'I'm telling you because they are a matter of mild historic interest. The first was with Pamela Harriman.' Once married to

Churchill's son Randolph, she was the aristocratic English femme fatale who bedded many of the world's richest men. She went on to become President Clinton's ambassador to France, where she died of a stroke in Paris's Ritz Hotel swimming pool.

And Clark claimed his second undeclared paramour was the actress Joan Collins – of whom Clark told me: 'If she is the age she says she is, she wasn't born when we made love.'

Clark died in September 1999 of a brain tumour. He left a farewell letter to Jane, describing her as 'the sweetest, kindest, most percipient, intelligent human being I would ever encounter. A hundred times I ask myself how I could have been so cruel to you. Fool, Clark, fool. *Nasty* fool too. What is the use of my saying you are and will always be the only true love of my life. If you should ever need me, I will, I hope, be possibly at certain known localities in the grounds of each property. Love, love, love from A xxx'

People's reactions to *Love Tory* were more divided than over any other programme I've made. Women were particularly split. Some thought Jane was a disgrace to her sex and allowed herself to be a male chauvinist's doormat; others admired the way she had carved out her own life in the castle, with the man she loved. One female friend said to me: 'I suppose if I'd met Alan Clark I would have had an affair with him too, because he was funny and self-confident; but I would have hated myself for doing so.'

But there was a hidden side to Alan Clark. We had filmed with him at Eriboll, his vast estate in Sutherland in the far north of Scotland. There, he would climb the mountains, walk the moors and talk to the animals.

'All the solitude and magic of the highlands is up here,' he told me as we filmed on his favourite moor. 'Everything in politics is so instant, so immediate – you judge things by the day, by the hour, by what's going to happen in the House that afternoon. But once you are here, you are conscious that we are all just grains of sand.'

CHAPTER 15

ALWAYS ON THE JOB

As a schoolgirl, Margaret Thatcher wanted to become an actress. And as Prime Minister, she was to play many different roles: Iron Lady, tearful mother, simple housewife, world statesman and war leader. She was a one-woman force field of energy, her head thrust forward as she bustled from meeting to meeting forever saying: 'There's work to do.'

Mrs Thatcher did not enjoy big set-piece TV interviews. But she saw them as a necessary evil for getting her message across, and she developed different ways of dealing with interviewers. Some she coated with honey – while she would bite the heads off others. As she put it: 'This animal, if attacked, defends itself. So when I come up against somebody who is out to do a very belligerent interview, I say to myself: by God, anything you can do I can do better – and I'm belligerent back.'

By her own admission, she would become very nervous before high-profile TV appearances – and the tension inside No. 10 was palpable. When I asked Mrs Thatcher what she thought about such TV interviews, she replied: 'I hate them, I hate them, I hate them.' The PM would rehearse for interviews with her blunt Yorkshire press secretary Bernard Ingham, who pulled no punches in playing the part of the interviewer.

On one occasion, as Sir Robin Day set off for one of his major *Panorama* interviews with Mrs Thatcher in Downing Street, he said to me: 'Why don't I start the interview, "Prime Minister, what's your answer to my first question?"' Robin felt he knew that whatever he asked her, she would come up with the sound bites she and her advisers had prepared earlier. But sadly, despite my prompting, he never did begin an interview in that way.

In 1984, Margaret Thatcher became the first Prime Minister to agree to appear on a chat show. The timing was no coincidence. The miners' strike was at its height. Although the opinion polls showed that a large majority of people blamed Arthur Scargill for the violent confrontations with police that dominated the TV screens, the attacks on Mrs Thatcher as dictatorial and callous were getting through. Her advisers calculated that she would benefit from appearing on a programme that showed her human side.

The chosen chat show, *Aspel and Company*, was presented on ITV by the former BBC newsreader Michael Aspel. Sharing the bill with the Prime Minister was the Marmite singer Barry Manilow. Aspel asked the PM whether, both living and working at No. 10, it was possible to feel at home there. The grocer's daughter replied: 'I sometimes feel as if I started life living over the shop and I live over the shop now. Because people always come up. Is it possible? Well, I'm always on the job.'

The studio audience fell about with laughter. The PM beamed with pleasure at the audience response, although she was patently mystified about what they had found funny.

Mrs Thatcher was the mistress of the unintended double en-
tendre. During the 1983 general election, she said of one hapless
aide: 'He couldn't organise pussy' – meaning arrange a saucer
of milk for the cat. She had to be delicately advised to use a
different index of incompetence. And on a celebratory visit to
the Falklands, she posed for the cameras sitting proudly on the
saddle of a field artillery gun at Goose Green. Encircled by top
brass and squaddies, she asked innocently: 'Is it safe? If I press
this button, will it jerk me off?' The rest of the conversation was
drowned in spluttering squaddie hilarity.

But there were no double entendres about the way she ran
her government. She had become self-confident and dominant.
According to one of her Cabinet ministers, Chris Patten, her
style was to start a meeting by stating her conclusions and then
challenging all comers to fight her. She herself said: 'I think
a Prime Minister should be strong – there is not much point
being a weak, floppy thing in the chair.'

Talking to Mrs Thatcher during the 1987 election, I said that
when I had first filmed her as leader the TV cameras seemed to
fill her with dread and it looked if as she wished they would go
away. 'That's absolutely true,' she said. 'But over the years I've
learned that what you people want is a positive answer – and
that is what I always give you.' And in a way she always did –
even when she was saying, 'No, no, no.'

The last time I interviewed Mrs Thatcher as Prime Minister
was when she was celebrating her tenth anniversary in No. 10. It
was a pretty surreal experience. She talked to me looking into the
middle distance, almost as if she were Joan of Arc hearing voices.

I had earlier asked Willie Whitelaw, her recently retired Deputy PM, how long he felt Mrs Thatcher would continue in office: 'Oh, she is very fit, very strong. I hope she'll go on for a very long time,' he replied.

'But she is not immortal,' I ventured to suggest.

'No, she is not immortal,' responded Whitelaw, before adding: 'But perhaps she is.' In No. 10, I recounted this exchange on camera to the Prime Minister. Reviewing the tape today is revealing. On freezing the frame at exactly the moment she hears my intimation of her mortality, a remarkable look comes over her face for an instant: an apparent mix of alarm and blinding revelation. Within a few frames it is gone, and she recovers her composure when I tell her that Whitelaw had said perhaps she was immortal: 'What a sweet thing of Willie to say. No, I am not immortal, and I don't know how long I will go on – and no one does.'

But troubles were piling up for her. Although she dominated her government, she was alienating some of her most senior ministers, including her Chancellor, Nigel Lawson. She had often praised him as 'my brilliant, brilliant Chancellor'. But as evidence grew that inflation was returning to the economy, she found Lawson secretive, and by her own admission she was reduced to ringing up 'my spies in the Treasury' to find out what his Budget plans were. It was even rumoured that she had bugged No. 11. 'She was slightly paranoid at that time,' Lawson told me in an interview for a film I made about the Treasury.

He strongly objected to Mrs Thatcher's personal economic adviser, Professor Alan Walters, who would have lunches with

City financiers at which he sharply distanced Mrs Thatcher's economic policy from that of the Chancellor. 'These were things that the markets noted, and it made it impossible for me to do my job properly,' said Lawson. Walters told me: 'I had no authority whatsoever; all I had was the Prime Minister's ear. And Lawson objected to me having her ear and pouring what he regarded as poison down it – what I regarded as the truth.'

The crunch came in October 1989 after a series of meetings in No. 10 between the PM and the Chancellor. He threatened to resign if she did not sack her adviser. The PM stood firm, and there was turmoil as the Chancellor chose to quit. Mrs Thatcher agreed to be questioned by her favourite TV interviewer, the former Labour MP Brian Walden. They had become good friends after past ITV interviews, and he had built up a stock of capital with her. He decided to blow it all in one go.

Walden tried to cajole the PM into telling him exactly why Lawson had resigned. It was a question she kept refusing to answer. Instead she would repeat two mantras: 'The Chancellor's position is unassailable' and 'Advisers advise. Ministers decide.' It was as if Lawson hadn't resigned at all. At one stage, after Walden had said that the PM was coming over as domineering and refusing to listen, she responded: 'Brian, if any one of us is domineering in this interview – it's you.'

In his final question, Walden said: 'Prime Minister, I think the impact of this whole interview will be to make many people feel that nothing that has happened has in any way shaken or chastened you, and of course that will worry some of them, and they will say the PM is absolutely unyielding about everything, and though she might have done a good job, we think it's time that we had somebody more yielding. Now, what do you say to that?'

'Nonsense, Brian, I am staying my own sweet, reasonable self – founded on very strong convictions which are a combination of reason and emotion. Because I held these passionate convictions and fashioned our economic policies on them reasonably, firmly, strongly...'

Walden interrupted her flow, as the programme was running out of time: 'Prime Minister, I must stop you there.'

'No, you will not,' said Mrs Thatcher. 'Strong leadership will continue.'

Brian Walden told me later: 'In the interview, Margaret denied that she knew why Lawson had resigned. I in effect said, nonsense, you had four one-hour meetings with him. Don't tell me you don't know – you do know. For some extraordinary reason, she had decided not to tell the truth. Certainly she got caught out. She was deeply unhappy about that. And she never spoke to me again.'

Mrs Thatcher's evasions confirmed the public impression that she preferred an adviser to a top Cabinet minister. Or as one Tory backbencher put it: 'She is going off her trolley.' After eleven years at the top, the Iron Lady was showing signs of metal fatigue. And famously, she was challenged for the premiership by another blond bombshell, Michael Heseltine. Mrs Thatcher won the first round of the leadership election but not by a large enough majority, and she had to decide whether to stand again in the second round. Most of her Cabinet thought she was finished and queued up to tell her so. At the back of the queue was her veteran votary, the Defence Minister Alan Clark. He told me how the conversation went in the Prime Minister's wood-panelled room in the Commons.

'You're in a jam,' he recalled telling her.

'I know that,' responded Mrs Thatcher.

'They're all telling you not to stand, aren't they?'

'I'm going to stand.'

'That's wonderful, that's heroic. But the party will let you down.'

'I'm a fighter.'

'Fight then, fight right to the end. A third ballot, if you need to. But you lose.'

There was quite a little pause, remembered Clark.

'It would be so terrible if Michael Heseltine won,' said the PM. 'He would undo everything that I fought for.'

'But what a way to go! Unbeaten in three elections, never rejected by the people. Brought down by nonentities!'

'But Michael... as *Prime Minister*.'

'Who the fuck is Michael? No one, nothing. He won't last six months. I doubt if he'd even win the election. Your place in history is towering.' Outside, people were doing that maddening trick of opening and shutting the door at shorter and shorter intervals, Clark told me.

'Alan, it's been so good of you to come in and see me,' said Mrs Thatcher.

After a long dark night of the soul in No. 10, the PM reluctantly decided the game was up. A decade after the first female

British Prime Minister was clapped into No. 10, she was clapped out.

For Ted Heath, who had scarcely spoken to her since his own defenestration, it meant what he himself called 'the longest sulk in history' – his own – was over. I said to Heath: 'I heard that when she fell from office you rang your office and said "Rejoice! Rejoice!"' These were the famous words Mrs Thatcher had used to celebrate early progress in the Falklands. Heath responded: 'I said it three times – Rejoice! Rejoice! Rejoice! She only said it twice.' And his shoulders heaved with laughter.

Bernard Ingham, the PM's fearsome press secretary, was particularly harsh on those who he believed had brought Mrs Thatcher down. 'Heaven preserve us from political axe-men in a state of panic,' he said. 'They would cut off their grandmas in their prime if they thought it would serve their interests. And so they cut off a grandma in her international prime by the stocking tops.'

In her last interview in 2003, Lady Thatcher said: 'If you are in politics you expect to be knifed in the back. What I will never forgive is that it wasn't by Parliament that I was thrown out. I was away in Paris signing treaties for my country for the end of the Cold War. And this was after nearly eleven years when I had taken Britain from the slough of despond to the heights. I shall never forget that. I shall never forgive.'

Her departure left a huge hole for political journalists. Once you had Margaret Thatcher in your viewfinder, she rarely failed to produce riveting images and powerful quotes. The modern media, which in any case tends to magnify personalities, had for the fifteen years of her Tory leadership been faced with a giant-sized one. Disraeli, Lloyd George and Churchill became Prime Ministers before the age of television. Margaret Thatcher did not, and she made sure we knew it.

CHAPTER 16

MAGGIE'S MILITANT TENDENCY

In the autumn of 1986, four years before Mrs Thatcher's downfall, I was in the dock of the High Court in the Strand along with three co-defendants from *Panorama*. The editor Peter Ibbotson, presenter Fred Emery, producer James Hogan and I had all received writs early in 1984 from three Tory MPs. They alleged we had libelled them in a programme, which was to become notorious, called *Maggie's Militant Tendency*. The libel case, which had finally come to court, was expected to run for eight weeks. I remember feeling a sense of unreality about the whole thing. This was the same courtroom where only a few weeks before, in a case against *Private Eye*, the gargantuan Robert Maxwell had theatrically shed tears at the very suggestion that the way he ran his empire might not be 100 per cent kosher.

Our programme had looked at attempts by extremist groups to infiltrate the Conservative Party. Every great political party faces the problem of people who do not share its views attempting secretly to leech onto it. There had been many television reports about the phenomenon in the Labour Party. Ten years earlier, one of the first *Panorama* programmes I made was called

'Are there Cuckoos in the Nest?' It brought viewers' attention to a then virtually unknown organisation called the Militant Tendency – a secretive Trotskyist group that was infiltrating the Labour Party. We discovered they had made inroads into constituency parties across the country. Labour set up its own investigation, and when Neil Kinnock became leader he famously kicked them out of the party.

In *Maggie's Militant Tendency*, I did a piece to camera in which I said: 'Attempted infiltration of the party by extremists is on nothing like the scale of that in the Labour Party. But our investigation revealed one organisation operating secretly within the Conservative Party with views that echo those of the National Front.'

In case people were sceptical about entryism by the far right, our report began with film of a self-proclaimed neo-fascist called Don Mudie. In his office, he had built a shrine to Hitler filled with Nazi regalia. Since he built the shrine, Mudie had stood as an official Conservative candidate in the 1983 local elections.

We then showed film of Thomas Finnegan, who had stood as the official Conservative parliamentary candidate for Stockton South in the 1983 general election. He had, however, previously stood twice in a different constituency for the National Front. Finnegan had concealed his past from his local Conservative association and party headquarters. When that was revealed during the election campaign, the Cabinet minister Sir Keith Joseph, who was Jewish, pulled out of speaking for him. Embarrassed and angry, the Conservative Party was forced to disown its own candidate – and Finnegan lost the marginal seat the Tories had been expecting to win.

Finnegan and Mudie were not isolated cases. We discovered that twelve senior members of the National Front had recently joined the Tory Party, and six of them had become Conservative local election candidates. Our investigation revealed a patch-work of connections between a number of extreme right-wing groups and the Conservative Party. One group was an organ-isation working within the party, called Tory Action. It was run by a former deputy director of MI6, named G. K. (George Kennedy) Young, who ten years earlier had stood as an official Conservative parliamentary candidate.

Young made the claim to be supported by two dozen Tory MPs, among whom, he said, were Harvey Proctor, who won Basildon in 1979, and the newly elected Neil Hamilton and Gerald Howarth. Young also claimed he had a network of local party activists holding high office in Conservative constituency associations across the country. His aim was to shift party policy to the far right. 'We are denounced as a sinister, all pervasive influence in the Conservative Party; we are doing our best to be just that,' said Young.

G. K. Young put out a regular internal bulletin for his sup-porters, whom he called correspondents. My producer, James Hogan, managed to locate copies of the bulletin which were meant to be kept confidential. One, dated autumn 1982, car-ried this commentary from its northern correspondent about a disappointing by-election in Moss Side, an inner-city area of Manchester with a large West Indian community: 'The result

was pretty dismal but, there again, with the extraordinary con-
centration of c**ns, and the proletariat, life's failures and human
seconds, little else could be expected.'

In another bulletin from Tory Action, Young attacked the
Queen for consorting with non-whites on her foreign trips: 'On
every occasion, the monarch has to be photographed beaming
at a piccaninny, while Prince Philip and Prince Charles caper
about in yarmulkes' – the skull caps worn by Orthodox Jews.
And he dismissed Mrs Thatcher's victory in the Falklands as
'just an expedition to put the Dagos in their place'.

One of the people I interviewed for the film had been in Tory
Action for the previous eight years. He was Jon Phillips, a Con-
servative local councillor who was seeking selection as a par-
liamentary candidate and had become disillusioned with Tory
Action. 'They are a very secretive organisation,' Phillips told me.
'They're not at all open like other pressure groups within the
Conservative Party. They are a Militant Tendency-type organi-
sation within the party. They're not as big or serious a threat as
Militant are to Labour. But they are a cancer that ought to be
cut out of the party.'

G. K. Young said the aim of Tory Action was to keep Mrs
Thatcher's government on target on major issues – of which immigration was the most important. Tory Action advocated the
compulsory repatriation of immigrants, and Young's long-term
vision was of a Britain peopled by white Anglo-Saxon Chris-
tians. But he said he feared that he could expect nothing from
a government whose leading lights were the Chancellor Nigel
Lawson and the Home Secretary Leon Brittan, both of East

European Jewish descent. He called them 'Latvian Lawson and Lithuanian Leon'.

When our film was transmitted, it was followed by a live interview in the studio with the then Conservative Party chairman, John Selwyn Gummer. Questioned by the *Panorama* presenter Fred Emery, Gummer described Tory Action as 'a thoroughly nasty group. We are talking about one of the most horrible things that a person can be and that is a racialist.' Gummer played down the extent of Tory Action's influence in the party: 'G. K. Young is opposed to everything the party stands for. I wouldn't trust his claims. If you go to an admitted racialist and say, "Do you have support in the Conservative Party?" of course he is going to say yes. It's the only thing that gives his little mind some support.'

Gummer added that Young had been removed from the Conservative parliamentary candidates list.

In the *Panorama* green room afterwards, the Tory chairman appeared to feel he had got off rather lightly. In a relaxed manner, he remarked to Emery: 'If you had seen the half of what we've got in our files at central office, then you would really have had a programme.'

The film caused a huge storm. The three MPs named in the programme as being on Young's mailing list issued libel writs. And the BBC launched an intensive inquiry, led by the Director-General Alasdair Milne, into the evidence for what we had said in the film. He pronounced it 'rock-solid'; also, the BBC's chairman Stuart Young and the board of governors backed the film. One governor said: 'The BBC cannot become a government mouthpiece. It's the job of *Panorama* to disturb governments of any colour.' Milne's assistant, Alan Protheroe, took over the task of seeking to negotiate a settlement of the libel cases without going to court.

Protheroe was a sinuous Welshman who doubled as a colonel in the Territorial Army. He said to me: 'I have one crucial question for you – did you speak to anyone from the security services while making this film?'

'Yes. I did,' I replied. That seemed to satisfy the man always known in the BBC newsroom as The Colonel.

Protheroe negotiated with Neil Hamilton and Gerald Howarth directly during a series of meetings at the Institute of Directors headquarters in Pall Mall. During one meeting, Protheroe was wired up with a concealed recorder, which ran out of tape at one point, causing the gadget to make a repetitive clicking sort of noise. The BBC man explained that it was a new type of telephone pager before making his excuses and retreating to the lavatory to fix it.

He felt he was making some progress to an agreed settlement when a new player came onto the stage. It was the right-wing billionaire businessman Sir Jimmy Goldsmith, who was determined to 'crush the communists in the BBC'. He had decided to finance people who were in legal conflicts with the Corporation.

Protheroe, who had expressed his confidence to us about reaching a last-minute settlement 'at the gates of the court', suddenly discovered what he called 'an insertion of financial backbone into the two MPs'. Goldsmith had promised to fund their libel action through the court. Protheroe returned from a meeting with Hamilton and Howarth saying: 'They are going to go all the way.' They were demanding damages, costs and 'a grovelling apology'. And, he added: 'There is no possibility of a settlement remotely acceptable to the BBC.'

In the autumn of 1986, the libel actions of Hamilton and Howarth were at last due to come to court. Earlier, Harvey Proctor in his own words 'had to sue for peace with the BBC' and received no damages or costs. But much had changed in the nearly three years since the programme had been broadcast, not least among the dramatis personae. The BBC chairman Stuart Young, who had been a strong defender of the programme, had died. Mrs Thatcher had appointed the former head of Times Newspapers, Duke Hussey, as the new chairman. Hussey had inherited a mess not of his own making, and his inclination as a newspaperman was to get it off his doorstep fast. A highly placed source in Conservative central office put it bluntly to me at the time: Hussey's job was 'to make it bloody clear' that change was urgently required at the BBC; he was 'to get in there and sort it out'.

It had also become clear to the BBC's legal team that our defence case had been weakened by the fact that a number of our witnesses had been heavily leant on by Conservative central office. Tory officials informed witnesses that any hope of becoming parliamentary candidates would disappear if they gave evidence for the *Panorama* team. As Richard Lindley put it in his history of the programme: 'After these conversations some of these witnesses said they would not after all be able to repeat in court what they had said to the BBC.'

But the barrister leading *Panorama*'s defence in court remained relatively sanguine. He was Charles Gray QC, later to become a distinguished High Court judge, who said: 'Though the BBC's defence was not without difficulty, my junior and I both thought the case was winnable.' The case, which was expected to last two months, opened with a lengthy philippic by Gray's opposite number, Richard Hartley QC. Speaking at dictation speed, he accused us of 'foul allegations and complete lies', claiming that we had built 'a stinking cesspit of unbelievable evil into which we had dropped Neil Hamilton'.

'The truth is', Hartley continued, 'that the members of the *Panorama* team should be kicked out of the BBC. The methods they used would make Dr Goebbels, the Minister of Propaganda in Hitler's Nazi Party, proud of them. They used all the tricks of disinformation and misinformation.' It wasn't much fun sitting in the dock listening to Hartley – but we were told it was the typical hyperbole of a libel case. However, the speech sent shivers down the spines of the BBC governors, especially when it was reported the next day in all the papers in big headlines. It was decisive in convincing Duke Hussey and his deputy, Joel Barnett, that they had to take action – fast.

Before the jury had a chance to hear the defence case and assess our still numerous witnesses and supporting documents, Hussey ordered Gray 'to settle this case for whatever you can manage'. Gray told me: 'I remember being surprised that the governors should be so naïve and react in such a panicky way to the opening speeches. Our advice was that this was the worst possible way to put out feelers for such a settlement.'

After just four days in court, I and my three co-defendants were summoned by Protheroe to the Corporation's headquarters at Broadcasting House. He told us that the BBC was abandoning us, and if we chose to fight on, we would need half a million in readies – and anyway our case would be fatally undermined by the Corporation's decision to settle. We were mortified.

On the following day, the lawyers on both sides met and reached a settlement. We had to sign a statement unreservedly withdrawing any suggestion that either Neil Hamilton or Gerald Howarth was a Nazi, a racialist or a member of any extremist organisation. The two MPs were awarded £20,000 each in damages, plus costs.

After the settlement details were published, my three co-defendants and I put out a carefully worded personal statement. It said that we had been told all along that if the case went to court the jury would be allowed to reach a verdict on the basis of all the evidence. We regretted that this had not happened.

The broadcaster Roger Bolton, a former editor of *Panorama* although not responsible for the programme, claimed: 'The BBC got the worst of all worlds. It settled too late to prevent the prosecution from making its case, and too soon to allow the defence to be heard.'

The case had been a horrendous experience. But in contrast to the usual BBC maxim in a crisis – 'assistant heads must roll' – this time it was the chief head that rolled first. Alasdair Milne, the DG who had constantly clashed with the governors over a range of controversial programmes, was unceremoniously given his marching orders by Duke Hussey. Milne's assistant Alan

Protheroe decided to take early retirement, and John Birt was brought in from London Weekend Television to transform the current affairs department.

A year after the settlement of the libel case, the BBC decided not to renew my *Panorama* contract – and I went freelance. It turned out to be one of the best things that had ever happened to me professionally.

CHAPTER 17

SEX ON TELEVISION

The first film I made as a freelancer was for Channel 4. It was called *Sex on Television – What's All the Fuss About?* The subject had become highly topical because Mrs Thatcher had embarked on a campaign to clean up television. In the 1987 general election she had, against the advice of her Home Secretary Douglas Hurd, promised to do something about what she called 'the deep public concern over the display of sex and violence on television'. I suggested to Channel 4 that I make a film looking at the history of sex on British television and also seek to interview Lord (William) Rees-Mogg, the first chairman of Mrs Thatcher's newly created sex and violence watchdog. He had not yet talked about the sex part of his remit. The film was commissioned immediately by the documentary maker Roger Graef, who had started a new arts programme on Channel 4 called *Signals*.

Our film started in Paris, where television had just been deregulated and a new programme called *Super Sexy* had just become a huge hit on the main channel. We filmed the latest episode being made, which featured a James Bond spoof where a young blonde woman strips naked to seduce the spy. I did a piece to camera which started on the stripper and pulled back to reveal me speaking next to her. 'This is the kind of thing', I said, 'that Mrs Thatcher wants to avoid and fears could happen to British television. The Prime Minister is determined that her plan for many new satellite television channels will not lead to a flood of gratuitous sex on our screens. And she has created a new council to police the portrayal of sex and violence on television. The question of how to control small-screen sex has been of overriding concern to the broadcasting authorities in Britain since the earliest days.'

I then went to film in the BBC's archives and discovered many files that revealed the constant battles the heirs of the Corporation's puritanical first chief, Lord Reith, fought to keep the screen clean. The BBC policy guide for variety producers carried a stern section headlined in large type: 'Vulgarity'. 'Programmes must at all costs be kept free of crudities, coarseness and innuendo,' it said. 'There is an absolute ban on the following: jokes about lavatories, effeminacy in men, immorality of any kind, suggestive references to honeymoon couples, chambermaids, fig leaves, prostitution, ladies' underwear, animal habits, lodgers and commercial travellers.'

A key figure leading the crusade against on-screen indecency was the chain-smoking head of BBC television programmes, Cecil McGivern. He sent a stream of memos to his staff: in 1951, he was particularly concerned about the actress Renée Houston. In a memo to the head of wardrobe, McGivern wrote: 'The amount of shoulder and chest on display by Renée Houston in

Charivari [a variety show] was definitely embarrassing. And the dress as it appeared should not have been passed. Also, did she wear a brassiere? She is the type who needs one. Please let me have a report on this.'

McGivern was also worried about male ballet dancers. 'The fact is', he wrote in a memo, 'that the male body in tights – especially white tights – is quite shocking to certain quite intelligent and ordinary people. The dressing of male dancers must be supervised,' instructed McGivern, 'and they must be shot in such a way that the risk of offence is minimised.'

But it was television drama that would cause the major problems. In the early days, most contemporary TV plays were set in the drawing room. But by the end of the 1950s, under its new Director-General Hugh Greene, the BBC shed its Reithian inhibitions. TV drama followed the theatre towards the kitchen sink, angry young men and sexual scenes. In reaction, Mrs Mary Whitehouse, a Shropshire school mistress, started a Clean Up TV campaign. A quarter of a century before Mrs Thatcher, Mrs Whitehouse called for the creation of a Broadcasting Standards Council 'to purge television of the sub-Christian standards to which it has sunk', and she gained the support of a number of Tory MPs. 'I think many of the programmes on the BBC are vile,' said Sir Charles Taylor MP. 'There's far too much vice. There's too much murder. There's too much violence, and there's too much fornication.'

I interviewed Hugh Greene, who told me: 'I refused to see Mrs Whitehouse. And I think that was right. It would only have given her publicity.' But in November 1965 came a moment of ultimate outrage for the Clean Up TV campaigners. A new satirical programme called *BBC-3* featured an interview with Ken Tynan, the sexually adventurous literary director of the National Theatre. I talked to the programme's producer, Ned Sherrin, who vividly recalled what happened: 'Ken Tynan was asked whether he thought the act of sexual intercourse was something which should properly be seen on stage in the National Theatre. And Tynan said, "I think so, certainly. I doubt if there are any rational people to whom the word 'fuck' would be particularly diabolical, revolting or totally forbidden. I think that anything which can be printed or said can also be seen."'

The F-word had never before been uttered on television, and I asked Sherrin about the reaction. 'Nothing in the studio at all. It was a conversation between consenting adults. But outside the studio all hell broke loose on the phone lines and across the country.' Conservative MPs put down four separate motions in the Commons attacking the BBC and calling on Hugh Greene to return to the high moral standards set by Lord Reith. The motions were signed by 133 Labour and Conservative backbenchers.

Tynan's wife Kathleen, an author and scriptwriter, told me: 'I remember it went on for ever. We had a secretary and Ken said: "You must keep a fuck file, dear." This poor, rather nervous girl had to come in every day with his large box of letters and press clippings.' In the face of concerted pressure, the BBC governors apologised for Tynan's four-letter word.

Mrs Whitehouse told me: 'I said at the time that Tynan deserved to have his bottom smacked. That was actually dealing with him on his own level. He was behaving like a naughty little boy – and what do you do with a naughty little boy but smack his bottom?' Ned Sherrin responded: 'Knowing Ken, he would rather have enjoyed that.'

Throughout the '60s, the BBC regularly aroused protests with strong social themes and more daring sexual scenes in the weekly *Wednesday Play*. 'People would stay at home specially to watch on Wednesday evenings,' said Hugh Greene. 'Mrs Whitehouse of course was among those watching, and very often disapproving.' Mary Whitehouse told me: 'The *Wednesday Plays* were central to our petition to Parliament about the attack on family life, because they promoted the idea that to sleep around was the thing to do – this was the way to have fun and all the rest of it.'

I discovered that both the BBC and ITV had special departments to decide exactly what sexual scenes should be shown on television – and what should be censored. The head of ITV's Film Centre, Ken Fletcher, told me how it worked: 'There are some films that are suitable to be shown any time, which we are satisfied do not show any form of nudity, male or female, nor contain any bad language – either real bad language or the lavatorial kind. From 7.30 in the evening standards become slightly more relaxed. We can then permit a flash of nudity, a touch of breast or buttocks. But nothing showing full-frontal or pubic hair – and certainly no form of lovemaking in the nude.'

After 9 p.m., continued Fletcher, 'because it's supposed to be an adult time, we can be slightly more specific. Here we can show nudity. But strangely enough, and I think it's a convention that has grown up in cinema and has been grafted onto television, we don't show the male member. We can, though, show a flash of pubic hair and we can show lovemaking, provided it's not too explicit – without seeing penetration or anything like that. And there's one word, strangely enough, or one compound word, that we would never allow to be said – and that is the Oedipal noun [motherfucker].'

'Even on Channel 4?' I asked.

'Oh, Channel 4 are their own arbiters.'

I asked Jeremy Isaacs, Channel 4's founding father and its first boss, about his approach to sex on television. 'Since sex happens in private,' said Isaacs, 'there always has to be the most overwhelmingly powerful artistic justification or expository justification for such depiction. But we started from the basis that sex couldn't be left out. And that it would therefore be in the programmes that we made and the films that we showed – provided they were films of merit and repute and not just dirty movies – we wouldn't try to take the naughty bits out: we'd leave them in. I wasn't in favour of ramming things down people's throats, but I am in favour of people having a choice.'

Isaacs came up with the idea of showing a red triangle before a film started, along with a message to warn viewers that they might find it too violent or sexually offensive. Mary Whitehouse made her own recordings of the red-triangle films and showed the most explicit sequences to Tory MPs in the Commons. I said to Mrs Whitehouse that the point of the triangles was to warn people in advance about films that might offend them.

'Aaah,' she replied, 'but it was so silly, wasn't it? The viewing figures went up from 800,000 to nearly 2 million. Now don't tell me that Channel 4, with all their experience, didn't know that if they put up a red triangle warning people off watching, the opposite would happen and people would want to see what it was all about: that's the nature of man and perhaps women as well.'

'She's right about that,' Isaacs responded. 'If you put out a warning just before a programme that it's a bit strong, people at home would yell out: "Come on, Granny, come downstairs, there's something interesting on!" This is because Mrs Whitehouse consistently misreads the views and preferences of the British public. She simply does not understand that people benefit from – and therefore welcome – frankness about difficult subject matter on television. And they don't want to be protected from it.'

At the BBC in the mid-1980s, a successor to *The Wednesday Play*, *The Singing Detective* by Dennis Potter, came under especially fierce attack for showing the most explicit scenes of lovemaking seen up to that time on British television. 'I remain firmly of the view', said the Tory MP Gerald Howarth in the Commons, 'that it is no part of the business of public service broadcasting which goes directly into people's homes to put on television explicit scenes of sexual intercourse.' 'Hear, hear!' chorused fellow Tories, and Howarth continued: 'Why is this happening in 1986, when for the past fifty years it has not been shown? The fact is the producers are always anxious to press further and further and further.'

We had the mischievous idea as we cut our film to run the soundtrack of Howarth's last words 'to press further and further and further' over the shot of the naked male bottom going up and down in *The Singing Detective*'s sex scene. It worked a treat in the cutting room, but we were stymied by the actor involved. Patrick Malahide refused to give permission for his bottom to be seen out of context, saying that was not how he wanted to be remembered. 'Quite right too,' remarked the *Sunday Times*, 'because Patrick Malahide deserves to go down in history for more than his bare cheek.'

Margaret Thatcher had taken the lead in opening British television up to competition for as many as twenty new satellite channels. But she was also greatly concerned to protect viewers from what they might show. There was evidently a conflict between the Milton Friedman side of Mrs Thatcher's brain and the Mary Whitehouse side.

To prevent a flood of gratuitous sex and violence on the new and existing channels, the PM's freshly created Broadcasting Standards Council was something that Mrs Whitehouse had been advocating for twenty-five years. The man Mrs Thatcher had appointed as its first chairman had been in the Oxford University Conservative association with her. Lord (William) Rees-Mogg was a Balliol man who had been editor of *The Times* and vice-chairman of the BBC. The father of Jacob, then a teenager, he was a Conservative Catholic and had a slight speech defect, which he called a lateral lisp. It meant he slurred the letters 's' and 'x', so when he talked of 'explicit sexual scenes' – as he did when I interviewed him – it came out as 'exshplishit shexshual sheenesh'.

Although Rees-Mogg had been often asked about violence on television, he agreed to give me his first TV interview about the sex part of his remit. I asked him what sort of sexual scenes he would not want shown on television. Rees-Mogg replied: 'I think first of all sexual scenes which are basically in the area also of violence: sado-masochistic scenes, rape scenes, offences against children and so on. I think then you've got the problem of what you could call erotic scenes. And defining the precise area in which you are dealing with the sympathetically erotic, and the precise area that would properly, naturally be regarded as pornography is, I think, inherently difficult. That's where the difficult boundary has to be drawn.'

'And how do you think you're going to overcome these difficulties and draw these boundaries?' I asked.

'Well, there are erotic scenes which are perfectly clearly all right to show. What you could call, broadly speaking, Romeo-and-Juliet scenes – romantic scenes. Then there are erotic scenes which raise very serious questions, where there is very explicit sex, and a very explicit view of the sex act. There are then...' – and Rees-Mogg's throat made a strange gargling sound as he audibly searched for *le mot juste* – 'gropings which occur in the middle. And these gropings are found to be very offensive by large numbers of viewers. There is a question which will no doubt have to be defined about those. There's an area in which there would be very considerable dispute between reasonable people about whether they were just on one side of the line or just on the other.'

When I put what Rees-Mogg had told me to Jeremy Isaacs, he said: 'I think there will be lovely arguments about this. And William and co. will have great fun watching everything six times to make sure they've got it right.'

When our programme was transmitted on Channel 4, it achieved an audience of 3 million – a record high for the slot. And in the House of Lords, Lib Dem Lord Bonham Carter picked up on Rees-Mogg's commendation of Romeo-and-Juliet romantic scenes as innocuous: 'The noble Lord neglected the fact that Juliet was underage. And in *Romeo and Juliet*, sex and violence are more intimately interlocked than in any other of Shakespeare's plays.'

As it turned out, Rees-Mogg, who had pictured himself as the chief censor of British television, fell short of his goal – partly because Mrs Thatcher failed to give the Broadcasting Standards Council regulatory teeth. But the noble Lord did become a much satirised figure on *Spitting Image* and in *Private Eye* – particularly for the G-word: 'gropings'. *Private Eye* produced a full-page take-off of our film headlined: 'That Rees-Mogg sex shocker in full!' calling him Lord Really-Smug and me Michael Cock.

CHAPTER 18

THE POWER BEHIND
THE THRONE

The next film I made as a freelancer was for Granada's *World in Action*. For my thirteen years on *Panorama*, the programme we used jokingly to call 'World in Acton' was our fiercest competition. My film was an investigation into the secretive honours system and how successive Prime Ministers from Lloyd George on used it to reward their friends and cronies. The film needed to be lawyered and the programme's editor called in a top libel QC, Richard Hartley. Ironically he had been the Silk against us in the *Maggie's Militant Tendency* case – and had colourfully described us as 'the heirs of Goebbels' who built a stinking pit into which we threw his clients.

After a sticky introduction, Hartley and I got on fine. And the controversial programme went out without attracting a writ, despite the ample evidence we showed linking big donations from industrialists to the Tory Party with subsequent knighthoods and peerages. We even managed to film one big businessman, the shipping magnate Kerry St Johnston, receiving his knighthood soon after his company contributed to Tory funds. As he showed me his award inside Buckingham Palace, I asked him on camera about the linkage. 'It's all a mysterious process – who knows how it works?' he replied. I met him again later and he bore no grudge about being doorstepped on his great day.

I wasn't sure what I would do next. But I read a piece in the media magazine *Broadcast* about the plan for a new BBC documentary unit in opposition to the traditional department. Based at the BBC's Elstree Studios, it was to be run by Paul Watson. He had effectively created fly-on-the-wall observational documentaries with his series *The Family* and had made many subsequent controversial programmes. Knowing him a bit, I rang and told him of my idea to make a profile of Willie Whitelaw. He had just stood down after ten years as Mrs Thatcher's Deputy Prime Minister and knew where the bodies were buried. Paul liked the idea and said he would talk to Alan Yentob, the then controller of BBC 2. Five minutes later my phone rang, and Paul said: 'I've talked to Alan and he has commissioned it.' So from being out of work and out of the BBC I was suddenly back in the fold.

I went to Elstree, the famous old film studios now run by the BBC: it was used for *EastEnders*, and variety and history programmes. I met Paul on the first-floor atrium of a big block which had a square of empty private offices. He said: 'You can choose your office – I've taken the best one for myself, but you can have your pick of any of the others.' I chose one diagonally opposite his – not too near and not too far.

It was the start of a new chapter. Paul is a great enthusiast and said I should aim to make a fresh shelf-ful of big political profiles – starting with Willie Whitelaw. I had known Whitelaw since he ran for the Tory leadership against Mrs Thatcher in 1975. He agreed to my making a profile partly, he told me later, because he wanted to make up for the way the Tory Party had treated me over the libel case.

We called the film *Power behind the Throne*. From the time Mrs Thatcher became leader, Whitelaw had been her ever loyal No. 2. Yet there was little surface evidence of how he became the most influential man in her Cabinet, as he operated discreetly and away from the public gaze.

Willie Whitelaw was a fascinating character. His father had been killed in the First World War soon after Whitelaw was born – and he never saw his son, who grew up an only and lonely child. He told me that at prep school he was bullied by the other boys. What did they do to you? I asked. 'Oh, you know, the usual things that little boys do – they made me eat stones and things.'

Whitelaw was schooled at Winchester, a traditional forcing house for sharp intellects, but he was no intellectual. Harold Macmillan claimed that Whitelaw was 'a Wykehamist who spends his life masquerading as an Etonian'. For all his noisy bonhomie, Whitelaw was a skilled political operator; he was a big bear of a man with a booming voice, who could move with surprising guile. 'I've always believed in politics that you have a little in reserve if you can appear slightly less intelligent all the time than you may be,' Whitelaw told me. 'I think it is a great mistake to appear to know all the answers in life, because then people like catching you out. If they think, "Poor old thing, he doesn't really understand these matters," you can perhaps get a good deal past them by the fact you actually do, even while you may be pretending otherwise. It's quite an art to underestimate oneself. Some people think I may have done it too much.'

Whitelaw served in the Scots Guards throughout the Second World War, winning a Military Cross in Normandy. In his very first battle, he saw many of his close friends killed in a matter of minutes – an experience which ensured he would become a dedicated supporter of European unity.

He spent nearly thirty years on the front bench as an MP and then in the Lords. Made Chief Whip by Ted Heath, he developed the skills of holding the party together as a conciliator and deal-maker. And he became known for his fierce loyalty to the party leader, whoever he – or she – was and managed the unique feat of becoming the most trusted confidant of first Ted Heath and then Margaret Thatcher. As Northern Ireland Secretary he met the IRA; he was Employment Secretary during the three-day week; and he was a member of the Falklands War Cabinet.

In 1982, an unemployed painter and decorator, Michael Fagan, broke into the Queen's bedroom at Buckingham Palace when Whitelaw was Home Secretary. Though the Queen was unharmed, the strong monarchist Whitelaw felt guiltily responsible for the security breach and that he had no choice save to obey the many calls for his resignation. But a note from a candid friend changed his mind. Whitelaw read it to me: 'Don't resign as everybody says you should. After all, if the Queen and the Prime Minister wanted a Home Secretary who would be good at getting over walls, running round the Palace gardens and catching intruders, the last person in the world they would have selected for the job is you – because nobody is less agile, nobody less likely to catch an intruder. So don't be so silly: that's not your job and people who say these things about resigning are absurd.'

Our film showed it was Whitelaw's sensitive political antennae, along with his role as a subtle Dutch uncle, that often saved Mrs Thatcher from her own impetuosity. I approached No. 10 for an interview with the PM about Whitelaw, fearing that because of the libel case I might be persona non grata. But rather to my surprise, she agreed to an interview.

In the White Drawing Room of No. 10, the Prime Minister told me: 'Willie had this fantastic capacity to distinguish between those things which I would like to happen and those things I would go to the stake for. And he knew when to say: "Now look, does that really matter?" In your team you have got to have some people who are prepared to practise the qualities of leadership and say: "This I believe and upon this I will not compromise." Some people in politics say: "Well, let's see what the people think and then we will follow it." But how can people know what they think unless really strong views are put before them and the reasons for it? And they see someone really prepared to stand upon that view – that is Willie Whitelaw.'

I interrupted her and said: 'That sounds more like a description of you.'

The PM gave a light laugh and after a long pause said: 'Oh, I had some of those qualities; Willie had them all.'

Mrs Thatcher's was the unlikeliest description of Whitelaw, who was known for his legendary skills as a negotiator, compromiser and fixer. I asked Whitelaw how he saw his role as Mrs Thatcher's Deputy Prime Minister. He replied: 'I have to go in and hose her down occasionally.' And on one occasion, while out of Mrs Thatcher's earshot he was heard shouting: 'That woman thinks she has a hotline to the British people. She doesn't!'

Mrs Thatcher laid on a lavish farewell dinner at the Tory Carlton Club for the retiring Lord Whitelaw. She said that she could not have achieved what she had without his invaluable support and advice. 'I would go so far as to say: "Every Prime Minister needs a Willie."' It was not clear that she realised at first what she had said. Then, as the assembled males broke up in laughter, she instructed: 'That is not to go beyond this room.' Happily it did, via me.

I also made a film about Mrs Thatcher's press secretary, Bernard Ingham, known as Maggie's Rottweiler, with whom I'd had numerous brushes. It had taken some time to persuade him to appear; eventually he told a friend: 'I've reached the age of irresponsibility; I'll do it with Cockerell.'

I did a number of other films for Paul Watson's new unit. Then the BBC 2 controller had a cunning plan. He worked out that if I did my next films not for the documentary department but for current affairs, he could get them for free as they would be paid for out of the news budget, not the BBC 2 budget. So, I was invited back to current affairs, which I had left five years earlier – and one of the executives who had given me my marching orders from *Panorama* went around saying: 'I am the man who got Cockerell back into current affairs.'

CHAPTER 19

THE RED QUEEN

I was happy to come back to a specially created unit within current affairs called 'political documentaries'. It was run by an old colleague of mine from Lime Grove days. Anne Tyerman was a multi-skilled producer and editor with great gifts in the cutting room. And she was very politically savvy. We were to work together for the next decade, which was the happiest of my professional life. Anne pulled together a wonderfully talented team of producers (including my future wife, Anna Lloyd), directors and researchers who made a range of sparky and revealing programmes about how politics and politicians really work.

One of the first films I made for Anne was about the woman who had for many years been tipped to become the first female Prime Minister: Labour's Barbara Castle. Peter Riddell of *The Times* wrote: 'Barbara Castle is a natural for the Cockerell treatment. She has the right mixture of vanity and candour. And she relishes re-fighting some long-forgotten battles with old adversaries.'

One of my favourite political books opens with the line: 'Barbara Castle was pacing up and down Harold Wilson's room, bullying him as usual.' I know exactly how Wilson felt, having made a number of TV programmes with Castle. She no doubt would have put it entirely the opposite way and said it was I who bullied her. But whatever the truth, there was no question that our relationship could be pretty rugged. You did not want to get on the wrong side of Barbara Castle: she took no prisoners.

I remember when I started asking about her early life for the documentary, she wanted to talk about the present and how much she hated John Major's Tory government. She said: 'If you think I sit here drooling in nice nostalgic memories, you're wrong. We've got too much to do in the modern world still. All these bastards to beat – haven't we?'

Barbara Castle was the first woman to break the sex barrier in British politics. It is astonishing to think of it now, but she was only the fourth ever female Cabinet minister. In 1964, Harold Wilson appointed her Minister for Overseas Development. Although she emerged in the age before spin, she was always very carefully protective of her image. Before a big speech or interview, she would spend so long in the Commons ladies' loo ensuring she looked just right that MPs called it 'Barbara's Castle'. And going to film her at Hell Corner Farm, her house in the Chilterns, involved a regular ritual. She would insist on the BBC sending a makeup artist an hour and a half in advance to do her hair and her face. One day, she asked me to arrive early so that I could brief her about the programme. Answering the door quite unselfconsciously, with her hair in rollers and completely unmade-up, Barbara Castle looked a tiny, pale shadow of the formidable figure I was used to. But once the process was completed, she came down the stairs transformed, with big hair and immaculate maquillage.

On film, she told me that she thought female politicians were judged by very different criteria from men. 'We do have a terrible time in politics because we are supposed always to look nice. I think actually that a lot of Margaret Thatcher's hold over her own party was her sexual attractiveness.'

I asked: 'Do you think that was the secret of your hold over your own party – sexual attractiveness?'

Mrs Castle replied: 'I think there is no doubt that if a woman cares about her appearance, it helps her up the ladder. I always found men vulnerable to a little femininity – and many are unable to cope when it is combined with some mental ability and with what is considered a masculine strength of will.'

As a former journalist herself, Castle had a keen appreciation of her market worth on television. She was the only politician I have ever known who actually sought to haggle over her fee on camera. I was filming with her and halfway through the interview, she said: 'I'm on such good form today, and you're covering so much more ground than I thought you would, if you want to do any more, then you'll have to up the fee.'

She was right, and we did. Like almost all politicians, Castle had a version of her life that she would trot out when journalists asked the usual questions. It was polished, sometimes nicely self-deprecating but often, when one went back to the original sources, subtly wrong. It can sometimes stop politicians in their tracks and make them think afresh when you query their well-honed autobiographical anecdotes. But it did tend to make for a bit of grit between Castle and me.

One such instance was when I asked about her early relationship with the former Labour leader Michael Foot. They had first met as struggling young left-wing journalists in pre-war London. They travelled together for a week's holiday in Brittany, at around the same time as the Prime Minister Neville Chamberlain was having his famous 'peace in our time' talks with Adolf Hitler in Munich. Exactly what went on in Brittany remained a subject of boundless dispute between Mrs Castle and the mischievous Mr Foot.

He told me: 'We went for a week's holiday. People didn't know what we were going for, but anyway we went and had a nice holiday.' Barbara bristled when I put to her what Foot had said. 'Well, so what, have you never been on a holiday with a woman without getting into bed with her?'

Foot riposted: 'Well, at any rate, I've made a joke about it ever since. Barbara thinks I'm not entitled to do it, but I do. I say, for me, "peace in our time" has a special meaning: it was when I got back after a week with Barbara.'

Her response was: 'Bloody cheek.'

My producer, Matthew Barrett, and I had lengthy discussions about what the title of our Castle documentary should be. We wanted something that would combine her red-haired glamour with her passionate socialist views and often autocratic style. Eventually, I landed on 'The Red Queen'. Why had we not thought of it before? I doubt if it was to her taste, and one of her oldest friends later told me we had got it wrong; it should have been 'The Red Empress'.

Like the later Iron Lady Margaret Thatcher, Barbara Castle was the product of a provincial grammar school and Oxford. But unlike the Tory grocer's daughter, she came from an ardently socialist family. She recalled how she and a girlfriend would display their political allegiances at school in Bradford, where she grew up. 'We used to put on huge red rosettes,' she said, 'and we would walk round the playground defiantly, arm in arm – a little nervously because I really thought people were going to throw things at us, they were so furious. These poor merchants' daughters decided we were just a couple of communists and we were probably going to leave bombs under their desks or something. But it was quite a frightening experience to be as hated as that. You could feel the intensity of the hate among that vast majority.'

After she left Oxford, the economic slump of the 1930s reinforced Barbara Castle's radical convictions. Her first job was selling sweets in a Manchester department store, but she soon came to London hoping to break into journalism. She fell under the spell of a leading left-wing journalist, William Mellor. He was twenty years older than her, and he tried to teach her to drive. 'William was married and he had a son,' Barbara told me. 'We would sit in the car with sort of electric currents radiating between us. But it was I who had to make the first overture.' They embarked on a torrid affair, and Mellor turned out to be the first great love of her life; but his wife refused to agree to a divorce. When we filmed Barbara looking at photos of Mellor, she was near tears and said: 'I would have loved to get married and have his child. But I wasn't going to split the marriage so long as his wife wouldn't accept it.'

Their love affair was to last for ten years, until William Mellor died during the war. Barbara was devastated and sublimated her passion into politics. Along with her fellow left-winger Michael Foot, she became an MP in the Labour landslide of 1945. 'Barbara had a fiery reputation even then,' Foot told me. 'And her red hair was even redder in those days – I'm not quite sure how red it is now. It varies I think from time to time. But in those days it was absolutely red hot and so were most of her socialist views.'

It was her tub-thumping oratory which first captivated Ted Castle, a *Daily Mirror* journalist, when he saw her speaking at a wartime Labour conference. They married in 1944, and Mrs Castle told me how very much they wanted to have children. But there were problems, and she talked frankly about how they tried to overcome them. 'Somebody gave us the name of a fertility expert,' she said. 'Well, he nearly ruined our marriage. I was told I must have a course of injections of hormones from pregnant mares. And Ted was told to produce samples for analysis – and we both revolted against it. Finally, Ted said: "I refuse to make love to any more jam jars," and I said: "I refuse to have any more painful injections, however great the pedigree of the pregnant mare." So we said: "Oh, let nature take its course."'

Without the distraction of children, Mrs Castle devoted herself single-mindedly to politics. In Labour's civil wars of the '50s, she was a comrade-in-arms with Harold Wilson as the left of the party, led by Aneurin Bevan, fought against the right, led by Hugh Gaitskell.

When Wilson became Prime Minister in 1964, he put Mrs Castle in the Cabinet, and over the following decade she was a highly controversial minister in a series of high-profile posts. I asked her about the speculation by some of her male colleagues as to why she seemed to exercise such a hold over Harold Wilson. 'Barbara only had to wiggle that bottom of hers to get her way,' one Labour MP told me when I was making a TV biography of her.

'Of course people used to think I must be his mistress or something,' said Mrs Castle. 'Harold never made any serious attempt to seduce me. In the nearly forty years I worked with him, all I can remember is one rather fumbling kiss. He liked a little flirtation, but it was verbal rather than physical. He would say "nice pair of legs" or something like that, or "I dreamt about you last night," but I don't think he was very unusual in that.'

Wilson made her Transport Secretary in 1965, even though she could not drive. She attracted the hatred of many who could by introducing breathalyser tests and compulsory seat belts. Three years later, as Employment Secretary, she tried to bring in reforms to curb the power of the trade unions. Her plan, called 'In Place of Strife', included compulsory strike ballots and a cooling-off period, which could have resulted in the jailing of recalcitrant strike leaders. It caused a huge row. Jim Callaghan, the Home Secretary and 'keeper of the cloth cap', led a Cabinet revolt which sabotaged Mrs Castle's plan. She never forgave him, and Labour lost the 1970 election.

Four years later, Barbara Castle was back in government as Health Secretary. She had long been tipped to become Britain's first woman Prime Minister – but now there was a new contender for the role. In February 1975, Margaret Thatcher saw off six male contenders to win the Tory leadership. Mrs Castle wrote in her diary: 'I can't help feeling a thrill. She is so clearly the best man among them. She is in love; in love with power, success and with herself. If we have to have Tories, good luck to her.'

A few months later, Mrs Castle was one of the leading anti-European Cabinet ministers in the referendum on Britain's membership. At a packed meeting in the Oxford Union, the Europhile Liberal leader Jeremy Thorpe said after her fiercely anti-EU speech: 'Holding these views as passionately and sincerely as she does, may we assume if the vote is "Yes" she will not stay on to administer these policies as a minister?' Mrs Castle riposted: 'If the vote goes "Yes", my country will need me to save it even more.' Cue hilarity.

Barbara Castle's estimation of her indispensability was not shared by the new Labour Prime Minister Jim Callaghan. He had taken over in 1976 when Harold Wilson had suddenly stood down. But Callaghan and Castle were long-time foes. They were very different types of people. Callaghan claimed she bullied Harold Wilson, which was 'very tiring for him', and when the new PM summoned Mrs Castle to No. 10, his long knife flashed.

We filmed her watching my interview with Callaghan, when I asked him why he had dropped her from the Cabinet. He had answered: 'I did not think she'd want to be there. She had never been strongly supportive of what I'd wanted to do.' Mrs Castle reacted: 'Uncle Jim – how he does smooth it all into a confused and untruthful picture. He had said to me: "I'm awfully sorry, Barbara, but I think it's time we make way for the young." And, you know, I thought one of the most restrained things I ever did in my life was not to retort: "Then why not start with yourself, Jim?"'

Mrs Castle left office proudest of having introduced the Equal Pay Act and having made family allowance directly payable to the mother. She had been happily married to Ted Castle for nearly thirty-five years when, in 1979, he suddenly died. She told me: 'I've been a very lucky woman because I've had two great loves in my life.'

Barbara Castle called her autobiography *Fighting All the Way*, and in our documentary we tried to reflect the feisty qualities as well as the charm and wit which had enabled her to make it to very near the top of the male world of politics. Her friends and even her opponents told us how well they thought she had come over. But Barbara saw it differently. She rang to tell me how little she liked the programme. I was somewhat taken aback and asked her what she objected to. 'When you filmed me walking into the Labour Party conference, you got a shot of me from behind – and it showed how creased my jacket was. And it was only creased because I had been sitting in the back of the car you sent to drive me up to Blackpool,' she said. 'Also, you said on the programme that I was eighty-five.'

I countered: 'I didn't say you were eighty-five, I said that you'd be celebrating your eighty-fifth birthday later in the year. Partly it's a BBC thing. You know how much they like anniversaries.'

'Well,' she snapped, 'people think I'm eighty-five because of your programme. I've already even had a telegram of congratulations from a German MEP.'

'But Barbara,' I said, 'I thought that at your age you'd be proud of how old you are and not want to be seen as younger.'

'It's not that,' she retorted. 'Don't you understand that if everyone thinks I'm already eighty-five, when it is my birthday later in the year I won't get another bite of the media cherry.'

Barbara Castle met every Labour Prime Minister there has ever been since she first canvassed for Ramsay MacDonald in 1924 at the age of thirteen. We filmed her first meeting with Tony Blair soon after he was elected Labour leader in 1994. 'It's really good to see you,' said Blair. 'You know, I'm a great, great fan. I always have been.'

She replied: 'You're so young. And you haven't made any serious mistakes – yet. I'm watching you, mind you.'

'Right,' said Blair.

But Tony Blair, like many Labour leaders before him, failed to live up to Castle's standards. Four years after he became Prime Minister, she launched an attack on him for running a presidential system and ignoring bread-and-butter issues at home in order to strut the world stage. 'Tony's Achilles heel', she pronounced with no sense of irony, 'is his self-love.'

Barbara Castle was still firing on all cylinders into her nineties. And when I last saw her, she refuted Enoch Powell's famous line that all political careers end in failure. 'Political careers don't end in tears,' she said, 'they end in fury.'

CHAPTER 20

MAJOR PROBLEMS

John Major had become Prime Minister at more or less the same time as Anne Tyerman's new political documentary unit was set up. His seven-year stint at No. 10 was to provide rich pickings for us. Major had a great advantage when, in 1990, he became Prime Minister: he was not Margaret Thatcher. His was a new administration, and he wanted it to look and sound very different from hers, partly so he could counter Labour's 'time for a change' strategy. He played up his humble roots as the son of a circus performer who'd fallen on hard times and taken to selling garden gnomes.

'I am who I am,' Major told me, insisting he would not be spun and promising to create a truly classless society. He lacked charisma on television and was lampooned on ITV's *Spitting Image* as a man with a totally grey face and grey suit, who ate dinner with his wife in silence, occasionally saying, 'Nice peas, dear.' The reality was sometimes not very different. When he flew to Riyadh, the capital of Saudi Arabia, before the first Gulf War, the British ambassador asked Major to sign the visitors' book. He wrote: 'John Major, 10 Downing Street, London

SW1A 2AA.' Probably the first Prime Minister to know his post code, let alone use it.

But he had a sense of self-mockery. At one Conservative council meeting he said: 'I regard it as a scandal that some 20 per cent of children leave school functionally illiterate – they can neither read nor write. What is to become of them?' He paused, then added: 'They can't all become Prime Minister.'

Famously, Major was a cricket nut – as am I. On *Desert Island Discs*, the luxury he asked for was The Oval cricket ground. He had himself been a pretty good club cricketer, but he had smashed his knee in a car crash when he was working for Standard Bank in Nigeria and was never able to play properly again. He is two years younger than me, and whenever we met he would ask: 'Are you still playing cricket at your advanced age?'

'Yes,' I would say. 'But having once been a fast bowler, I have gone down first to a medium pacer and then a slow bowler. Now I like to bowl up the hill and into the wind and the batsmen often play too early.'

'And you can still reach the wicket, can you?' Major would respond.

He told me about the one time he did play in a big game of cricket after his injury. It was at the Commonwealth Prime Ministers' Conference in Zimbabwe in 1991, before President Mugabe had become public enemy No. 1. A charity match was arranged at the Harare Club stadium between a Commonwealth Prime Ministers' XI and a Zimbabwe youth team. Major had agreed to play but, as he put it to me: 'I approached the occasion with the greatest trepidation.' He was afraid that he was so rusty he would be humiliated: out first ball for a golden duck. But Mark Williams, one of Britain's top diplomats in Harare, told me how he came up with a cunning piece of match-fixing. He wrote a memo to No. 10 saying: 'There is no obligation for the Prime Minister to bat, but he might wish to face at least a token ball. A bowler who can be relied on to bowl a slowish long hop outside off stump will be carefully chosen. It would ensure an excellent publicity photograph. No running between the wickets would be required, although the Prime Minister might care to amble a single to chalk up $250 for charity.'

The game attracted a big crowd, and Major walked out to open the batting with Bob Hawke, the Labor PM of Australia. Hawke was a former trade union leader, good at cricket and as tough as they come. Major told me that after his token first ball, Hawke would hog the bowling and take a single off the last ball of each over, so that he would also face the start of the next one. 'After a few overs,' said Major, 'the wisdom of the Hawke strategy was revealed: "Off you go," said the umpire, waving us off the pitch as he added, rather pointedly: "It's time for the real cricketers." A roar of applause greeted our departure.'

Hawke had scored over twenty, whilst Major had fewer than ten. 'Did you know we didn't have long?' Major asked Hawke as he walked disconsolately back to the pavilion. 'Jeez, yes,' admitted Hawke. 'Didn't you know, John? Arh, heck – I thought you did.' Major told me: 'Not for the first or last time, I noted that Australians play hard.'

Bob Hawke was a larrikin. As a Rhodes scholar at Oxford he set a record for drinking a yard of ale in just eleven seconds. At the liquid launch of his biography in London, I asked Hawke a question that I would not have put to a British Prime Minister. I said I had heard that when he was at Oxford, Hawke had a white van that he would use when he dated young women – and it was called the shag wagon. He replied: 'Jeez Michael, if you are in politics you expect to be insulted. But it wasn't called the shag wagon. We had more class than that. It was called the fornicatorium.'

In the 1992 general election, the Tories had a poster which asked: 'What does the Conservative Party offer a working-class kid from Brixton? They made him Prime Minister.' Major binned the cosy images of 'Citizen Major' and 'Honest John' so carefully crafted by Tory election planners and took to campaigning passionately with a megaphone on a soapbox in the street. It looked and sounded authentic and helped see off the Labour leader Neil Kinnock.

But Major was soon in trouble with Black Wednesday, when Britain was forced to crash out of the European Exchange Rate Mechanism and interest rates rose to 15 per cent. He told me later in a TV interview that he felt totally let down by the German Chancellor, Helmut Kohl, whom he'd seen as his good personal friend. He had rung Kohl personally asking him to prop up the pound. Kohl promised to get back to him, but when after a long delay he did, it was too late: 'I was extremely angry and frankly I thought it was unforgivable,' said Major.

I asked the PM what effect he thought Black Wednesday would have on his reputation. 'I had no doubt that Black Wednesday would haunt me for the rest of my premiership – it was a fundamental reversal.' Major had lost the Tories' trump card of economic competence, and he also came under bitter attack from the growing number of Eurosceptic Tory MPs.

The PM's years in office were plagued by splits in the Cabinet over Europe. TV microphones picked up a conversation with ITN's political editor, Mike Brunson, after Major had finished an interview and thought he was no longer being recorded. Major was lamenting how difficult he was finding life because of 'the poison being spread to the media against me over Europe'. The PM said to the TV man: 'Where do you think most of this poison is coming from? From the dispossessed and the never possessed. You and I can both think of ex-ministers who are going around causing all sorts of trouble.' Brunson asked Major why he didn't sack the Eurosceptic Cabinet ministers who were making his life hell. Major responded: 'We don't want another three more of the bastards out there.' And the recording was leaked.

Major came consistently under attack from the normally Tory-supporting press. He said later that he was 'much too sensitive' about the press. 'God knows why I was, but I was. It was a basic human emotion to get a bit ratty about it.' He described reading the newspaper each day as 'a source of wonder', though not in a good way. 'I discovered what I thought, which I didn't think; what I said, which I didn't say; and what I was about to do, which I wasn't about to do.'

To rebrand the party at the 1993 conference, Major made a speech calling for the country 'to go back to basics' – meaning a simpler, kinder way of life. But the Tory Party's head of press briefed journalists that the speech was about sexual morality, family values and an end to permissive society. It gave the media a field day as they scrabbled to find examples of philandering by his ministers. They didn't have to look far; a succession of Tory ministers and MPs were forced to quit following strings of sexual and financial scandals. Labour made hay with what they called 'Tory sleaze'.

Major later talked about the 'routine' with which he would be telephoned over the weekend to be warned of the latest embarrassing story due to break in the Sunday papers. He became obsessed with the media. One of his aides told me that Major would insist on seeing the *Evening Standard* the moment it arrived in No. 10 at around midday. Officials would hide it from the Prime Minister for as long as they could, otherwise no work would get done until he had gone right the way through the paper. In the light of revelations after he left office about his love affair with Tory MP Edwina Currie before he became PM, he may well have been looking for any hint that the story might be about to surface.

The story only came out five years after Major lost the 1997 election, when Currie revealed their affair in her published diaries, describing Major as 'the big man in blue underpants'. In his sole comment on it, Major said that he was 'ashamed' of the affair and that his wife had forgiven him. In response, Currie, whom I later made a film about, retorted: 'John wasn't ashamed of it at the time and he wanted it to continue.'

'Now we know what John Major did after he sank a few pints of his favourite warm beer – he went for a Currie!' miaowed one letter-writer to *The Guardian*.

After a ruthlessly well-organised Labour campaign against 'Tory sleaze', John Major lost the 1997 election by a record margin. He went off to The Oval and wrote a poem which he called 'The Cricket Prayer'.

> Oh, Lord, if I must die today,
> Please make it after close of play.
> For this I know, if nothing more,
> I will not go without the score.

Throughout his time as PM following the 1992 election, Major had a slim majority which was steadily being whittled away. It meant that he was always on the edge in any crucial divisions in the House – and his survival would depend on the shadowy, powerful cohort of MPs of which he was once a member: the Tory Whips' Office. They were notoriously camera-shy, but in 1995 I embarked on trying to make a film about them, which we planned to call *Westminster's Secret Service*.

CHAPTER 21

THE SECRET WORLD OF THE WHIPS

In 1995, I set out to make a film about the highly secretive Conservative Whips' Office and the way it operates. With John Major's government engaging in civil war over Europe and a slew of Tory MPs' sex and money scandals, the whips were accused of deploying all the dark arts of their trade to keep the party in power.

The Whips' Office is the nerve centre of the Tory body politic. But its workings have always been shrouded in masonic mystery: discretion is like the calcium in the bones of a Tory Chief Whip. Unlike other ministers, Chief Whips take their official papers with them when they leave office, and they swear a vow of what one of them called *omertà* – the Mafia code of silence – about their work.

Along with two producers in the political documentary department, Alison Cahn and Manisha Vadhia, I set out to try to find Conservative whips past and present who might agree to appear in our documentary. Every Chief Whip heads a sixteen-strong team of whips, and Alison and Manisha spent many hours at the Tory Party conference and in the House trying to persuade serving and ex-whips to talk.

Once the then Chief Whip Richard Ryder learned of our plans, he summoned all living Tory government Chief Whips and their deputies to a meeting. There, as we later discovered, they agreed to a complete boycott of our film: none of them would speak to us on or off the record nor give us any help in making the programme.

This led to some comic, surreal meetings. One was with the former Deputy Chief Whip Lord (Bernard) Weatherill, who had gone on to become Speaker of the House. He had replied to our written request for him to participate saying: 'The work of the whips is imperfectly understood, I will be happy to talk to you and help you making your film. Indeed I would go so far as to say that you wouldn't be able to make the film without my cooperation – which I gladly give you.' So, we went to a pre-arranged meeting with him in his room in the Lords. We said how pleased we were that he had agreed to an interview, and he replied: 'Err… um…' We explained in more detail what we were planning, and he said: 'Err… um…' This went on for about five minutes, including us quoting from his acceptance letter – to no avail. In the end, we decided to leave and said goodbye, and the noble Lord said: 'Err… um…'

We subsequently worked out that Richard Ryder's meeting of senior Tory whips agreeing their boycott must have happened after Weatherill had sent his letter of agreement to cooperate – and he felt bound to keep the fact of Ryder's secret meeting secret from us. Hence, the most extraordinary meeting without words I had ever had.

Yet we were able to make the film because our blanket approach had paid off. In all, we contacted some eighty whips, most of them below the level of chief. Almost all refused to talk to us. But a handful agreed to speak off the record and another half-dozen agreed to take part. We had also located one of Major's serving Cabinet ministers who had been a whip and who agreed to appear. And I persuaded Willie Whitelaw to give us an interview. He had been Ted Heath's Chief Whip in opposition from 1965 to 1970, and Ryder had not thought to invite Whitelaw to his boycott meeting.

The origin of the term 'whip' comes from the hunting field: the whipper-in is the huntsman who has to keep the hounds hunting as a pack and round up the strays. In the documentary, we cut from a pack of baying hounds to a pack of baying backbenchers. The main task of the Whips' Office is to ensure the government gets its business through the House and to maintain party discipline. The Tory whips prefer to carry out their work away from the public gaze. As one of them put it to me: 'Whippin', like strippin', should be done in private.'

Each whip is responsible for a group of some forty MPs, known as their flock, who represent a specific area of the country. Until Mrs Thatcher came to power, the Tory Whips' Office tended to be run on military lines and was peopled by middle-aged former army officers. But in more recent times the office became a political training ground for bright young men.

The always outrageous Alan Clark said: 'The concept of having clever, tough, congenial people in the Whips' Office is relatively new. In former times they were just field sport enthusiasts whose last and only fulfilment period had been bullying (and in some cases buggering) Lower Boys at Eton. Now it is recognised as a nursery for junior ministers.'

And not just junior ministers. Over a third of John Major's Cabinet, including himself, Ken Clarke, Michael Portillo and John Selwyn Gummer, served their apprenticeships in the Whips' Office at 12 Downing Street. It was in that house of secrets that they learned where the bodies were buried – and, indeed, how to bury them. Major's survival skills as Prime Minister owed much to his whip training.

The Tory Camorra likes to preserve its mystique. 'We are the last safe house in Europe – more secure than MI5,' Tristan Garel-Jones, Mrs Thatcher's Deputy Chief Whip, told me. Another recent ex-whip said: 'I cannot discuss with an outsider what whips do; it would break our code of honour and confidentiality.'

Since the whips deal daily with MPs and their problems, a quasi-Hippocratic code about individual cases is understandable – but they extend it to every aspect of their work. When the then National Heritage Secretary Stephen Dorrell, a whip from 1987 to 1990, agreed to give us a filmed interview, a serving whip, Andrew Mitchell, went up to him in the Members' Lobby of the Commons and hissed 'traitor'.

As in the grander London clubs, at the time we were filming in 1995, no one could become a whip unless the other whips approved – one blackball excludes. Former Tory whips told me how they were inducted into the club. 'I had to be security cleared,' said Sir Hugh Rossi, who was a whip in Ted Heath's government from 1970 to 1974. 'I was asked to go to No. 12 and a very tall man with a long face walked in wearing a black suit and a wing collar. He sat down and said: "We can find nothing against you in security terms and we are reasonably satisfied. I have only one piece of advice to give you – don't go to bed with a Russian of either sex." And he walked out.'

Sir Michael Neubert, who became a senior whip in a five-year term under Mrs Thatcher, told me: 'I had gone out to have a haircut and was just walking back across St James's Park and suddenly one of the most senior whips spotted me. He took me by the arm and held me in a vice-like grip and said: "Don't move," and I realised that I was to be invited to join the government Whips' Office.'

According to Tim Fortescue, a senior whip under Heath, 'the Tory Whips' Office is a self-perpetuating oligarchy: there is no nonsense about democracy'. And Cecil Parkinson, who was a whip under both Heath in government and Mrs Thatcher in opposition, said: 'We don't roll our trousers up or pin knives to our breasts or anything of that kind. It is just people who spend a tremendous amount of time together and are privy to a lot of the innermost secrets of the party and the government.'

The one group of Tory MPs persistently blackballed from the Whips' Office – again in shades of clubland – were women. When we made our film, there had never been a female Tory whip. Michael Neubert explained: 'I think when men get together they have different interests and priorities from women:

that's the essence of manhood. And mixing the two might get in the way of some of the more masculine activities of the Whips' Office.' What does that mean? 'Well, the general badinage might be more difficult to sustain. Sometimes it was found when Mrs Thatcher, as Prime Minister, came to see the whips, she might not always appreciate a man's joke and think it frivolous or trivial.'

Cecil Parkinson provided a glimpse of these masculine activities. Three times a year, there are black-tie dinners for whips only, at the Carlton Club or in Downing Street. 'These dinners are a chance for the whips to let their hair down, to have a clubby-type evening, perhaps drink a little bit more than usual and play whips' games,' said Parkinson. 'These games are not smashing the furniture but just drawing up lists of people and having a bit of a laugh. But I'd be drummed out of the club if I told you more than that.'

On their little lists at dinner are the whips' least favourite MPs, both on their own benches and among the opposition. And, like White's Club, they nominate an overall 'Shit of the Year'. At the first whips' dinner Parkinson attended in the Carlton Club in January 1974, the Prime Minister, Ted Heath, himself a former Chief Whip, arrived, picked up the list and remarked: 'Still the same old names, I see.'

Heath was the first chief, as they are known, to move two doors down the road from No. 12 to No. 10. But the inspiration for the most notorious Tory chief turned Prime Minister – Francis Urquhart in *House of Cards* – was said to be not Heath but Tristan Garel-Jones. Dubbed 'The Prince of Darkness',

Garel-Jones became Deputy Chief Whip under Mrs Thatcher and reputedly knew as much about the private lives of Tory MPs as their bank managers or their wives – in some cases more.

'Tristan fostered the image that he was up to all sorts of tricks,' Cecil Parkinson told me, 'and he doesn't deny the fact that he loves conspiring. He'd sit in the tearoom and say: "I am only in politics so that I can be Chief Whip when Chris Patten goes to No. 10."' Garel-Jones had two different faces when talking about the Whips' Office and his role in it. Privately, he explained that the whips' sinister public image actually serves their purpose – 'for once the media's exaggeration actually helps because it terrifies new MPs'. On the record, he was more down to earth and told me: 'The only reason you journalists are so fascinated by the Whips' Office is because it's the only secure part of Parliament; it's the one part of Westminster that does not leak. It doesn't tell anybody – and certainly I'm not going to tell anybody – how it works and what it does. In fact the essential job of the whips is a rather dull one – they make sure that MPs turn up for work and they put out the lights after everyone has gone home at night. And they manoeuvre with skill around that no man's land where the rights of the executive, the opposition and Parliament meet.'

But in his more Urquhartish moments, Garel-Jones claimed that the whips know more, do more and have more influence than any outsider can imagine. The problem, he maintained, is that if what the whips actually do is exposed, the system will no longer work.

I had been on friendly terms for some years with Richard Ryder, the Chief Whip. But he told me he could not possibly comment on his methods, arguing that he was only following a well-established convention and adding with a light laugh: 'And because I am a real bastard.' The joke about the boyish-looking Ryder was that he wore his watch face inwards because he did not regard the time of day as public information.

One of the chief's central tasks is to act as the Prime Minister's eyes, ears and nose: to sniff out conspiracies and revolting elements in the parliamentary party. 'You've got to be totally straight with your Prime Minister and very close, and he or she has to trust you completely,' former Tory Chief Whip Willie Whitelaw told me.

Although not formally a member, the chief attends all Cabinet meetings and key Cabinet committees. He has regular scheduled meetings with the Prime Minister and could slip in unobtrusively to see him (or her) at any other time through the interconnecting corridor between No. 10 and No. 12. The Whips' Office is a two-way conduit between the leadership and the backbenchers, and Prime Ministers rarely attempt to second-guess the chief's headcount on a controversial bill.

'We need to know whether an individual MP is likely to vote against or abstain and what are the reasons,' said Hugh Rossi. 'Some reasons may be political; some may be due to purely personal problems.' So how do you find this out? 'Gossip. I can't think of a more gossipy place than the Commons.' In their role as intelligence gatherers, the whips seek to make friends with as many MPs as they can, and an effective Whips' Office always has its members in the tearoom and the bars, lobbies and committee rooms of the Commons.

'If three or four MPs are gathered together, one of them is always going to be loose-tongued', said the former Tory leader Iain Duncan Smith, 'and is going to say something which gets passed back to the whips or [they] will seek to buy favour by telling the whips what is going on.' Like the police, the good whip has a network of informants – from MPs to Commons door keepers – who are known as 'whips' narks'.

Once they learn of a potential rebellion, the whips deploy every weapon in their armoury to quash it. Stephen Dorrell claimed: 'The most widely used method is actually the best one: to persuade on the merits of the argument. And if you can't, then you can always appeal to party loyalty. For a party divided against itself is one that is not going to stand well in public opinion.'

Another persuasive weapon is patronage. The Chief Whip's official title is Patronage Secretary, and the whips pride themselves on their skills as political talent-spotters. A whip sits on the front bench, following every speech that is made in the Chamber and in committees. At their weekly meetings, they compare notes about potential high-flyers and ministers who are not cutting the mustard. The chief passes the assessments to No. 10 and has considerable sway in ministerial appointments.

Every reshuffle is a whips' reshuffle, claimed Tristan Garel-Jones. And Tim Fortescue admitted that the whips would remind potential rebels of their powers of patronage. 'Oh, very subtly indeed, we'd say: "You're ambitious, aren't you – you'd like to be a minister? I'll make a note of that,"' Fortescue said with a knowing grin.

Whips' blandishments include the prospect of honours (a knighthood for a male MP means his wife becomes a Lady), exotic parliamentary trips and, at the time we were making our film, appointing the chairs and members of Commons Select Committees. The whips also control the allocation of MPs' offices in the Commons. A ruling tenet of the Whips' Office is that almost every MP wants something; the few who do not they refer to as 'whips' nightmares'. Sometimes the designations are less courteous.

'Oh, there is a shits' whip,' said the then Tory MP Rupert Allason, who himself would sometimes ignore a three-line whip – a mandatory written instruction to vote for the government which is underlined three times. Allason told me: 'In the Whips' Office in the Commons there is a blackboard with a curtain across it, and on it is the shits' list. I was once shown it by a whip just to demonstrate that I hadn't achieved membership of the list.'

The point of such designations is for the whips to know where to concentrate their persuasive efforts; they target the potential waverers or 'wets' (a term ironically first invented by the whips during the Heath government) and tend to ignore the long-term rebels who are unbiddable. The whips like to match their approach to the individual, varying from the psychological to the physical. Most Tory MPs seem to get on well with their individual whips. But in the early '90s, things came to a head during the debates on the famous Maastricht Treaty, which Tory Eurosceptics saw as an attack on Britain's sovereignty and as the roadmap to a federal Europe.

The Eurosceptics accused the whips of going way over the top in their prolonged efforts to propel the Maastricht legislation through Parliament. One whip they often fingered was David Lightbown, a notorious bruiser who weighed an estimated twenty stone. His intimidating presence reportedly reduced some young Tory MPs to tears during Maastricht. In a rare on-the-record comment, Lightbown said: 'I think most people I deal with understand my powers of persuasion. And they are not all sticking them up against the wall and putting the knee in. I sometimes kiss them better.'

One former Tory minister, Nicholas Fairbairn, said openly what many other Eurosceptics claimed privately during Maastricht: 'I am appalled at numerous reports that the whips saw fit to threaten to expose extra-marital conduct by backbench colleagues in order to persuade them to abandon their consciences. There has been, so far as I am aware, no denial of these reports.'

Whips told me that they did seek to know all about the lives of their flocks – not for purposes of blackmail but because they want to understand any political or personal pressures which might affect voting intentions. We discovered that the whips would enter details about the private lives of Tory MPs in what they call the Black Book or the Dirt Book, which was kept locked in the Chief Whip's safe. 'The Dirt Book is just a little book where you write down various things you know or hear about people,' said Whitelaw. What kind of things? I asked. The Delphic Whitelaw replied: 'Oh, I think you could make a very good guess. Things that are happening in life to varying people that you have heard about or know about, which may be true.'

Tim Fortescue was more forthcoming about what went into the Dirt Book: 'Oh, scandalous stories. Which are possibly not accurate. But you say Member Bloggs told me at dinner this evening that Member X is seeing a lot of somebody's wife, not his own. That would go in.' I asked Fortescue what the Dirt Book's purpose was. 'So that we know everything about everybody, because we are a very efficient organisation. And when you are trying to persuade a member to vote the way he doesn't want to vote on a controversial issue – which is part of your job – it is possible to suggest very mildly that perhaps it would not be in his interest if people knew something or other.'

Fortescue continued: 'Anyone with any sense who was in trouble would come to the Whips' Office and tell them the truth: "I am in a jam, can you help me?" It might be debt, it might be a scandal involving small boys or any kind of scandal which a member might be mixed up in. They would come and ask us to help, and if we could, we did. [This quote from Fortescue would be widely recycled twenty years later during the parliamentary paedophile scandal.] And we would do everything we could, because we would store up brownie points. That sounds a pretty nasty reason, but it's one of the reasons. Because if we could get a chap out of trouble then he'll do as we ask for ever more.'

But Rupert Allason claimed that the modern Whips' Office was 'full of thrusting, ambitious young men – about the last people to whom you would wish to confide some kind of infidelity or indiscretion'.

When I asked Stephen Dorrell about the use of the Dirt Book as a whips' weapon, he responded with a half-smile: 'I think that most whips know rather less about their colleagues' lives than their colleagues might think – like all police work, it's based to some extent on a confidence trick.' Another former Tory whip, who didn't want to be identified, put it more starkly: 'It's like the Society of Jesus in the eighteenth century: you show them the Bible but also the instruments of torture.'

Tristan Garel-Jones had a different perspective: 'Never repeated by this loyal brotherhood of whips are the thousand acts of unremarked kindness they perform as part of their stock-in-trade for Tory MPs who face personal problems.' He went on to claim that 'the whips are the unsung heroes of British democracy', and he added a quote from Enoch Powell: 'Westminster without whips would be like a city without sewers.'

One former Tory Chief Whip who did not want his name mentioned later explained why the whips observe *omertà* about their work. He said: 'A Conservative Chief Whip is a bit of a Father Confessor, and we deal with a lot of personal problems – and not just the usual myths of whipping and throwing people off the roof of the Commons [what Francis Urquhart did to his mistress]. Therefore, Chief Whips would never be trusted by our flocks if they thought that at some future date a chief would spill the beans and they might be revealed, however tangentially. There has only ever been one Conservative Chief Whip who wrote a book and revealed whipping information. He has never been invited to any whips' function since.'

The only chief to fit that description was the late Tim Renton, Margaret Thatcher's final Chief Whip, who died in August 2020. His book gave little away, but it was enough to make him persona non grata with the brotherhood. And the entertainer Gyles Brandreth, who was a junior whip under Major from 1995 to 1997, wrote a book about his time in the Whips' Office called *Breaking the Code*. On the day it was published, Brandreth says he received a large envelope, hand-delivered to his home. He opened it, and inside was another envelope which he opened, and inside was yet another envelope. He opened it and inside was a double-folded piece of paper which he carefully opened. The paper was blank, except in the middle there was a black spot.

CHAPTER 22

A VERY SOCIAL DEMOCRAT

For the next of my candid portraits of top politicos, Anne Tyerman, the head of political documentaries, and I came up with Roy Jenkins. Widely known as Woy, he was a coal-miner's son who became Labour Chancellor of the Exchequer, Home Secretary, first and only British President of the EU Commission, a founder of the Social Democratic Party (SDP) and high on the list of candidates for best Prime Minister we never had. We were also to discover he had a fascinating love life.

I first met Roy Jenkins on a cricket pitch in 1954, when I was fourteen. He and a number of other members of the centre-left think tank the Fabian Society were playing against a Surrey village, and I was roped in to make up the numbers. I still have the team photo, which includes Bill Rodgers, who was later to help Jenkins create the SDP. I was the only one wearing cricket whites. We managed to beat the village, partly due to Jenkins's cunning left-arm spin bowling. Many years later, I filmed Jenkins playing croquet at his house, where he demonstrated a sharp eye for angles and a ruthless instinct. 'The object of the game', he told me, 'is to keep your own two balls together and separate your opponent's balls.'

In filming our Jenkins profile, I witnessed a pretty scene at the National Liberal Club in Whitehall in May 1996. Helena Bonham Carter, the chattering class's favourite actress, was at the feet of Jenkins, looking up admiringly as he made a speech. Other members of the formidable Bonham Carter clan, as well as Liberal grandees and assorted glitterati, were assembled to celebrate the publication of Helena's grandmother's diaries. Lady Violet Bonham Carter was the daughter of Asquith, the Liberal Prime Minister whose biography had been written by a young Jenkins, and the Bonham Carters were Jenkins's intimate friends.

After an elegantly witty speech, Jenkins moved off rapidly. He was due at Buckingham Palace for a banquet in honour of the French President, Jacques Chirac. Dame Jennifer Jenkins, his wife, had advised her husband that it would have been inappropriate to appear at the publishing party in the full fig of white tie and tails with decorations; after a quick change, he joined the Establishment in its full splendour.

The Rt Hon. Lord Jenkins of Hillhead OM felt quite at home. He told me afterwards that the Bordeaux at dinner, an '88 Pichon Longueville, was rather better than was usual on such state occasions.

At the age of seventy-five, the coal-miner's son still retained a singular capacity for calling forth vitriol from his many detractors – on both the right and the left. They accused him of class betrayal, Europhilia, arrogance and snobbery. 'The only

thing Woy ever fought for was a table for two at the Mirabelle,'
claimed one of his senior Labour colleagues. But his image as
a claret-quaffing, duchess-loving Establishment pillar missed
many aspects of the man.

He was no Tory. His instincts were libertarian, internation-
alist and radical; he was something of a political gambler. He
was also a politician with a hinterland: he wrote award-winning
biographies of great men, including Gladstone, Asquith and
Churchill. And he had many eccentricities.

When my producer, Alison Cahn, and I filmed him at his
country house in the Cotswolds, we saw bizarre evidence of
this. Although he was surrounded by picturesque countryside,
Jenkins chose to take his pre-breakfast walk on his tennis court.
He marched round and across the court in what he called 'an
elaborate series of zig-zags'. It was surreal to watch, but he explained it logically: 'I walk for exactly forty-five minutes: shorter
would be too short and longer would consume too much time.
It makes me feel rather virtuous – and it relieves me of the need
to take any further exercise for the rest of the day.'

He kept lists of the exact number of words he wrote every
day and used to enjoy swapping railway timetables and cricket
statistics with Harold Wilson in No. 10. One of his former civil
servants told me that Jenkins was the only minister he had ever
worked for who knew exactly how long it took for the main
traffic lights to change in every major city in Britain. You could
almost call him an anorak – except that Jenkins would scarcely
have recognised such a garment, still less have been able to pronounce it. Harold Macmillan, the Old Etonian Prime Minister

who married a duke's daughter, once asked about the young Roy Jenkins: 'Who is that grand fellow who makes me feel so common?'

But Jenkins was not born to the purple, and much of the criticism of him and his manner stemmed from the peculiarly British resentment of people who are seen to have moved out of their class. He had working-class origins many other would-be Labour leaders would kill for. His birthplace was the South Wales coal-mining valleys, and he was the only child of a pit-face worker. But Arthur Jenkins was a pretty unusual miner. He had studied at the Sorbonne in Paris and at Ruskin College, Oxford. A year after his son was born, he never hewed another lump of coal again.

Instead, he became a leader of the local mining union and then Labour MP for Pontypool. When we were filming there, Arthur Jenkins was more fondly remembered than Jenkins's mother, who was upwardly mobile enough to be nicknamed 'The Duchess'. Roy Jenkins claimed that his father had a greater influence on him socially than his mother: 'Insofar as some people think I've got slightly grand, Whiggish tastes – they came more from him than from her.'

To his father's delight, the Abersychan Grammar School boy won a place at Balliol College, Oxford, where one of his tutors described him as 'nature's Old Etonian'. There, Jenkins first developed the voice – once described as like gargling in treacle – that would lay him open to ridicule in later years. But Jenkins told me: 'A whole variety of people – like the old Lord Salisbury

– haven't been able to pronounce their 'R's very ruggedly. That's perhaps a word I oughtn't to use too much,' he added ruefully.

Jenkins gained a first in politics, philosophy and economics. His history tutor had told him: 'I am not sure how much you know, but you write it in a fine style – which I couldn't teach you, and which will be of more value to you than anything I could teach you.'

He was still at Oxford when he met the woman to whom he was to be married for nearly sixty years. Jennifer Morris was a Cambridge undergraduate from a professional family. She told me: 'Roy has always been the most engaging companion I've ever known; many other attractions, too. It has always been better to be with him than with anybody else.'

Recruited into army intelligence during the war, Jenkins worked as a codebreaker at Bletchley Park, seeking to decipher top-secret German signals. 'It was the most frustrating mental experience of my life,' Jenkins told me. 'Particularly as the act of trying almost physically hurt one's brain, which became distinctly raw if it was not relieved by the catharsis of achievement.'

Three years after the war, he had become the youngest MP in the House at the age of twenty-seven. Ironically, he started on the left and wrote a *Tribune* pamphlet advocating a stringent wealth tax, satirically entitled 'Fair Shares for the Rich'. But he soon fell under the spell of the rising star of the Labour right, Hugh Gaitskell, who won the party leadership in 1955. 'Hugh was the one person in politics I have not merely liked but have loved,' Jenkins told me. 'He really did have an inspirational effect on me as a leader.' In the internecine battles against the left-wing Bevanites, Jenkins became a key member of the Gaitskell set. It combined high living with high politics and wanted to transform Labour into the natural party of moderate government.

When Harold Wilson was elected Labour leader after Gaitskell's sudden death in 1963, Jenkins thought of leaving politics altogether. But within three years he had become minister for the swinging '60s in the Wilson government. As a young Home Secretary, he encouraged radical reforms of Britain's social and sexual laws. Divorce was made easier, homosexuality and abortion were legalised and theatre censorship was abolished altogether. 'I am a libertarian, and I was trying to make Britain a more liberal and open society,' Jenkins told me.

He was regularly tipped as a future Labour Prime Minister. When he moved from the Home Office to become Chancellor, he revived the economy after the trauma of the 1967 devaluation of the pound. But there were many in his party who saw him as the best Tory Chancellor since the war and who deeply distrusted his lifestyle. 'Roy is a very impressive figure with a lot of friends and social contacts,' said Harold Wilson in interview. 'He still felt that it was all like Asquith's day, where everything is done over a rather lush dinner table with good claret. But I never thought the Labour Party could be run on the basis of dinner parties. I hardly had any at Downing Street – a sandwich occasionally.'

For his part, Jenkins told me that he had only ever had a sandwich for lunch once in all his professional life, 'and I never repeated the experience'. A beleaguered Harold Wilson was becoming increasingly convinced that Jenkins was using his social contacts to seek to replace him as Prime Minister.

It was a hysterical era, when all kinds of lurid rumours about conspiracies against Wilson were circulating, many involving high public figures such as Lord Mountbatten. A classic case that sparked Wilson's suspicions came in July 1966. Jenkins had gone to stay for a country house weekend with Ann Fleming, the society hostess wife of writer Ian Fleming. He was the creator of James Bond and she had been Gaitskell's mistress.

Barbara Castle, a fellow Cabinet colleague of Jenkins, recounted in her diary a conversation with Wilson where he fingered Jenkins: 'The interesting thing was Harold's obsession with plots against him. He dilated to me about ministers who went a-whoring after society hostesses. He mentioned Lady Pamela Berry, whose parties Jenkins attended. And Harold said: "Mrs Ian Fleming is another one. If any of you knew your job, you would find out who attended that weekend meeting at her place when I was in Moscow."'

Jenkins laughed off the idea when I put the quote to him: 'That was pure paranoia on Wilson's part. Ann Fleming was a friend of mine, but the idea that she could have been a significant factor in a plot to change the leadership of the Labour Party is absolutely insane fantasy. If I was engaging in a plot to make myself leader, I don't think the way I would go about it would be to go a-whoring or anything else after society hostesses.'

Wilson's charge, though, had special resonance in a party weaned on tales of its leaders, from Ramsay MacDonald onwards, being seduced by the upper classes to betray a Labour

government. The PM's suspicions about Jenkins's social connections were fuelled both by security service reports and by
Colonel George Wigg MP (known as Earwig), Wilson's baleful
bloodhound who saw his job as digging up the dirt on fellow
Cabinet ministers. For there was no doubting Jenkins's attraction for the discreet charms of the aristocracy. And while I was
making the film about him, I discovered that over the years
he'd had a number of unpublicised love affairs with high-born
women.

The idea of Jenkins as a serial swordsman was a novel one,
and I knew I had to ask him about it. But how to raise it in interview? I thought I would take my cue from his own approach
as a political biographer. Years earlier Jenkins had been commissioned by his great friend Mark Bonham Carter to write the life
of his grandfather H. H. Asquith, the Liberal Prime Minister
from 1908 to 1916.

Jenkins had to decide how to treat the question of Asquith's
love life. It was rumoured that while in No. 10 Asquith had a
long affair with a society beauty, Venetia Stanley. Jenkins had
been given access to a huge tranche of hitherto unseen love
letters that the sexagenarian Prime Minister had written to his
would-be mistress, who was thirty-five years his junior. The letters were strong stuff and showed Asquith had become obsessed
with Miss Stanley. He would send her as many as three letters a
day – sometimes even writing them during meetings of the War
Cabinet. Jenkins had to choose: should he use the letters and
risk the wrath of his friend's formidable mother, Lady Violet –
or should he ignore them? He decided on disclosure.

That seemed a good example for us to follow. We had discovered that Jenkins had had a series of love affairs, some of them with the wives of his best friends. They included Caroline Gilmour, daughter of the impossibly rich Duke of Buccleuch and wife of Tory MP Ian Gilmour. And secondly, Leslie Bonham Carter, a Condé Nast heiress who, ironically, was the wife of Jenkins's publisher Mark Bonham Carter. Both the husbands learned about Jenkins's affairs with their wives and acquiesced in them, partly because it gave them carte blanche to have liaisons of their own.

I thought the best way into raising the subject with Jenkins was to talk to him about writing political biographies and how much they should include details of private lives. With his customary precision, Jenkins answered: 'Well, these things tend to go in waves. It used to be the case that there was nothing at all about the private lives – but more recently the pendulum has swung the other way – perhaps too far.'

'I am interested you say that,' I responded, 'because in your own autobiography you make no mention of the series of affairs you have had, often with the wives of your best friends.'

The room fell very silent, then Jenkins said: 'I've never commented on these things because I think on the one hand if you deny something, it's rather ungallant. But if you confirm something, it's like Budget secrets – best not talked about.' And he stonewalled further questions.

We subsequently learned that Jenkins had succeeded in keeping his love affairs out of the media by swearing friends to secrecy until his death. And both he and his wife managed to remain good friends with his lovers and their husbands. It was what Jenkins might have called an agreeable and civilised throwback to the Bloomsbury Set and Edwardian England.

When Harold Wilson suddenly resigned as Prime Minister in 1976, Jenkins stood for the party leadership. By then, though, he had become disillusioned with Labour. Also, the left's dossier of his crimes against the party included his austere regime at the Treasury and his voting with the Heath government in favour of Britain's entry into Europe. He came a poor third behind James Callaghan and Michael Foot. 'I think by that time it wasn't in the stars I was going to win,' Jenkins told me. 'I wanted to win, but the result didn't shatter me.' Shirley Williams said: 'If Roy had gone on looking as if he came from that Welsh mining valley, I think his route to the premiership would have been unstoppable.'

Jenkins left the government to become President of the European Commission in Brussels, where his grand ways gained him the nickname '*Le Roi Jean Quinze*'. He presented an incongruous spectacle when he appeared as a jogger in the Parc du Cinquantenaire behind the commission building, wearing a tracksuit but smoking a cigar. As President, he relaunched the idea of European Monetary Union – to which he remained totally committed.

But he was back in Britain after only four years, with an ambitious plan to break the mould of two-party politics. He told me: 'I thought the Labour Party had got itself into an appalling mess. I didn't in the least like Thatcherite Conservatism, and I thought there ought to be a third route.' It was a phrase he used long before Blair ever talked of the Third Way.

Jenkins and three other former Labour Cabinet ministers, Dr David Owen, Shirley Williams and Bill Rodgers, known as the Gang of Four, came together to create a new centre party – the SDP. The aim was to attract moderate Tories disillusioned by Mrs Thatcher, and Labour voters alienated by the Bennite left, along with people who had never taken an interest in politics.

The new party took off like a rocket. Thirty MPs, twenty-nine from Labour and one Conservative, crossed the floor to join. In by-elections, Shirley Williams won the safe Labour seat of Crosby and Jenkins took a seat in Glasgow and became the party's first leader. At the time, Bill Rodgers even suggested to me that I might like to consider standing as an SDP parliamentary candidate. I thanked him and said I preferred filming politics to doing it.

In early 1982, the SDP briefly topped 50 per cent in the opinion polls, while Mrs Thatcher was ranked the most unpopular PM since polling began. There was even fervid talk of Roy Jenkins becoming the next Prime Minister. But then came the Falklands – and Mrs Thatcher's landslide election victory the following year. The SDP was left with just six MPs. The party's middle-class image and fuzzy policies had led to them being ridiculed as the soggy Dems. And Roy Jenkins resigned as leader.

Yet from the beginning, the new party contained the seeds of its own destruction. 'Roy was just an old man in a hurry,' Dr

David Owen told me. 'He saw the SDP as a disposable vehicle for his ambition to become Prime Minister.'

'Nonsense,' responded Jenkins. 'If anyone disposed of the SDP, it was David Owen.'

The Labour left's view was that the sole effect of the SDP on British politics was to help keep Mrs Thatcher in power for a decade. *Au contraire*, Jenkins told me in 1996: 'The SDP had a profound shock effect in causing the unelectable Labour Party to reform itself. I think Tony Blair's New Labour owes a great deal to the SDP. Nothing does the Labour Party more harm than when it turns on itself in a mood of proletarian sullenness. Blair epitomises the reverse of this.'

Jenkins also paid his protégé the ultimate compliment, by calling Blair the best Labour leader since his idol Hugh Gaitskell.

Jenkins held many of the great public offices – though not the top one. But in his mid-seventies he had become a mentor to the man who was odds-on favourite to be the next Prime Minister, the leader of New Labour, Tony Blair. Blair came to lunch at East Hendred, Jenkins's country home in Oxfordshire, where the new leader hung on the old statesman's words. At that stage Blair had never held government office and, remarkably, had only once set foot inside No. 10, while Jenkins was the biographer of numerous Prime Ministers, and arguably knew more about the job than anyone else who had never held the post.

Jenkins both helped augment Blair's sense of history and familiarised him with the ways of modern Whitehall. And he told me he arranged discreet dinners at one of his clubs for Blair and top mandarins, including the Cabinet Secretary Sir Robin

Butler. Blair and Jenkins established an easy intimacy in their regular phone conversations, with the Labour leader normally initiating the call. 'I like Tony Blair,' Jenkins told me. 'I find him engaging – he is not too serious, not politically obsessed.'

Jenkins's close relationship with Blair meant that he might still have become an éminence grise to a new Labour government, although that was some way from holding the top job. 'Of course I would have liked to be Prime Minister,' Jenkins told me. 'But I don't think I had the necessary ruthless steel to seize the job. As I look around, I think I have a rather happier and more agreeable life in my seventies than most of those who have been Prime Minister.'

Jenkins had become a figure of pervasive, if discreet, power and influence: leader of the Liberal Democrat peers, Chancellor of Oxford University and a member of all the most select political clubs (the rules of one state: 'The names of the Executive Committee shall be wrapped in impenetrable mystery'). Even some of those who were once among his powerful right-wing detractors, such as Sir Peregrine Worsthorne, now admitted: 'He is the last of the grand old men who live up to one's idea of what a grand old statesman should be.'

When Roy Jenkins died in 2003, among those who came to his crowded funeral were the Prime Minister Tony Blair, as well as both his paramours, Caroline Gilmour and Violet Bonham Carter. Jennifer Jenkins wrote a poignant note with her flowers: 'To Roy, my only love. Sixty-two years and five months.'

CHAPTER 23

TB OR NOT TB

The first time I pointed a TV camera at Tony Blair was at a by-election in 1982. He was standing as the Labour candidate in the true-blue seat of Beaconsfield in Buckinghamshire. One of my first lines in the final film was: 'The Labour candidate Tony Blair looks exactly like the kind of young man that the matrons of Beaconsfield would be happy to see escorting their daughters to the Young Conservatives Ball.'

His multi-toothed grin made him look younger than his twenty-nine years. The Beaconsfield constituency housed the country churchyard where Gray had written his celebrated elegy. One couplet resonated with me:

> Full many a flower was born to blush unseen,
> And waste its sweetness on the desert air.

It seemed to me to sum up Blair's chances in the by-election, and I told him later that was why I used it in the film. He responded: 'I learned from that never to be filmed in front of a graveyard.' It was a good line, but we never actually filmed him in front of a graveyard.

We did, though, film him going to have lunch in a local pub with the Labour leader Michael Foot. When Foot emerged, I asked him about Labour's chances in the by-election. 'Tony Blair is a wonderful candidate – one of the best possible candidates there could be. And whatever the result here, he is going to have a big future in British politics.'

It was not a belief I shared at that time. I thought Blair was a public-school boy with a big grin and our paths were unlikely ever to cross again. At Beaconsfield, Labour's share of the vote halved as the Falklands factor boosted the Tories, and Blair was beaten into third place and lost his deposit.

But the following year Blair included in his application to stand for the safe Labour seat of Sedgefield a transcript of what Foot had said. He won the nomination against a strong field, and Foot's comment may well have hastened Blair's elevation to Westminster.

Blair remembered that one of the first people he met in the Commons after Mrs Thatcher's landslide victory in the 1983 election was the former Prime Minister Ted Heath. He was in his customary gracious form and said to Blair: 'You, an MP? What party?'

'The Labour Party,' replied Blair.

'Well, you don't look it. Or sound like it,' laughed Heath, shoulders heaving.

As an MP, Blair was swiftly presented to the country as the acceptable face of Labour by the party's new communications director, Peter Mandelson. Blair told me: 'Every time the Labour Party said: "Let's address the public," they wanted someone who looked vaguely respectable and could talk in a language the public might find appealing. So I was wheeled out – I was very lucky, I was the beneficiary of that.'

When he won the Labour leadership in 1994, Blair was determined to transform the party's image and disenfranchise the so-called 'loony left'. His private pollster Philip Gould told me that when he asked Blair what the heart of his strategy was, 'Tony's reply was emphatic: reassurance, reassurance, reassurance.'

Blair had taken as his role model the charismatic American President Bill Clinton, whose media techniques he emulated. Clinton had won power after twelve years of Republicans in the White House partly by rebranding his own party as the 'New Democrats'. Labour had been in opposition for a decade and a half when Blair became the first leader of 'New Labour'. In the following years, the two lawyers Clinton and Blair, both educated at Oxford, would unblushingly lift each other's rhetoric – with a little light polishing. Clinton promised in a speech: 'Not bigger government, more effective government.' Echoed Blair: 'Not bigger government, better government.' 'Opportunity and responsibility: they go hand in hand,' proclaimed Clinton; Blair's version was: 'And in return for those opportunities – responsibility.' 'New ideas for new challenges,' said Clinton. 'New challenges, new ideas,' said Blair.

Sometimes, Blair would come up with the line first. In September 1996, with Labour still in opposition, I watched Blair wowing his party conference when he proclaimed: 'At the time of the next election there will be just one thousand days until the new millennium: a thousand days to prepare for a thousand years.'

In his State of the Union Address four months later, President Clinton declared: 'Tomorrow there will be just over one thousand days until the year 2000. One thousand days to build a bridge to a land of new promise. My fellow Americans, let us seize those days and the century.' The US President was only one tenth as ambitious as the putative British Prime Minister; Clinton only sought a century, while Blair wanted a New Labour millennium (with unfortunate echoes of the Thousand-Year Reich).

When I asked Blair about the verbal cross-pollination with the President, he was unapologetic: 'We are two leaders facing many of the same kinds of problems and both looking for similar new, modern ways of dealing with them.' Clinton echoed that thought. Standing next to Blair at a televised press conference in the Downing Street Rose Garden after New Labour's 1997 landslide, the President said: 'All governors should borrow shamelessly from one another.' The Tory Rottweiler Norman Tebbit was less gracious: 'Blair is just Clinton with his trousers zipped up.'

I had been seeking to make a genuine access film about Blair from almost the moment he was elected Labour leader. It took six years for Blair and his chief spin doctor Alastair Campbell to agree. New Labour had developed the slickest publicity operation up to that time in British politics. The Conservative attack line that the government was all spin and no substance was gaining traction. Blair and Campbell agreed to give Anne Tyerman and myself access to film New Labour's news management machine behind the scenes at No. 10. 'I may be making the biggest mistake of my professional career in letting you in,' Campbell told me and Anne.

For us, it represented a great challenge: how to prevent the king of spin putting the spin on us? In his diary, Campbell wrote: 'Cockerell was a bit pushy but I felt on balance it was right to get some kind of film which showed what we actually did, as opposed to all the bollocks written about us.'

Campbell's deputy, Lance Price, used rather saltier language in his diary to explain why we were being let in to film: 'The idea is to show that lobby journalists are a bunch of wankers, interested only in trivia and personalities.' Both Blair and Campbell felt convinced that the political journalists known as the lobby were, in the PM's words, 'corrosively cynical'. Campbell said: 'The press – hand-in-hand with the Conservatives – say that everything we do is just spin. It is all part of their strategy to say "you can't trust the Prime Minister; that this guy doesn't really stack up, doesn't stand for anything".'

We were given unprecedented access to Blair, Campbell and the No. 10 media operation for three months. They made no prior conditions and had no editorial rights over the finished film. For the first time, we were able to film Campbell's twice-daily anonymous briefing to the lobby journalists, which had until then always been shrouded in secrecy. What we captured on camera was a state of bitter conflict between No. 10 and the media – with each side accusing the other of faking the news and with both sides convinced they were more spinned against than spinning.

But as the filming went on, Campbell became increasingly concerned in his diaries about the decision to give us access. 'I had the nagging feeling that letting Cockerell in was a mistake,' wrote Campbell one week. He followed it up the next by saying: 'TB is very sensitive to the possible thesis that he could not do anything without being directed – that he couldn't cope without me.' The following month Campbell noted: 'TB was antsy and hoping to get Cockerell out of our hair.'

Probably the best spontaneous moment came when we filmed the shirt-sleeved Prime Minister coming into the smartly suited Campbell's office in No. 10, looking rather like the nervous schoolboy entering the headmaster's study. As Campbell put it in his diary: 'I was behind my desk with TB looking on a bit anxiously. It looked like I was the boss and he was explaining himself, which got me worried.'

Lance Price's diary version was: 'TB was effectively ambushed when he walked into AC's office while Cockerell was filming.' The PM certainly looked a little startled to see us but recovered his composure when I asked how important Campbell was to him. 'I think I've hired the best in the business. At least, I hope I have,' replied Blair. 'But a lot of twaddle is written about us – it's said that we spent our last summer holidays together. Well, you know, much as I like him…'

I asked the Prime Minister why his government placed such importance on its relations with the media and on presentation. 'It's just modern government,' replied Blair. 'In the past twenty years the media has intensified. It's quicker and sharper than it used to be. So you have to have the means to get on top of it – insofar as it's possible. Otherwise, a story can be out there saying you are doing something that you are not doing at all. And these stories take on a life of their own and start running away into the far distance. And you have to be able to say: "Hang on, the facts are X and Y."'

But, I said, what about the recent report that he and Campbell spent their whole time planning how they could spin it to win the next general election? 'That's rubbish,' said Blair. 'I'd be the happiest person in the world if I didn't have to give another thought to what the presentation was. That's not what motivates us and it must not disturb me from doing the things which are really important for the country. People can believe that or not as they want – that's what I spend my time thinking about.'

The impact of his impassioned peroration was somewhat blunted when Alastair Campbell interjected on camera: 'So that's why you've spent the last seven minutes talking to Michael Cockerell.' I subsequently learned that was the moment Campbell wished he had bitten his tongue. He wrote in his diary: 'The press went in droves to the preview of the Cockerell film which I watched in the office. It seemed fine: neither great nor disastrous. The only moment I cringed was when I seemed to be taking the piss out of TB.'

He continued: 'There was a real sense of access. It certainly wasn't a hatchet job. But some felt it made TB look weak and me look strong. TB said we had just about got away with Cockerell, but that was enough.'

The image of Campbell as the dominant partner in the relationship with Blair was one that the impressionist Rory Bremner had already seized on. By chance, I was playing in a charity cricket match with Bremner on the day after the documentary went out and he told me: 'I've been studying your programme frame by frame.' His TV sketches impersonating Blair and Campbell became deadly accurate in terms of the way they spoke and their body language. But having filmed over three months in No. 10, I got the sense that the two men each increasingly felt about the other: 'I can't live without him, but I can't live with him.'

Throughout his time as PM, Tony Blair regarded his own personal relationship with the US President as key. Sir Christopher Meyer, who became the British ambassador in Washington in 1997, recalled the instruction he was given by Blair's chief of staff, Jonathan Powell. In the characteristically laddish style of New Labour's No. 10, Powell said: 'Basically, Christopher, what we want you to do is get up the arse of the White House and stay there.'

Blair had to change arses in midstream when George W. Bush won the 2000 presidential election. The Republican Texan neocon was seen as a very different figure from both Blair and Clinton. And there was much speculation about how the two leaders would get on. At the press conference after their first meeting at Camp David, Dubya was asked whether he had found any personal interests he had in common with Blair, 'maybe religion, sport or music?' 'Well,' responded the President, 'we both use Colgate toothpaste.' Blair laughed and said: 'They are going to wonder how you know that, George.' Afterwards Blair told me: 'The really alarming thing about that was it happened to be true. I went back and checked my toothpaste, and it was Colgate.'

In the early months after that meeting there was little to suggest the Bush–Blair relationship had a genuine ring of confidence about it. But then came savage September. When the terrorist planes crashed into the Twin Towers, the PM was in Brighton addressing the TUC conference while Jonathan Powell was in his No. 10 office.'In the immediate aftermath,' Powell told me, 'I suddenly realised how little we knew about the Taliban: we hadn't really had them on our radar at all. So I walked down Whitehall to the Waterstone's on Trafalgar Square and bought all the books I could find on the Taliban. And the only one that was any use was by Ahmed Rashid, which was about the Taliban and the fight with the warlords. So, I sat at my desk and read it for the next twelve hours – the whole book. And Alastair and Tony became very jealous and wanted to have my copy, but they had to wait. Alastair I think read it first and Tony after that: so then we were all the experts on the Taliban.'

In the summer of 2002, nearly a year after 9/11, I made a film about the so-called Special Relationship between Britain and the US. With war in the air but No. 10 insisting no decision had been taken about the rumoured invasion of Iraq, I interviewed Blair in Downing Street. I put to him the definition of the Special Relationship given by a former US Defense Secretary. Robert McNamara said that from America's point of view it means: 'At a time of crisis, are the Brits prepared to send troops, are they prepared to pay the blood price?' Blair replied without hesitation: 'Yes. What is important is that at moments of crisis they don't need to know simply that you are giving general expressions of support and sympathy. That is easy, frankly. They need to know, are you prepared to commit, are you prepared to be there when the shooting starts?'

Blair added: 'We are not at the stage of decision on Iraq, and there are all sorts of different ways in which we might decide to deal with this Iraq problem in the end.' 'Blair: We'll pay the blood price' was to lead the TV news and the front pages.

I left the interview in the Cabinet Room convinced that we would be at war within months. I remembered what Blair had said after he first stood, unsuccessfully, for Parliament twenty years earlier. The Beaconsfield by-election had been dominated by the latest news from the South Atlantic as Margaret Thatcher sought to reverse the Argentinian invasion of the Falklands. And Blair's former Foreign Secretary Robin Cook revealed to me that Blair had told him: 'The thing I learned from Beaconsfield is that wars make Prime Ministers popular.'

But after the invasion of Iraq, Blair learned that wars can also take a great toll on the popularity of Prime Ministers – and on their health. In late 2003, I made a documentary about the mental and physical strains of the premiership called *The Downing Street Patient*.

CHAPTER 24

THE DOWNING STREET PATIENT

In October 2003, nine months after he had ordered British troops to invade Iraq, Tony Blair woke up at Chequers with chest pains and a racing heart. He was rushed to hospital, where he was anaesthetised and given electric shock treatment to restore his heart to its normal beat. It was an event diametrically opposed to the optics about his health he had always sought to present to the public.

Blair had come to power in 1997 aged forty-three, the youngest PM since Lord Liverpool nearly two centuries earlier. Bursting with robust health and youthful energy, he felt that you can only cope with the demands of the modern premiership if you are in top shape. He was the first Prime Minister to have a rowing machine installed at No. 10. 'I do the gym three times a week,' Blair told me. 'It helps me deal with the stress of the job.' He sought to personify the notion of 'fitness for office' with regular physically active photocalls, including a heading contest with the England football star Kevin Keegan.

Lewis Moonie MP, a doctor and a minister under Blair, said

to me: 'It's all part of the manipulation of a media image. If the prime ministerial image is generally one of a young, bouncing superhero then intimations of mortality are the last things he needs if he wants to keep that image of himself in the public eye.'

David Owen, a former doctor and at one time a would-be Prime Minister, told me: 'Political leaders are usually, by nature of the office they hold and the greasy pole they have climbed to get there, exceptional people. They want to appear super-fit supermen or superwomen. So when they are unwell, they want to give the impression that they're still healthy.'

It is a pattern I recognised after looking at the true state of health of many of our post-war Prime Ministers. For when medical doctors get together with spin doctors to issue bulletins from No. 10, they have rarely taken a truth drug.

One of the classic cover-ups came nearly seventy years ago. Winston Churchill had returned to power at the age of nearly eighty and continued to run on the diet of brandy, cigars and midnight oil that had seen him to victory in the Second World War. But, in 1953, he suffered a stroke while hosting a dinner at No. 10. Officials managed to manoeuvre Churchill out of the room, but his condition was so severe that his doctor, Lord Moran, did not expect him to last the night.

A compliant Fleet Street, largely run by proprietors who were personal friends of Churchill, agreed to toe the official line. The papers printed a statement from No. 10 saying simply that the PM was 'taking a rest'. According to Moran: 'It was a medical communiqué that didn't include any medical facts.' With the PM out of action for weeks, his son-in-law, Christopher Soames, signed official documents with his own version of Churchill's signature, and the public was none the wiser.

Churchill's successor, Anthony Eden, came to power suffering from the after-effects of a botched operation on his gallbladder, as well as extensive surgery to correct it. He was to preside over the Suez debacle while sometimes running a temperature of 106.

'Eden's problem during Suez was that he was on really very high dosages of amphetamines, in addition to his bile duct complications,' said David Owen, who made a special study of the health of political leaders. 'And there was very little doubt that he was taking decisions at a time when he was not fully well. I'm not saying he was deranged – but he was right on the edge.' Eden resigned after Suez, citing poor health.

Harold Wilson came to power in 1964 at the age of forty-eight, at that time the youngest Prime Minister of the century, claiming he was 'as fit as a flea'. His press secretary Joe Haines said: 'Harold would always brace himself and go up stairs two at a time in a public place as if to say: "I'm on top of the job; I'm Superman."'

But in fact in 1974, while he was Prime Minister, Wilson suffered from a similar racing heart complaint to the one that would afflict Blair in 2003. And as we saw earlier Haines had no qualms about misinforming the press, given Labour's meagre majority of three and the country's dire economic state.

On his return to No. 10 in '74, Wilson was already showing signs that his fabled memory for detail was beginning to fail. His principal private secretary, Ken Stowe, said it was becoming pointless to show the PM documents for decision after five o'clock, because of the brandy bottle and his state of mind. And Robin Butler, then a more junior private secretary, believed he saw signs of early onset dementia.

The former Tory leader William Hague explained to me the psychology behind always wanting to project an image of glowing health: 'It's important for a political leader not to betray any sign of physical weakness. I was conscious in the 2001 election that it would have really been a blow to get a cold in the middle of the campaign and suddenly to be struggling with one's voice. Because then it would allow people to say: "They're having such a bad time that even he's become ill!"'

Tony Blair took a more hands-on approach to government than any of his predecessors. The last thing he wanted was any suggestion that, after nearly seven years in office, those hands might be trembling.

It was in the months following the hugely controversial invasion of Iraq in March 2003 that people started to notice a marked change in the Prime Minister's physical appearance. 'The stress and fatigue was starting to show on Blair,' said William Hague. 'This is not a criticism: anyone would be the same in that situation, because of the pressures of jet lag, conversations round the clock, and the need to think so hard about such a pressing problem.'

By chance, in September 2003, the month before Blair was rushed to hospital with a racing heart, he had visited a newly refurbished cardiac unit at King's College Hospital in London. We filmed him watching as a surgeon scanned a patient's heart using ultrasound, and the PM seemed to take an especially keen interest in what might be called the state-of-the-heart technology. Blair asked the doctor: 'So does that mean when you open a patient up you can go straight to where you want to operate on the heart, without any collateral damage?' The Prime Minister was obviously still in war-talk mode.

A month later, Blair was having to depend on cardiac technology himself. After waking up at Chequers with his heart problem, he was whisked to Hammersmith Hospital in London. The doctors diagnosed supraventricular tachycardia. They anaesthetised the Prime Minister, who was unconscious for twenty minutes while he received electric shock treatment to restore his heart to its normal beat. He had to spend five hours in hospital before he was discharged.

That night, No. 10 put out a statement designed to reassure. It gave very few details beyond saying that the PM had been 'feeling under the weather' with an irregular heartbeat, and that a 'cardioversion was administered to regulate it'. The PM was suffering from a common complaint that had been simply and successfully treated. Downing Street repeatedly denied that Mr Blair had any history of a heart condition.

Medicine, of course, like politics, is an inexact science. But Blair's former minister Dr Moonie, who had suffered from the same condition as his boss, decried No. 10's attempt to suggest that the procedure carried out on the PM in hospital was a minor one: 'Anaesthetising somebody and giving their heart electric shocks is not something you just do in the routine run of medical practice. Anybody with the slightest knowledge of medical procedures knows it's not nothing when that's done.'

Questioned by political journalists the following day, the PM's spokesman was anxious to quash the suggestion that Blair might become a lame duck Prime Minister. He said that the PM's heart scare was 'just one of those things. It's something that had never happened before and there is no reason why this should re-occur. The Prime Minister does not have, has never had, a heart condition.'

But that version was contradicted by two very highly placed sources. One came via the *Sunday Mirror* editor, Tina Weaver, who revealed a face-to-face conversation she'd had with Blair's friend, ex-President Bill Clinton: 'Clinton said, "Tony Blair told me that he had also suffered from this heart problem some years earlier – and it was brought on by too little sleep and too much caffeine."' And a week later, an undercover newspaper reporter who had gained employment as a royal footman reported the Queen saying Blair had told her he'd had similar complications with his heart in the past. When asked about it, Blair said that he would not go into details of his conversations with the Queen, but he added: 'I have never had this condition before. It happened. I stopped work for one day. I think I have had one day off through illness in seven years, which is not bad really – and even then I was working for most of it. When you are in my position, if you have a moment's illness it is translated into a major crisis.'

But Blair's Home Secretary and close ally David Blunkett later revealed a conversation he'd had with Blair after he had left hospital: 'Tony told me when I spoke to him on the telephone that he had had the heart problem, on and off, for fifteen years.

But this time he had to go into hospital, which is why it became public knowledge.'

For Prime Ministers, the fear that power, credibility and respect will seep away if ill-health is revealed remains. Not just the electorate will lose faith – but also your Cabinet colleagues may sniff a succession. Blair's reluctance to reveal his heart issues stemmed from the angst that his once best friend, the Chancellor, Gordon Brown, might take advantage.

Prime Minister Blair well knew from his own experience that ill-health is the malign and unpredictable joker in the political pack. The sudden and unexpected death of Labour leader John Smith in 1994 had given Blair the chance to seize the crown. As Alan Clark had once put it with his customary black cynicism: 'In politics where there's death, there's hope.'

CHAPTER 25

HOW TO BE HOME SECRETARY

I made a number of programmes about Tony Blair – including a three-part series called *Blair: The Inside Story*, transmitted just before he left office. The programmes went down well with the audience, the press and inside the BBC. Perhaps the most gratifying response was from George Entwistle, who was head of current affairs. He sent me a text saying: 'Thanks for your series – I much enjoyed it and it got a very good audience too. It's a pleasure to have you on the channel.' So, when I received a call a few days later asking me to come and see George, I imagined he wanted to congratulate me in person and discuss what I should be doing next. To my astonishment, he told me instead that the BBC was having to make cuts, so they would not be renewing my staff contract. I was shocked and hurt. The previous time they let me go they could at least say that my programme had caused a huge row.

This time I was being given the order of the boot despite having a big success. George was sad-faced and hesitant. And he later told a friend that sacking me was the hardest thing he'd ever had to do in his career. He was soon to find even harder things to do, when he was himself sacked over the Jimmy Savile sexual abuse affair after only a few weeks in his job as the new BBC Director-General.

Though I no longer had a staff contract, which on paper saved the Corporation money, happily for me the BBC has many mansions. So, I could operate as a freelancer and I found supporters. One was the new head of current affairs, Clive Edwards, a talented programme-maker whom I'd worked with previously. He set himself the task of bringing me back into the fold. The new controller of BBC 4 wanted a film made inside the most controversial, secretive and accident-prone department in Whitehall: the Home Office, long considered a graveyard for ministerial careers. I worked hard on a proposal and was commissioned to make the film. At that moment in 2009, the Prime Minister, Gordon Brown, was having a big reshuffle and was about to appoint a new Home Secretary.

I rang one of my best contacts, the Health Secretary, Alan Johnson. We had known each other since I'd interviewed him in 1994 for a film I was making about political lobbying. He was at that time a trade union leader and had come over so well as an articulate, modern figure that Tony Blair encouraged him to become a Labour MP. Once in the Commons, he rose so fast through the ranks that he seemed certain to get one of the top jobs in Brown's reshuffle.

I said to him: 'I've heard that you are in the frame for Home Secretary. I'm making a film about the Home Office. Could I ask if you do get the gig, can we film your first meeting with your new Sir Humphrey, the Permanent Secretary at the Home Office?'

Johnson replied: 'Not for the first time, Michael, you seem to know more about my life than I do. But if I get the job, I'm happy to let you film, so long as you can square it with the Perm. Sec.'

I said: 'I've already done so. I met him yesterday and he's happy to let us make a behind-the-scenes access film at the Home Office – so long as the new Home Secretary agrees.'

'Agreed,' said Johnson.

The following day we were in the basement car park of the Home Office with Sir David Normington, the Permanent Secretary, awaiting the arrival of his new ministerial boss, Alan Johnson. Normington had agreed to wear a personal microphone so we could hear their first conversations. Johnson was coming from King's Cross station, having taken the train down from his constituency in Hull, where Gordon Brown had appointed him by phone. As Johnson got off the train at King's Cross, he had his first taste of his new job. He told me there were four policemen with sniffer dogs and five plain-clothes security officers. The protection officers told the new Home Secretary where to sit in the back of his new bullet-proof black Jaguar 'to avoid assassination'.

When Johnson's limo swept into the basement car park, his first words to Normington were: 'It was a strange journey coming down from Hull. I was thinking, when I get to King's Cross I'll be taken into custody for the next few years – at least I hope the next few years.' The next person he met was the Home Office head of communications, Simon Wren, who along with Normington briefed Johnson about what he should say to the press pack waiting outside. 'They are not expecting you to know anything at the moment,' said Wren with a laugh. 'Other than what you already know. So: pleased to be here, great honour, that kind of thing.' Normington added: 'The agenda is protecting the public, being very clear about what the public's concerns are – crime, immigration, security.'

One journalist asked whether Johnson had hesitated about taking the job, which was known as a poisoned chalice. 'It's not a poisoned chalice,' responded Johnson, 'it's a three-course meal with dessert and coffee. It's a really great honour and privilege. And it's a challenge to make people feel safe and secure in their homes and on the streets – and give the public a reason to vote Labour.'

At that, Normington's personal microphone picked him up saying to Wren: 'How are we going to get him out from there?' Johnson spotted Wren's cut-throat signal, and he walked back into the Home Office – and into the most politically hazardous role in government.

He was the sixth New Labour Home Secretary in twelve years, and half had 'left the office feet first', as one of them put it to me. The Home Office had been living up to its reputation as a glittering coffin for ambitious politicians. From the end of the Second World War until 2009, only one Home Secretary had become PM – Jim Callaghan – unless you count Winston Churchill, who had been Liberal Home Secretary before the First World War.

Partly this is because disastrous, career-ending events can suddenly come at you out of a clear-blue sky. Ken Clarke, a former

Tory Home Secretary, told me: 'Someone's escaped from prison; there's been some great police scandal; someone's broken into Buckingham Palace; somebody's been deported and has been instantly shot upon arrival in his own country. All these things, some of them serious, quite tragic cases, suddenly explode in the Home Secretary's area.'

'This is the job where you get to know your own country most closely,' said another former Tory Home Secretary, Douglas Hurd. 'You tend to see the bad bits of it: rundown housing estates, drugs, prisons, riots, terrorism. Horrors of all kinds, drabness of all kinds, wickedness of all kinds come your way as Home Secretary more than in any other job.'

I discovered that every new Home Secretary is astonished by the extraordinary range of their responsibilities. Along with law and order, immigration and the security service MI5, they include au pair girls, nuclear bunkers, nudist beaches, wild birds, swearing in new bishops, emergency planning and falling satellites.

Jack Straw, who was New Labour's first Home Secretary, told me: 'One of my Conservative predecessors gave me a gypsy's warning about the job. He told me the thing to remember is that at any one time there will be fifty sets of officials working on projects that will destroy your political career. And the worst thing is that not only do you not know who they are, but they don't know who they are.'

Forty years ago, the Home Office moved into new headquarters. Its brutal concrete and glass exterior seemed to reflect the distinctive culture that had grown up among its civil servants

– secretive, defensive and designed to repel boarders. 'It used to be a real fortress of a department,' Douglas Hurd said, 'which rejected outsiders and erected fortifications to prevent people knowing what was going on inside the castle.'

Sir Hayden Phillips, a long-time Home Office mandarin, told me: 'There was a sense of being bunkered – always being got at and not being understood – with people not appreciating you were trying to do a good and honest job.'

Jack Straw said that he and his officials would refer to the Home Office building as if it were a KGB jail: 'We used to call it Lubyanka. It was like a prison and with little cells. As Home Secretary you could go up to your office in the ministerial lift – you had your own loo. And with a bit of luck you'd never be contaminated by any other form of human life – except in a meeting. And later you'd go down in the lift and leave.'

Relations between Home Secretaries and their permanent officials are key to understanding how the Home Office operates. While some ministers and mandarins have got on well, others have been at daggers drawn with their senior officials about their respective roles. Like Jeeves and Bertie Wooster, there is a certain uncertainty about who is really the boss.

Sir Brian Cubbon served as Permanent Secretary for ten years, from 1979 to 1988, under three different Home Secretaries. I asked him about the reputation the Home Office had that its officials would always want to continue with the policies they felt had worked over the years – whoever was Home Secretary. 'Oh, there is always inertia in every institution,' said Sir Brian. 'One of my tasks as Home Secretary was to…'

'Freudian slip,' I said.

Sir Brian threw his hands in the air and restarted: 'One of my tasks as *Permanent* Secretary was to explode occasionally and say: doesn't the office realise there's been a change of government – there's been a change of Home Secretary?'

Michael Howard, who became John Major's Home Secretary in 1993, told me that journalists would ring the Home Office to ask about policy, and officials would say: 'Well, the Home Office policy is this – however, the Home Secretary thinks...' Howard had come to the job with a hard-line agenda to cut crime. But he came up against the Home Office's own distinctive view that had developed over the years. He said: 'I was shown charts which showed crime rising inexorably, and the officials actually said to me: "It is going to continue to go up and the first thing, Home Secretary, that you have to understand is that there is nothing you can do about it."'

Howard felt that in his four-year term he had managed to change that world-weary culture and was saddened to hear from me what his successors had found. 'I hate to agree with Michael Howard about this,' said David Blunkett, Blair's second Home Secretary. 'But he and I shared the view that the Home Office didn't really believe that they could change the world – that they could really make a difference in reducing crime.'

And Jonathan Powell, Tony Blair's chief of staff, recalled the presentation the Home Office gave to the New Labour Prime Minister: 'They presented projected figures that showed crime inexorably rising during our years in government. And they said this was a result of the economy improving, and as the economy improved there'd be more stuff to nick and therefore there'd be more crime.

'We were a bit bemused by this and I asked what would happen if the economy turned down and we suffered a recession rather than a growing economy. They said: "Oh, well, crime would go up; there'd be more people to nick things."'

Former Cabinet Secretary Lord (Richard) Wilson, who was the Home Office's top mandarin under both the Tories and New Labour, explained the official mindset: 'In the Home Office, you do have a sense that you are the Department of Law and Order, in an age when authority may not be the most fashionable of the roles to play. They feel that, faced with the growth in crime, this is the sum total of endless other failings which no one Home Secretary – however brilliant and however powerful – has the capacity to tackle.'

Tony Blair came to feel that his first Home Secretary, Jack Straw, had fallen prey to a defeatist Home Office orthodoxy on crime. 'I did get irritated with Tony sometimes,' Straw told me, 'and I used to say to him: "I think you're asking me to push water uphill, aren't you?"'

To encourage a new approach, Blair brought into No. 10 the controversial former BBC Director-General John Birt, as a 'blue skies thinker on the causes and cures for crime'. I asked Straw what he thought of the appointment: 'Not a lot. I groaned. I dutifully cooperated with these blue skies and the thinking. John Birt began life as an engineer and he was famous for wiring diagrams. I'm sure he was very good at technical drawing at school, so we had loads of wiring diagrams, and end-to-end solutions and stuff.'

The report has never been published in full and I asked Straw what he thought of Birt's ten-year plan when it finally reached him.

Straw made an odd popping noise. 'I'm afraid... um... pop... pop... a serious admission. I remember remarkably little about it except thinking, we'll study it with great care.' And Straw made such a determined attempt not to smile, his mouth actually turned down.

One of the Home Secretary's key responsibilities is MI5, the security service with its HQ at Thames House, just upriver from Westminster. Its critics claim that over the years it has acted as a secret state within a state. And a number of the Home Secretaries I talked to felt they were not kept up to speed with the operational activities of the secret world.

Roy Jenkins, who was twice Home Secretary, told me: 'I did not, I'm afraid, form a very high regard for how MI5 discharged their duties. There was naturally a secretive atmosphere, but they were secretive vis à vis the government as well as vis à vis the enemies of the state.'

I said: 'You mean that you as Home Secretary didn't necessarily know what MI5 was doing?'

'No, one always felt a certain lack of frankness,' replied Jenkins. 'I also thought that living one's life in this sort of spybound world gives people a distorted view of things. If you are not careful you get into a sort of Alice in Wonderland world in which truth is falsehood and falsehood is truth and nothing is in real contact with reality.'

I put the same question to the man who, in 1976, succeeded

Jenkins as Labour Home Secretary, Merlyn Rees. He said: 'No, I did not know what MI5 was doing – and nor can any Home Secretary.' Other Home Secretaries told me that they felt they knew what they needed to know. But, I asked, if it's MI5 which itself decides what it is they are going to tell you, how can you know what they are keeping from you? 'We don't talk about the workings of the security service,' they all answered in a single voice.

David Blunkett shed a further chink of light. He talked about his meetings as Home Secretary with the then head of MI5, Sir Stephen Lander: 'Stephen is what's known as a spook. Spooks are spooks. They are in a world which is very different. The security services do a phenomenal job – much more than I ever envisaged when I came into office. But it is a world apart by its very nature. And Stephen Lander speaks in riddles. He put things in the kind of way that you read in John le Carré novels. I was reading a couple of them when I was Home Secretary and I noticed the particular nuances. With all these spooks you always have to learn to read the print that's disappeared between the lines.'

In his time as Straw's successor, Blunkett told me that he thought being Home Secretary was 'not a bundle of laughs', and he came to feel increasingly frustrated by what he saw as the sclerotic bureaucracy of the Home Office. And as his private life became entangled in official business, he felt that even the run-down building itself was in revolt against him. 'I went in one morning and the building was creaking – it was beginning to fall apart, a kind of metaphor really,' said Blunkett. 'I walked into the upstairs toilets, and I was very quick on the uptake in realising there was something amiss here. And I was very glad I did, because I called in one of the private secretaries: he declared with an entirely straight face that the sewage system had obviously gone into reverse and the whatsit was now in the washbasin and the bath area rather than down the toilet. And I thought, well that just about sums it all up.'

After Blunkett resigned, the Home Office moved to shiny new hi-tech headquarters. Charles Clarke was the new Mr Fixit. He was to have a series of clashes with his top mandarin, Sir John Gieve. Clarke told me: 'I thought the first thing the Permanent Secretary said to me was disgraceful. He said, "You've just got to accept that this is a job where things come along, and whatever disasters happen you just have to deal with them as best you can."' When I asked Gieve about that first meeting with Clarke, he said: 'Well, knowing Charles, I suspect he told me first what the nature of the job was – and he had been a junior minister at the Home Office. Of course there are events that happen. It's not a department where you can set out your plan on 1 January and then stick to it.'

It was not a promising beginning. The two men soon became embroiled in a huge political row when it was revealed that the Home Office had, over six years, released a thousand dangerous and violent foreign prisoners – including murderers and rapists – without them being considered for deportation. The Home Office had no idea where the men were, nor how many more such cases there were.

Clarke told me that the scandal was a result of the 'absurd

and ridiculous system' in which one part of his sprawling empire did not know what the other part was doing. And in our film he took the highly unusual step of publicly pointing the finger at his top mandarin. 'I made the mistake of relying on Sir John Gieve, who had assured me that he'd got the matter in hand in terms of dealing with the immediate situation – which turned out not to be the case.'

Gieve responded: 'We should have dealt with the thousand cases better over six years – actually before I was there as well as when I was there. But obviously Charles Clarke had doubts about me, and, um…' After a lengthy pause, he added: 'And I about him.'

'You had doubts about him? Why?' I asked.

'I'm not going to say any more about that. In fact, I'm scarcely going to say any more about anything.' And he stood up with the words: 'I'm due to be at lunch in Baker Street.' Doubtless off to see Sherlock Holmes, I checked myself from saying.

John Gieve had left the Home Office by the time Charles Clarke was, as he puts it, 'sacked' by Tony Blair over the foreign prisoners fiasco. The new Home Secretary was the Glaswegian hard-man John Reid. And the new Permanent Secretary was David Normington, who told me: 'John Reid came in like a whirlwind. He was put here to steady the ship and take a grip.' Normington was at Reid's side in the Commons when the new Home Secretary famously described his division's dealing with asylum and immigration as 'not fit for purpose'.

'I agreed with his analysis,' said Normington, 'but I wished he hadn't used the "not fit for purpose" phrase, because of course that then became the label that attached to the Home Office for the next several years – and to some extent still is – when we run into heavy weather.'

But what, I asked Normington, had the phrase done at the time for morale in the Home Office? 'Morale was low because the previous Home Secretary [Charles Clarke] had lost his job. That was the result of something that we had done wrong. We're here to serve our Home Secretaries, not to cause problems for them. Departments can lose their reputation in a moment and on that day our reputation was absolutely in shreds.'

Although Normington had strong personal reservations, he went along with the plan hatched by Tony Blair and John Reid for the biggest shake-up in the Home Office's history. The department was split into two ministries on continental lines: criminal justice, prisons and probation were handed over to the newly created Ministry of Justice; and the Home Office became effectively the ministry of the interior, responsible for internal security, law and order, immigration and terrorism.

Reid resigned when his old Scottish rival Gordon Brown became Prime Minister. And following Jacqui Smith's unhappy interregnum, Alan Johnson became David Normington's fourth Home Secretary in the space of four years. We filmed as Johnson addressed his first mass meeting of Home Office staff, crowded onto the floor and the balconies in the atrium of the new building. 'I asked if I could have a quiet and intimate word with the staff,' said Johnson to laughter. 'I am a huge believer in the civil service. We can have our internal discussions about what happens here, but I am the public face of this department.

And I will take the rap if things go wrong – and I'll take the credit, obviously, when they go right. I am a politician after all.'

The decision to split up the Home Office and create the new Ministry of Justice led many former Home Secretaries and leading officials to wonder whether the Home Office any longer deserved its designation as a great office of state. I put the question to Johnson. 'Yes, I do think it does. And it had better stay a great office, now that I have reached it.'

But any future incumbents would be wise to heed the words of a beleaguered Home Secretary who wrote in a memo to his Sir Humphrey sixty years ago: 'Poor old Home Office, we don't always get it wrong. But we always get the blame.'

CHAPTER 26

NOT FLASH, JUST GORDON

I had long found Gordon Brown an intriguing figure and wanted to make a behind-the-scenes profile of him. He had appeared as co-star in two other films I had made: one with Blair and one with his then opposite number, Michael Portillo, the Tory shadow Chancellor. Every time we met, Brown said to me: 'Are you still making those documentaries?'

I replied: 'Yes – and I'd love to make one about you.'

He said: 'That'll require some thinking about.' Over the following years when we bumped into each other in the Commons or at party conferences, the conversation was verbatim the same – he was still thinking.

He finally achieved his life's ambition and became Prime Minister at the end of June 2007, after an uncontested election for the Labour leadership. He had once had a proper job – he had been a television reporter – but whatever communication skills he had learned then had long fallen into disuse. He was a man of great intellect but had little ability to get through to ordinary people. As he put it to me: 'I was brought up to contain, even suppress, my inner feelings in public.' Having been at

daggers drawn with Tony Blair throughout the latter's premiership, Brown now decided to disown his former best friend
altogether.

Nick Pearce, who was the head of Brown's policy unit, told
me: 'Gordon Brown came to No. 10 with a very clear sense of
it not being Tony Blair. There would be an end to so-called sofa
government. He would have a very different set-up on the whole
spin agenda. It was very defined in antithesis to Blair.'

It all began so well for Prime Minister Brown. He enjoyed a
honeymoon period, during which he confidently handled various small-scale crises: a limited outbreak of foot and mouth,
some flooding in the Midlands and a botched terrorist attack.
He received A++ glowing press – even from the *Daily Mail*. Yet
Brown's brother, Andrew, told me that the new PM felt very
frustrated, because the detailed plans he had long worked on
for his first weeks in office kept having to be postponed by what
Harold Macmillan once called 'events, dear boy. Events.'

About a year before Brown moved into No. 10, a very senior
mandarin who had worked closely with him said to me: 'Gordon
will hate being Prime Minister, it's everything he loathes:
making quick decisions, going on daytime TV, sucking up to
foreigners.' When I asked another senior official, who had served
both Blair and Brown, about the two men's approaches to the
job of PM, he gave me an interesting scenario, saying: 'Suppose
the King of Jordan was coming on an official visit to No. 10.
If it were Blair, he would wing it between a Cabinet meeting
and sub-committee, and as he walked to the meeting with the
monarch he would say to his foreign affairs adviser: "Just fill me

in on where we are on the Middle East peace process." He has a lawyer's ability to pick up a brief at pace. But if it were Gordon he would say: "Meeting with the King of Jordan? Cancel it – I need to read the whole history of the Middle East before I can see him.'"

But with the opinion polls turning in his favour, Brown nurtured press speculation that he was planning to call a snap general election in the autumn of 2007, just four months after coming to power. At his party conference in Bournemouth, Labour's new ad agency, Saatchi & Saatchi, came up with a slogan approved by the PM. 'He's not flash, he's Gordon' sought to make a virtue of Brown's perceived lack of charisma compared to his predecessor.

Though the pundits and the bookies felt an election was a racing certainty, at the last moment the PM got cold feet. He told an incredulous TV interviewer that however good the polls were, he would carry on with his duties as Prime Minister. And he desperately tried to convince a sceptical press lobby that the thought of such an election had never even crossed his mind.

The opposition leader, David Cameron, made hay at PMQs. Said Cameron: 'The Prime Minister was asked, "If the polls showed a hundred-seat majority, would you have still called off the election?" And he said: "Yes." He's the first Prime Minister in history to flunk an election because he thought he was going to win it.' Wholescale mirth and mockery ensued.

The Tories sent a number of their activists dressed in brown beer bottle costumes to sing in unison outside the gates of No. 10, 'Ten brown bottles hanging on the wall'. For months afterwards the Prime Minister was regularly taunted as Bottler Brown. And his wife Sarah admitted: 'Gordon is finding the job much harder than he thought it would be. It is a big step up – bigger than he realised.'

Brown became increasingly indecisive in No. 10. According to one of his top officials, he virtually never completed his red box and big issues would pile up. 'Put simply, he was the most chaotic Prime Minister in modern British history,' declared his authoritative biographer, Sir Anthony Seldon. And Brown's Chief Whip, Geoff Hoon, said: 'Gordon wants to interfere in everything. He's temperamentally incapable of delegating re-sponsibility. So he drives himself demented.'

I remember talking to Brown and seeing that his fingernails had been gnawed down to the quick. I felt that he was being eaten up from the inside by his years of bileful resentment against Tony Blair, and he was eating himself up from the out-side. It was painful to watch.

One day in the Commons, he seemed momentarily to have forgotten what job he now held. The Speaker announced: 'State-ment – the Prime Minister', which prompted Brown, as he had regularly done for the previous decade, to get up from the front bench to walk out of the Chamber rather than stay and listen to Blair. There was much amusement from both sides when Brown suddenly recalled he was now first among equals and U-turned back to his seat.

He took Prime Minister's Questions very seriously. While Blair would spend two hours on the Tuesday and two hours the following morning preparing for the session at noon, Brown originally spent much of Monday, much of Tuesday and all Wednesday morning prepping. By his final year, he was doing roughly the same as Blair. And ironically, his advisers felt that the less time he spent preparing, the better he performed.

The PM decided he needed to change the way he was running No. 10. He took inspiration from a visit to Michael Bloomberg, the Mayor of New York and former financial trader turned billionaire media mogul. Brown was impressed by his open-plan office, which was a mix of trading floor and newsroom with giant TV screens. Brown brought the mayor's concept back with him across the Atlantic. He had his own office and senior staff moved down the linking corridor from No. 10 to No. 12 and created what he called the War Room.

Peter Mandelson, who had become Brown's No. 2 after having patched up their fifteen-year 'uncivil war', told me: 'Gordon put himself with his top officials, political advisers and speech writers all round a bank of computers and workstations with huge TV screens – BBC in front and Sky News behind. Gordon was in the middle. He was mission control, he was the pilot, the commander in the field as he saw himself, driving everyone, responding to things very quickly and taking thoughts from the TV output and sending his orders.'

Nick Pearce said: 'If he heard something on the TV news that he didn't like he would shout at the screen and order his people to get straight on to the broadcaster.'

Brown's initial pledge to avoid a Blair/Campbell-style spin operation was a distant memory. Working with the PM in the War Room and trying to dominate the round-the-clock news media was Damian McBride. A former Treasury official, McBride had been hand-picked by Brown for his aggressive mastery of the black arts of spin. He was quickly dubbed Damian McPoison. Having spent much of his time as Chancellor obsessively plotting to replace Tony Blair, Brown was now spending much of his time as PM tormented by the fear that his closest Cabinet colleagues were obsessively plotting against him.

McBride knew his master's mind and used the unattributable lobby system to plant negative stories undermining two senior ministers whom Brown saw as prime contenders for his job. One was the Foreign Secretary and unreconstructed Blairite David Miliband. The other was Brown's long-time close friend and ally the Chancellor Alistair Darling, who said that being the target of No. 10's character assassination was like having 'the forces of hell' unleashed on him.

But in April 2009 Damian McBride himself became the victim of a devastating leak – of one of his own private emails. It revealed that he was planning a sexual smear campaign against the top two Tories. The plan was to plant scurrilous false stories about both David Cameron and the wife of the shadow Chancellor George Osborne.

Brown publicly denied all knowledge of the plan and stubbornly refused to apologise for his top aide's activities – until under mounting pressure he felt he had no alternative. 'When I saw this first I was horrified,' said Brown. 'I was shocked and I was very angry indeed. The person who was responsible lost his job and went immediately.' In fact, it had taken five full days for the PM to say sorry and for McBride to go. And when McBride said: 'You prove your loyalty to GB by your brutality,' it suggested that Brown knew rather more than he admitted about his Machiavellian spin doctor's exploits.

The PM also had a ferocious temper. A graphic instance of this came from his long-time senior adviser, the Oxford academic Stewart (now Lord) Wood. Before a big European summit, Wood had arranged a lunchtime reception at No. 10 for EU ambassadors in London. It was agreed that the ever-busy PM would join the envoys for coffee. Wood was to brief Brown on whom he should talk to first. But the PM was out of sorts when he arrived, and outside the meeting he raged at Wood: 'Why are you making me meet these fucking people? I don't want to meet these fucking people!'

The son of the manse had come a long way from the manse. The terrible irony of Brown's journey was that when he finally got the job he had always craved, he was temperamentally completely unsuited for it. For much of the time he seemed swamped by the range of demands on a modern Prime Minister. But there was one notable exception: the great banking crash of 2008.

Following the collapse of Lehman Brothers, it looked as if the world's biggest and most famous banks were on the edge of the abyss. Brown, as Britain's longest serving Chancellor since the 1832 Reform Act, had encouraged the boom that had led to the bust. While still at the Treasury in 2004 he had opened Lehman's flashy new HQ in London and paid glowing tribute to the bank's 'buccaneering approach that contributed so much to Britain'. But when Lehman went belly-up four years later,

Prime Minister Brown was uncharacteristically sure-footed and determined as he put together a huge rescue package to bail out Britain's banks. And he managed to persuade initially sceptical Europe and America to follow the British model. He had made full use of the contacts and skill sets he had honed in the Treasury. Ironically, Brown was at his best as Prime Minister when he could revert to being Chancellor, faced with a single impending calamity rather than a hundred urgent matters which all demanded his attention at the same time.

He celebrated his rescue package in the Commons with a Freudian slip. Under fire from free-market Tories, the PM announced: 'We saved the world.' He had meant to say: 'We saved the banks.' Amid an outburst of jeers and gesticulation, instead of trying to laugh off his slip, Brown repeatedly attempted to make himself heard – to no avail.

Watching and talking to Brown, I saw him becoming increasingly Eeyore-ish as the election of 2010 approached. 'I felt I was running out of time,' he said. He thought he was a 'politician out of season' who had failed to master the necessary skills of modern communication. 'No matter what I did to get my message across, I often fell short,' said Brown. 'I'm the son of a Church of Scotland minister. I was brought up to believe you get on with the job, you don't show your feelings, you are actually reticent and undemonstrative. I am not a touchy-feely politician and perhaps in the social media age and the television age that's the more difficult thing to be.'

His ex-spin doctor Damian McBride told me the reason why, despite encouraging words, they had never agreed to let me make an access documentary with Brown: 'We thought that if we let you into No. 10 to film, you might find Gordon having one of his tantrums and we knew that was something we couldn't control.'

The 2010 general election put Labour behind David Cameron's Tories in a hung parliament. Brown stayed put inside No. 10, desperately hoping to construct a last-minute deal that would keep him in office. His chief negotiator, Peter Mandelson, recalled to me the moment he came into the PM's office and found Brown on the phone to the Liberal leader Nick Clegg. 'I listened in on the extension phone,' said Mandelson. 'It was perfectly clear that Clegg and Cameron were going to form a coalition and they needed to get on with it.'

Mandelson, the renowned Prince of Darkness, continued: 'I said to him: "Gordon, this is it. You shouldn't really be hanging around waiting interminably for these two guys to make up their minds. And you certainly shouldn't be hanging around with the result that you might end up leaving No. 10 at nine or ten at night – in the dark. Gordon, is that the way we want people to see a Labour Prime Minister to be leaving Downing Street after thirteen years in power – in the dark?" I didn't like that at all.'

'The thing about politics', said Brown after he left office, 'is that there is only a particular shelf life that you have. I know media interviewers last a long time, but people get fed up and bored with a politician. My problem was that I'd been Chancellor for ten years. So I had been at the top of politics with Tony all that time. And I think when I took over from Tony it was very difficult for people to see it was a complete change from what had happened before. And I also wanted to emphasise continuity. But you can't assume you are going to have a long shelf life at the top of politics – and I didn't have one.'

And Brown ended by referring obliquely to the length of time that Blair had made him wait before handing over the crown. 'Perhaps if we had changed over a bit earlier things might have been different.'

CHAPTER 27

THE MAN WHO DID
THE DIRTY WORK

In October 2015, Denis Healey died at the age of ninety-eight. He had been the last surviving member of Harold Wilson's first Cabinet and was often seen as the best Prime Minister Labour never had. A politician with what he called 'a hinterland', Healey was a fine photographer, pianist, painter, author – and he was also a key player in a number of the twentieth century's most turbulent events. In a relatively rare fit of BBC percipience, two years before Healey's death the then controller of BBC 2, Janice Hadlow, had asked me to make an obituary of him.

I decided to approach the matter delicately with Healey. I had known him well over the years, and had made a previous television portrait of him. When I rang him I did not at first mention the O-word, but said the BBC had asked me to update my profile of him. 'Oh,' he responded immediately, 'you mean you are doing my obituary?' 'You've got it in one, Denis,' I said. He agreed to let me film and interview him at his home.

The first profile I had made of him in 1979 began with him saying: 'When I was a student communist at Oxford we would have debates about who would do the dirty work under social-ism. I discovered in later life the answer was Denis Healey.'

He was dead right. He spent most of his career in a tribal battle with the hard left for the soul of the Labour Party. One young activist who would regularly seek to shout Healey down at rallies was Jeremy, later eponymous leader of the Corbynistas.

Healey was a lone wolf in politics. In a world of Gaitskel-lites, Bevanites, Jenkinsites and Bennites there had never been a major grouping of Healeyites. 'I've been a loner in the sense that I've never tried to organise a group of people to achieve an objective for myself personally,' Healey told me. 'I've never been a plotter.' His fellow Labour Cabinet minister Shirley Williams said, 'Denis wasn't a schmoozer, he was an anti-schmoozer. What he hadn't got was an ability to create a world with disci-ples around him; friends yes, but disciples no.'

'I didn't build a carapace around me,' said Healey, 'but I have tried to preserve a personal life with my family and friends and a space for my love of poetry, music and literature. And the one thing I would never do is allow politics to destroy that space – because I think it would destroy me as a human being – and I've seen politics destroy human beings.'

Healey had Irish blood and grew up in Yorkshire, where both his parents were school teachers. 'From quite a little boy, he always knew he was right,' said his mother in a TV interview. He was also very bright and won a scholarship to Balliol. There two other grammar-school boys, Ted Heath and Roy Jenkins, were his contemporaries – and the trio were to remain friends and rivals for life. Healey took a double first in classics and joined the Communist Party. He went on anti-war marches and saw the Soviet Union as a bulwark against the threat of Nazi Germany. 'I was just misguided about communism, of course,' he told me. 'But I would reply with George Kennan [the US diplomat] I'd much rather do something to stop Hitler than sit around picking lint out of my navel.'

When the war started, he resigned from the Communist Party in protest at the Russians signing a non-aggression pact with the Nazis. As a Royal Engineer, he saw action in North Africa and the allied invasion of Sicily. Lieutenant Healey was also the military landing officer, the beachmaster, for the British assault brigade at Anzio in 1944. He had become used to being under fire. 'I wasn't panic-stricken,' he told me. 'I mean, if you're being dive-bombed and you've got something coming out of the sun screaming at you, you're bloody well frightened. But it didn't interfere with what I did.'

As he and his men fought their way up the spine of Italy in the terrible winter of 1944 – with, said Healey, 'the Germans fighting every inch of the way' – they increasingly felt they had become the forgotten army. 'We were bitterly resentful when Lady Astor, who was a Conservative MP, called us "D-Day Dodgers". And we sang a song someone had written, to the tune of "Lili Marlene", which was very rude about Lady Astor.' I asked Healey to sing it and we filmed as he obliged:

Old Lady Astor, please listen, dear, to this,
Don't stand upon the platform and talk a lot of piss.
You're the nation's sweetheart, the nation's pride,
But your bloody big mouth is far too wide,
That's from the D-Day Dodgers – out in Italy.
If you look around the mountains in the mud and rain,
You'll find the scattered crosses, some which bear no name.
Heartbreak and toil and suffering gone,
The lads beneath them slumber on,
For they were the D-Day Dodgers, who'll stay in Italy.

Healey's voice broke and there were tears in his eyes as he delivered the last lines. 'I'm sorry,' he said, 'I get too moved by these things. You know that sort of poetry may not stand up to Palgrave's Golden Treasury, but there's genuine feeling there – and you can get it, don't you think?' he asked.

Healey ended the war as a major and joined the Labour Party. Wearing his uniform, he spoke at the 1945 victory conference, as Labour was elected to government. 'I made a fiery speech,' he told me, 'and I said a thing, which I deeply regret since, that the upper classes in Europe were dissolute, depraved, and decadent.' Healey was congratulated by a fellow delegate for his 'wonderful gift of vituperation'. It was a gift he was to deploy in the Labour civil war of the 1950s.

Elected as a Leeds MP in 1952, the now fiercely anti-communist Healey became a bare-knuckle fighter against the left. When Labour returned to power twelve years later, Harold Wilson made Healey Defence Secretary. The first ex-communist to hold the post soon became a target for opponents of Britain's nuclear weapons and for demonstrators against the American war in Vietnam. Wilson's government supported the war and Healey, who privately deplored America's military methods, was not prepared to speak out against the US. I asked him why not. 'I don't think us speaking out would have made any difference, and of course the Americans deeply resented that we didn't give them physical military support.'

But you never as Defence Secretary ever said in public what you thought in private? 'Well of course not, my dear boy. You don't as Defence Secretary speak out against an allied government which your own government is supporting.' Even if you were convinced that what they were doing was completely wrong? 'No – but I did it in private.'

After Labour lost the 1970 election, Healey, who had been seen as a dry technocrat at Defence, set about humanising his own political image. At Labour Party constituency meetings across the country, he would tell his favourite off-colour story: 'In many ways I felt my job as Defence Secretary was rather like having a love affair with an elephant. It involved a great deal more pain than pleasure; I was in constant danger of being overlaid; and if I ever did conceive a good idea, do you know it took twenty-seven months to bring it to birth.'

Healey was made shadow Chancellor in April 1972, and the man who had become a hate figure for the left now seemed to revert to his pre-war Marxist roots. He never actually said, as was regularly reported: 'I am going to squeeze the rich till the pips squeak.' But I filmed at Labour's 1973 conference, where he declaimed: 'We're going to introduce a tax on wealth. I warn you there are going to be howls of anguish from the 80,000 people; people who are rich enough to pay over 75 per cent tax on the last slice of their income. Comrades, the battle begins here in this hall this week. Let us make sure we win it.'

Healey was achieving his aim of becoming an instantly rec- ognisable public figure, partly because his luxuriant black eye- brows were a gift for the cartoonists. He had also taken on the time-honoured role of the Labour bogeyman of the moneyed classes, as the country under Ted Heath was descending into ungovernable chaos.

On becoming Chancellor of the Exchequer in 1974, Healey inherited an economy pulverised by the three-day week and the fourfold rise in Arab oil prices. With inflation soaring at an un- precedented 30 per cent a year and with the government seeking a deal with the trade unions, Harold Wilson suddenly stunned the political world by resigning as Prime Minister in March 1976. It was the worst possible timing for Healey's chances of winning the party leadership.

In the run-up to the leadership election, he had been involved in a blazing row on the floor of the House of Commons with hard-left MPs. 'What happened is that one of them cast doubt on my paternity so I praised his virility,' said Healey with mas- terly understatement. In fact, the left-wing MPs called Healey 'a Stalinist bastard' and Healey yelled at them repeatedly, 'You fuckers, you're out of your tiny Chinese minds.'

At the time Healey tried to laugh it off when he said in an interview: 'Well, we have a very turbulent and boisterous love

Libertine Alan Clark and his long-suffering wife Jane at his castle in Kent, where we filmed for the documentary *Love Tory*.

I interviewed Denis Healey at his Sussex home who told me he was the man who did the dirty work for Labour. The director, who had cast off her shoes, is Habie Schwarz.

I interviewed Tony Blair on the sofa in his Downing Street den – the seat of New Labour's notorious sofa government.

Prime Minister Tony Blair comes into his spin doctor Alastair Campbell's office during our fly-on-the-wall documentary *News from Number 10*.

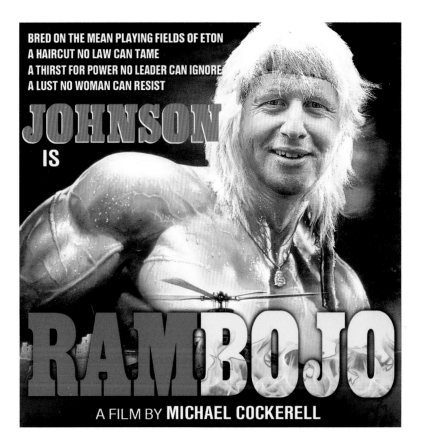

How the *Sun* newspaper billed my Boris Johnson documentary.

Filming for *Dave Cameron's Incredible Journey*.

Off to film Johnson playing tennis with his siblings for *Boris Johnson: The Irresistible Rise*.

I am the first journalist to ask Boris Johnson whether he drafted two articles on Brexit to help make up his mind: one in favour of staying in the EU; the other for getting out.

life in the Labour Party, you know, and these hard words get exchanged from time to time, but the bruises wear off quite quickly.'

He told me later: 'It didn't in fact make me unpopular with the left of the party, but I think it did scare a lot of middle-of-the-road MPs.' Healey easily lost the leadership election to Jim Callaghan.

Healey remained Chancellor, and in the autumn of 1976 the world's money markets were causing him nightmares. He was about to fly off to an international finance ministers' conference when he heard on the car radio that the pound was plummeting on the foreign exchanges. 'The only time I was really shaken as a minister', he told me, 'was that famous day when the pound collapsed and I had to turn back from the airport to deal with it rather than go on to the Philippines, where I would have been out of touch with Whitehall for seventeen critical hours. And I felt the world was collapsing around me.'

To bail Britain out, the government applied for a huge loan from the International Monetary Fund and Healey drove up to the Labour conference in Blackpool to confront his sceptical party. I was filming there, and I remember the atmosphere in the hall was like a bitterly divided football stadium as Healey strode to the lectern. There was heavy booing, jeering and counter cheering as the Chancellor sought to persuade his fractious party to accept deep public spending cuts as the price of the IMF loan to prevent Britain going bust.

He bellowed: 'Now I tell you, comrades. I am going to negotiate with the IMF on the basis of our existing policies, not changes in policies. It means sticking to the very painful cuts in public expenditure on which the government's already decided.' Shouts of 'Resign!' came from the audience. 'That's what it means and that's what I'm going to negotiate for – and I ask the conference to support me in that task.'

After a mammoth series of Cabinet meetings that eventually approved much deeper public spending cuts than Healey had promised the conference, he finally reached a deal with the IMF. 'Denis negotiated with the IMF, and he went much further than his brief that I had given him,' Jim Callaghan told me. 'He threatened the negotiators that if they didn't agree on what he was ready to go for, then we would have a general election. Denis had got no authority to say that but told me: "We're going to have a general election." I said: "Oh. Thank you very much!" But I didn't mind, because I knew it was a negotiating tactic.'

When I asked Healey about his tactics, he said: 'The proof of the pudding is in the eating. The IMF dropped its demand for an extra billion of spending cuts. We got the deal through, and from that moment on I was walking on water.'

'In what sense?' I asked.

He said: 'In the sense that the international community thought I was the best thing since sliced bread. One American financial journal had a cover story of the five best Chancellors in the world and I came top – and all the other four were working in dictatorships. And it's not difficult to be Finance Minister in a country where you can use electrodes applied to the sensitive parts of the body as a means of persuading people.'

When Callaghan resigned as Labour leader after losing the

1979 election, the party reverted to its default position of internal fighting, with Tony Benn leading the left and the position of leader of the centre-right vacant. 'It was a really horrid time,' said Shirley Williams. 'It was a sort of party civil war. Many MPs looked at Denis, the bully and the battler, as their natural leader. They thought of Denis as the sort of Sir Galahad, a white knight, one who would take on the far left and never turn back.'

But Healey decided that as favourite, his best chance was to do and say nothing publicly, believing the leadership would fall into his lap. Some right-wingers like David Owen felt Healey no longer had the stomach for a stand-up fight with the left. Healey's low-profile strategy was to do him no good, and he lost to Michael Foot by 139 MPs' votes to 129.

'The election became a "Stop Healey" campaign,' Healey told me. 'The left had always wanted to stop me, and they were very powerful. Another important factor in the campaign was the number of enemies I had made by the many unpopular measures I had been obliged to take as Chancellor. But in the words of an unsuccessful presidential candidate: "I would rather that people wonder why I am not President than why I am."'

The great bruiser of the Labour Party retired from front-line politics to what he called his 'earthly paradise' – his substantial house with a large swimming pool and a glorious view over the South Downs in Sussex. Sitting in the sun outside the house for my first profile of him in 1989, I began our interview: 'It's a nice place you've got here.' He nodded but declined to respond, and I said: 'There are people in the Labour Party who would say, what is he doing living in a house that grand?'

'Well, they say that about television presenters and popstars, don't they?' countered Healey.

His wife Edna added: 'Somebody once said to me, if a Chancellor at the end of his career can't live in a decent house, what hope is there for the rest of us?'

When I arrived at the house to film a last interview for his obituary, he was nearly ninety-six and had just finished his daily summer swim in his outdoor pool. 'Every time I go in I reckon to do twenty lengths,' he told me. 'It's not the swimming that's the difficulty – it's getting into the pool.'

Healey was famously happily married to Edna, whom he had first met at Oxford in the late 1930s. What did he see as the secret of a happy marriage? 'Well, we loved one another,' he said, 'it was as simple as that. And we shared the same love of music and poetry; and a pleasure shared with someone you love is a pleasure doubled, because you not only enjoy it yourself but you enjoy seeing your wife happy.'

Edna Healey was a distinguished biographer and wrote a book about the wives of famous men which she was tempted to name *I Didn't Know He Had a Wife*. She told me: 'Denis is basically an extraordinarily happy man. He does sing in the morning and sometimes he's a little too boisterous. He has this enormous energy and vim and vigour. He can be a bit rumbustious from time to time. But he's easy to live with, and it's a lovely marriage.'

They had celebrated their sixty-fifth wedding anniversary in the Sussex house. In 2010, soon after their anniversary celebrations, Edna died in her sleep. 'Oh, it was terrible,' said Healey.

'Edna was half of my life and when she died, that half which was the better half disappeared. But my family has kept me going and my love of music and poetry keeps me going as well.'

In a house filled with books, Healey found that the ones he would return to again and again for consolation were the poems. I asked which poets meant the most to him. 'Well, Maggie Thatcher once said, "Every Prime Minister needs a Willie." She meant Willie Whitelaw, but many people misunderstood her. I myself in politics have always had four Willies: William Shakespeare, William Blake, William Wordsworth and William Butler Yeats. And each of them in my mind is absolutely wonderful and I learned a lot of them by heart.'

Healey kept a shelf of *Spitting Image* puppets as latex mementoes of his turbulent political life – among them Margaret Thatcher, Michael Foot, Neil Kinnock and David Owen. As he picked up the Owen puppet and squeezed to make it squeak, I quoted Owen's view that when Healey stood for the Labour leadership in 1980 he 'didn't have the guts to take on the left wing of the party'. 'That's absolute bollocks,' snorted Healey. 'David Owen was a very self-centred person. He was good-looking, he was intelligent, he had immense charm and all these presents were given to him by the Good Fairy and then the Bad Fairy came along and tapped him on the shoulder and said, but you'll be a shit.' Healey's gift for vituperation was still in good working order.

I asked Healey if he regretted the fact that he never became Prime Minister. 'I do a little bit now. I never wanted to be Prime Minister at the time. I was in politics because I wanted to do something, rather than be something. But of course Prime Ministers have to do a hell of a lot as well as being a lot. And I wish now that I had gone on to No. 10.'

As we left his house after filming, Healey's last words to me were: 'Now you sod off and I'll nod off.' A few weeks after we finished cutting the film, his daughter Jennifer, who had been tremendously helpful to us in providing photographs and documents, rang and asked if it might be possible for Denis to see the film. I told her that *en principe* the BBC never allows the subjects to see their obituary. But I said I would ask if an exception could be made, as this was a rather special case. Rather to my surprise the Corporation's powers that be said yes, so long as Healey kept it strictly under wraps.

A few days later Jennifer rang again. I asked if her father had seen the film. 'Oh yes, he put it on as soon as he got it. He was glued to it, and he watched it almost reliving his life – sometimes laughing and sometimes crying, especially the part about Mum. He really liked the film. So much so that he immediately watched it all again.'

Denis Healey had held many of the toughest jobs in politics and had helped save Britain from bankruptcy. In a monochrome age, what Professor Peter Hennessy called 'Denis's special combination of brain and brawn' made him stand out as a Technicolor politician. Throughout Healey's career his capacity to divide his party and country was greater than his ability to unite it. But he should be remembered not in a sad way, as the nearly man of British politics, but rather by a great 'what if?' Wouldn't we have been in for a terrific helter-skelter ride if Denis Winston Healey had had a crack at the premiership?

He died in his sleep, aged ninety-eight, in the autumn of 2015. The Prime Minister David Cameron said: 'We have lost a huge figure of post-war politics. A hero in World War Two and a brave politician who always told his party hard truths. We should give thanks for all he gave our country.'

CHAPTER 28

CALL ME DAVE

When I made a TV portrait of David Cameron, I was struck by the fact that every previous leader I had made a film about became leader and then got themselves a spin doctor. Cameron was the ultimate identity bender: the spin doctor who became leader. All his previous political career had been about presentation and how to play things as a special adviser to various Tory panjandrums – among them John Major, Norman Lamont and Michael Howard. He'd had one job outside Westminster, when he became media adviser to a media company.

He had watched with growing admiration the presentation skills of the New Labour troika of Blair, Campbell and Mandelson. Cameron and his fellow modernisers regarded the revealing book about the making of New Labour by Blair's pollster Philip Gould, *The Unfinished Revolution*, as their bible – and they referred to Blair as 'the master'.

At a private lunch, Cameron described himself as 'the heir to Blair'. He meant he planned to detoxify the Tory brand. It would be transformed from what many people, according to the former party chairwoman Theresa May, called the 'Nasty Party' into the new Conservatives – modern, tolerant, youthful and diverse. And they would also, said Cameron, stop banging on about Europe.

When he was still Leader of the Opposition, I asked Cameron my favourite question: do you have any doubts about your ability to fulfil the role of Prime Minister? 'Look,' he replied, 'if I had major doubts I wouldn't have put myself forward to lead my party in the first place. You have to be absolutely ready to take the difficult and big decisions you would have to take as Prime Minister, including sending troops to war. And I decided I was ready for that.' Of all the future Prime Ministers who have answered that question, Cameron was the least self-doubting.

His wife, Samantha, said: 'Dave is the most glass-half-full person in the world – he's ridiculously optimistic.' But I was increasingly getting the impression that he was actually rather less self-confident and more insecure than the chillaxing image he liked to project.

At the age of forty-three, he had in 2010 become the youngest PM for almost 200 years. Like Tony Blair, the premiership was the first and only ministerial job he had in government. He recalled that when as opposition leader he had stood up to question Blair at PMQs: 'I had only ever spoken from the despatch box three times before.'

Cameron had often worked on preparing questions for previous Tory leaders, and for his debut as opposition leader in 2005, he and his team had come up with a telling quasi-spontaneous line. In his first question, Cameron offered to cooperate with the PM on an education Bill. Blair replied with a question of his own. Cameron responded: 'It's only our first exchange – and already the Prime Minister is asking me questions. This approach is stuck in the past; I want to talk about the future. He was the future once.' Blair's face took on a look of rueful poignancy.

Just as Blair had appointed Alastair Campbell, a former political editor of the *Daily Mirror*, as his director of communications, Cameron appointed a former tabloid editor to the post. But Andy Coulson had form. He had resigned as editor of the *News of the World* following the reports of phone hacking, while swearing he knew nothing about it. Cameron accepted his word, and when more allegations came out against Coulson, the PM stood stubbornly by his chief spin doctor. 'I choose to judge Andy Coulson', said Cameron, 'by the work that he has done for me, for the government and for the country. He's run the No. 10 press office in a professional, competent and good way. And if you compare that with the days of the dodgy dossier and Alastair Campbell and Damian McBride and all that nonsense we had from the previous government, he's done an excellent, excellent job.'

But as fresh revelations against the former *News of the World* editor piled up, Cameron reluctantly accepted his spin doctor's resignation. Coulson quit No. 10 with a last sound bite: 'When the spokesman needs a spokesman, it's time to go.'

Coulson was subsequently given an eighteen-month prison sentence for phone hacking. His last key task in No. 10 had been to help find a replacement for himself. Coulson texted a very experienced TV man, Craig Oliver, to see if he might be interested in the job. Oliver, who had been a high-up BBC and ITV

News executive, came for an interview at No. 10 with the Prime Minister and the Chancellor George Osborne. And a week after Coulson had left the building, Oliver was announced as his successor.

Cameron was determined to keep as tight a grip as he could on the modern media. The PM told his journalist cousin Harry Mount: 'The pressure to respond to every news event is immense. When I take people into the Cabinet Room, I say, this is one of the rooms where, for five days in May 1940, Churchill and others decided that Britain should fight on against Hitler. Imagine if that happened today – after half an hour, Alastair Campbell or Craig Oliver would pop his head round the door and say, "Sky News are outside. What do I say? Are we fighting on or are we surrendering?" You've got to use your time to make long-term decisions for the good of the country. That was one of the biggest lessons I learned from Blair.'

Cameron agreed to let us film him when I made a behind-the-scenes film about the House of Commons and the way Parliament works. It had taken six years and many hours of detailed negotiations to persuade the political parties and the Commons authorities to give us access. For the first time, we were allowed to film anywhere in the House, including in the Chamber, without restrictions. And we were able to see the whites of the eyes of MPs as they debated, rather than the tops of the heads that the fixed, unmanned official cameras often capture.

The one time of the week when the Chamber is full to overflowing is Prime Minister's Questions. In his grand, wood-panelled office in the Commons, David Cameron told me: 'There isn't a Wednesday that you don't feel total fear and trepidation about what is about to happen. I'm normally sitting here preparing for PMQs and about five minutes beforehand you think: "Oh no, have I got to do this again?" And I think Prime Ministers have always felt that.'

I put to Cameron Tony Blair's heartfelt description of Prime Minister's Questions as 'a nerve-racking, discombobulating, nail-biting, bowel-moving, terror-inspiring, courage-draining experience'. 'I think that about sums it up,' responded Cameron. He said that sometimes the noise was so great he couldn't actually hear the question properly and gave the answer to what he presumed the MP would be asking based on what he knew about the questioner.

'The noise can be deafening,' Ed Miliband, then Leader of the Opposition, told me. 'There are not many jobs where you go to work and have at least 300 people trying to shout you down.'

Our film revealed that the Prime Minister had little need to fear the questions from his own MPs. We discovered that Cameron's own parliamentary private secretary, Gavin Williamson (who was later to be sacked from Theresa May's Cabinet for leaking, only to be resurrected as Prime Minister Boris Johnson's accident-prone Education Secretary), would regularly get a group of Tory backbenchers together before PMQs to rehearse chants and gestures for use against the Labour leader. And each week Williamson would email a list of suggested questions and sound bites to Tory backbenchers.

We filmed the Tory MP Andrew Percy showing me the emails containing subjects to ask about, along with the approved wording for questioners – like 'our long-term economic plan is working' and 'this government is on the side of people who work hard'. When I suggested to Cameron this made a mockery of question time, the PM responded: 'If you are saying it's appalling that Tory MPs should possibly use any of these phrases, I would say that politics is about the team putting across team messages. So people shouldn't be too worried about that happening in PMQs.'

But that wasn't how the late Charles Kennedy, the former Liberal Democrat leader, saw it: 'I just can't understand how anybody can get elected to Parliament and then just read out a couple of sentences they've been given: "Doesn't the Prime Minister agree he is doing a great job this week and he will do an even better one next week?" It is always so obvious when they're doing it and it's pathetic.'

So how did Cameron rate the Labour leaders he had come up against at PMQs, as Prime Minister and earlier as opposition leader? Ed Miliband, said Cameron, was 'annoyingly good' at landing class-themed blows. Gordon Brown was 'tough, but you could get around him'. And Tony Blair was 'superb' and 'played the Chamber like a music-hall star'.

I asked Cameron what he thought of the Commons as an institution. He told me: 'You do feel a real sense of history in this place. It's half like a museum, half like a church, half like a school.' Clearly an unusual school where three halves make a whole.

Cameron was getting a kick out of being Prime Minister. Asked in opposition why he wanted the job, he had replied:

'Because I'd be rather good at it.' And once in No. 10 he said he saw himself as 'a political decathlete, switching from one discipline to the next trying to give every single one of them my best'.

Professor David Runciman, the Cambridge political scientist who was Cameron's contemporary at Eton, said: 'Much of what David Cameron relishes about being Prime Minister – and he clearly does relish it – is the range of tasks it demands: from mundane party management to high political gossip, from the grandest foreign trips to the most routine constituency visits, from interpreting economic forecasts to summarising legal briefs, from dealing with terrorists to dealing with his colleagues.'

For the five years after 2010, when Cameron won power in a hung parliament, he ran a coalition with the Lib Dems. Before the election, he had asked Angela Merkel, who was accustomed to coalitions in Germany, how they worked. She summed it up succinctly: 'Well, David, the way it works is that if things go well, then the big party gets the credit – and if they go badly, the small party gets the blame.'

'Sounds a good idea to me,' responded Cameron. And when the 2015 election came, he confounded the pundits and pollsters to win an overall majority. He looked forward optimistically to the prospect of being able to govern untrammelled by Lib Dems.

But Cameron had chosen to entrust the biggest foreign policy decision for a generation to a referendum. The question of Britain's relationship with Europe had long been a festering sore on the Tory body politic. It was the issue that would not go away and had helped bring down the previous two Conservative PMs. Cameron was later to admit that because of what Europe was doing to his party: 'Not once during eleven years as Conservative leader did I feel secure for any length of time.'

Ignoring the advice of his closest political ally, Chancellor George Osborne, Cameron decided that the only way to assuage his increasingly Eurosceptic party and counter the threat of UKIP was by an in/out referendum on Britain's membership of the EU. It was to be held in the summer of 2016. There were two top Tories the Prime Minister desperately wanted to have on his side in the referendum campaign: Michael Gove and Boris Johnson. He had known them since their Oxford days three decades back and regarded them as his very good friends. The Camerons and the Goves would holiday together, and Gove's wife, Sarah Vine, was godmother to the Camerons' youngest daughter. But the PM doubted he could fully trust either Gove or Johnson. He recalled that in a Cabinet reshuffle two years earlier, Gove had gone back on his word. He had accepted the job of Chief Whip, which he had said he wanted, but the next day tried to withdraw his acceptance.

Cameron had sent Gove a text saying: 'You must realise I divide the world into team players and wankers. You've always been a team player, please don't become a wanker.' In his autobiography, Cameron confirmed that text, but when he was filmed for the TV version of his book, the ex-PM refused point-blank to say the W-word on camera.

Having been led to believe by Sarah Vine that he would have her husband's support in the referendum campaign, Cameron tried to get a definitive answer from his elusive friend. 'Michael has been like a cat on a hot tin roof,' said Vine. 'Locked in an internal struggle of agonising proportions.'

Gove admitted he was moving towards Leave, but he promised Cameron: 'If I do decide to opt for Brexit, I will make one speech. That will be it. I will play no further part in the campaign.' As it turned out, Gove was to become a leader of the Leave campaign, touring the country and making evangelical speeches and broadcasts galore.

Failing to land Gove made Cameron all the more determined to bag Boris. Johnson was doubling as a Tory MP and Mayor of London, and he had become the most marketable politician in the country. The PM had long envied his fellow Etonian's charisma and campaigning skills, and he was convinced that for the Remain side to win the referendum, he had to have Johnson on his side. But BoJo was proving maddeningly and characteristically difficult to nail down. So, exactly who was the man the PM regarded as so indispensable for his cause?

CHAPTER 29

BORIS – THE IRRESISTIBLE RISE

Boris Johnson cuts an extraordinary figure on the tennis court. On a cold, bright morning in the spring of 2013, I filmed him playing doubles, partnering his sister Rachel against his brothers Leo and Jo. He wore red shoes, black socks, below-the-knee cargo shorts and a beanie hat bearing a Union Jack. He is a take-no-prisoners player who leaps in the air to smite the ball, grunting like a gorilla.

He was pretty good – especially as he was playing with a warped wooden racquet that must have been old when Fred Perry was young. It had the advantage, though, that it despatched the ball at wildly unpredictable angles – rather like Johnson himself. When Jo Johnson, then a Tory MP, had to leave early, I took his place. Boris said to me later that he was very worried about the film I was making about him. 'Why?' I asked.

'Well,' he said, 'I kept trying to hit the ball very hard straight at you to knock your head off when you were at the net – and you were somehow getting it back. You might cut the film to make it look as if you were better than me.'

'Perish the thought, Boris,' I said.

I had long wanted to make a TV portrait of Johnson, but I knew that apart from his self-presented *Who Do You Think You Are?*, he had turned down all requests to cooperate with a film about his life. I sent him a handwritten letter, and it was six weeks before I got a response. Eventually, he rang me with a question. Without committing himself either way, he wanted to know what would happen with the film if he refused to be in it. I told him we would go ahead and make it anyway, but that of course I would much prefer it if he did cooperate. He then said: 'That's a bit like a *News of the World* journalist ringing me up late on a Saturday afternoon and saying' – and he put on a thick Cockney accent – '"Mr Johnson, we have a story going in the paper tomorrow, and we thought we'd give you a chance to tell your side."'

'I'm glad you see it like that, Boris,' I replied. And he agreed to give my producer Adam Grimley and me access and do interviews for the film.

The setting for Alexander Boris de Pfeffel Johnson's entrance into the world was the New York Public Hospital, in summer 1964. 'Boris was a champion when he was born,' his mother, the painter Charlotte Johnson Wahl, told me. 'Not only was he very big and looked as though he was ready for prep school, but he had thick yellow hair. The Beatles had just arrived in New York, and he got called the blond Beatle. All the expectant mothers were brought in to see him.'

Johnson says his origins are like the supermarket honey that is labelled 'product of more than one country': Turkish, English, Russian, French and German, as well as Muslim and Jewish.

The blond gene, he claims, came from a flaxen-haired Cappadocian girl, whom one of his ancestors bought at a slave market. Johnson asserts: 'He said, "Wrap her up and I'll take her" – and later they married.'

Boris was the first of numerous blond Johnson children who grew up in a super-competitive household. He points the finger at his sister Rachel: 'My life was one of blameless, panda-like passivity until my younger sister arrived,' he said in our first interview. 'I had everything an eighteen-month-year-old [*sic*] could possibly desire, and suddenly I found that I had this competition – and it was necessary to exert myself for food, for attention, for everything else.'

'Boris knows that life is a competition, and he always wants to be top,' Rachel told me. 'As he was growing up, whenever anyone asked him what he wanted to be, he would answer: "World King". He thought it was an actual job and one that he could do, and that he fulfilled every criterion.'

The Johnson family moved house thirty times in fifteen years. It made for what Rachel calls a 'rackety childhood' – exacerbated when their mother began suffering from obsessive compulsive disorder and was away from her four children in a psychiatric hospital for the best part of a year. Boris Johnson later learned that his parents were getting divorced. His mother told me: 'I've often thought that his wish to be World King was to make himself unhurtable, invincible from the pains of life: from the pain of your mother disappearing for eight months – and the pain of your parents splitting up.'

Aged thirteen, Johnson was sent on a scholarship to Eton, the school that has produced one third of all Britain's Prime Ministers. It was there that Johnson first met David Cameron, who was known as 'Cameron minor' as he had an elder brother at the school. 'I do remember Dave,' Johnson told me. 'Someone once said to me, "That's Cameron mi" – and there was this tiny chap.'

For his part, Cameron says: 'I remember Boris at school because he was so striking. He was dishevelled. I remember watching him play rugby. He was ferocious – built like a second-row forward.' Over the following four decades, the two Etonians' lives would regularly intersect – and would eventually change the course of British history.

At Eton, Johnson was so brutish on the rugby field that he broke his nose four times. And he learned a rather more subtle skill on a different school stage. 'Boris discovered he could make people laugh,' Rachel told me. 'He was in a Molière play and he hadn't bothered to learn his lines. So, he hid behind a pillar reading them out, which was obviously much funnier.'

I asked Johnson if he had learned a lesson for the future about the advantages of not learning your lines. 'As a general tactic in life, if that's what you are getting at,' he replied, 'it is often useful to give the slight impression that you are deliberately pretending not to know what's going on – because the reality may be that you don't know what's going on, but people won't be able to tell the difference.'

When Johnson left Eton, he pasted in the leavers' book a photo of himself posing on a pillar like a Ruritanian dictator. Underneath, he wrote that his ambition was 'to achieve more notches on my phallocratic phallus'. That organ would lead Johnson a merry dance in the years to come.

He won a classics scholarship to Balliol College, Oxford – the alma mater of Asquith, Macmillan, Ted Heath, Roy Jenkins, Denis Healey, Chris Patten and Yvette Cooper. He had developed what he calls 'Tory tendencies'. Already a skilled and witty debater, Johnson was determined to be elected President of the Oxford Union, seen as a key apprenticeship for Westminster. But having lost at his first attempt, he sought to broaden his appeal by letting people think he was a fan of the new centre-left Social Democratic Party – the SDP. 'They were in search of a candidate,' Johnson told me. 'And it would be fair to say that while I never identified myself as a supporter, when asked if I would accept SDP support, I did not demur.' This time, with a new campaign manager called Michael Gove, he won the presidency.

Johnson was also elected a member of the now infamous Bullingdon Club, the exclusive drinking and dining club for opulent students famed for their rowdy behaviour – including trashing restaurants after their formal dinners. We filmed Johnson looking at the notorious group photograph of the members in their navy-blue tailcoats with velvet collars and ivory silk lapels, monogrammed buttons, yellow waistcoats and light-blue bow ties. In the photo, Johnson, David Cameron and the other members all looked as if they'd stepped straight out of *Brideshead Revisited*. The two would-be PMs had long sought to have the photo airbrushed from history.

When we flashed it up on the screen we were filming Johnson watching, he exclaimed: 'Aha! I congratulate you on defying the censors and bringing this appalling image once again into public view. It is a truly shameful vignette of almost superhuman undergraduate arrogance, toffishness and twittishness. But it was great fun at the time.' He paused. 'Or was it? The awful truth is that you kind of felt very posh and it was wonderful to be going round swanking it up. But actually, I remember the dinners being incredibly drunken.'

'Ending with smashing up restaurants,' I prompted.

'Yes,' said Johnson, 'but the abiding feeling was of deep, deep, deep self-loathing.'

'I've talked to a number of people who were with you in the Bullingdon.'

'Oh God. Have you?'

'They say when you see them these days, you greet them saying: "Buller! Buller! Buller!"'

Johnson laughed. 'It may be that I do – in a satirical way.'

For his part, Cameron says: 'When I look now at the much-reproduced photograph taken of our group of appallingly over-self-confident "sons of privilege", I cringe. It's cripplingly embarrassing. If I had known at the time the grief I would get for that picture, of course I would never have joined. The Bullingdon has haunted me for most of my political life.'

After leaving Oxford with a 2:1 in classics, Johnson joined *The Times* as a trainee reporter, but he was soon sacked for making up a quote from a distinguished academic who was his own godfather. He resurfaced in 1989 as the *Daily Telegraph*'s man in Brussels and began to make his name by going against the pro-EU orthodoxy of the resident UK press pack. Johnson ridiculed the Brussels bureaucrats — and helped provide ammunition for the Eurosceptic cause in Britain. 'Brussels recruits sniffers to ensure Euromanure all smells the same'; 'Threat to British pink sausages'; and 'Snails are fish, says EU' were headlines on just three of the stream of stories he produced. And he had a big scoop claiming the Berlaymont building, HQ of the European Commission, was to be blown up (the building still stands). Fellow correspondents claimed that Johnson would take a story containing a grain of truth and hype it up beyond recognition.

'There's a bit of pots and kettles going on there,' responds Johnson. 'Yes, there were one or two stories that perhaps in retrospect were a little bit over-egged. But I'm very proud of my coverage in Brussels.' Chris Patten, then an EU commissioner, says: 'Boris was one of the first exponents of fake journalism.'

Johnson returned to London as a star *Telegraph* columnist, where he was invariably late in filing his copy. He seemed to regard a deadline as merely a basis for negotiation. I asked Johnson about his habit of leaving things to the very last minute, so that, for instance, he would still be writing a speech on the menu card during the actual dinner where he was the key speaker. 'That's all to do with adrenaline,' he replied. 'You can only really perform at your best if you're under pressure. The ability to think of what to say doesn't happen until the heart rate starts to climb a bit.'

As a TV interviewee, Johnson differs from all the other politicians I have encountered on camera. While they are endlessly concerned to ensure they do not have a hair out of place, Johnson starts an interview by ruffling his blond mop and goes on doing so.

After his first marriage to his Oxford girlfriend broke down, he married Marina Wheeler, a left-wing lawyer and daughter of the BBC's Charles Wheeler. But, in 2004, the tabloids reported that Johnson was having a love affair with Petronella Wyatt, a fellow journalist at *The Spectator*, where was Johnson was now editor. He was also a Tory MP and shadow Arts Minister and he dismissed the reports out of hand, saying: 'I have not had an affair with Petronella. It's complete balderdash. It's an inverted pyramid of piffle. It's all completely untrue and ludicrous conjecture; I'm amazed people can write this drivel.' But when the affair was confirmed, the Tory leader Michael Howard sacked his shadow minister for lying to him.

One of Howard's advisers was David Cameron, who had become an MP in the same 2001 intake as Johnson. I asked Cameron at the time whether he thought it was a good idea for Howard to sack Johnson. Cameron's face reddened and he was less than fluent: 'I think, um, er, that's one for him rather than for me. I think there's a very difficult issue when you have said one thing publicly and then you have to say something else publicly. And you know, if it's about your private life, if you are talking to the press it becomes part of your public life. And that's incredibly tough, but I think that's something you have to deal with one way or another.'

But, I said, you haven't answered my question as to whether you thought the sacking was a good idea. 'Well, the short answer is yes – given the circumstances, that was the right decision. But, you know, Boris is a very close friend and colleague. And it was obviously a very tough time for him as well.'

Johnson seeks to apply a self-denying ordinance, or what might be called a blanket ban, on discussing his love life – even when it has caused clear political fallout. He repels personal questions, saying: 'The difficulty is that one line of enquiry invariably leads to another.' I asked whether this was because he did not want to lift any stones: 'If you talked about your private life, more interesting things would come out?'

Johnson gave a throaty laugh and said: 'It is quite amazing how little the public are interested in that side of things.'

But in 2004 his love life had cost Bonking Boris, as the tabloids dubbed him, his front-bench job. And he watched as David Cameron dramatically overtook him by winning the Tory leadership the following year. Johnson was excluded from the Cameron inner circle; the new leader was having quite enough trouble playing down his own privileged image without promoting another Etonian – especially one so difficult to control as Johnson.

But having failed to find a suitable Tory candidate to stand for Mayor of London, Cameron sounded Johnson out. He was initially dead against the idea. One of those closest to him told me: 'Boris thinks it's all a plot by Cameron to get him out of the way, because he'd have to resign as an MP if he were to become mayor.' Sir Max Hastings, who had been Johnson's editor at the *Daily Telegraph*, told me: 'I remember when Boris was trying to decide whether to run, he asked me out to lunch, and I said I thought he should go for it. He asked whether I had any advice, and I said: "Yes, lock up your willy."'

After much dithering, Johnson finally decided to run for mayor. Many people at the time thought it was a hopeless cause. London was traditionally Labour, and the incumbent Ken Livingstone was seen as unbeatable. 'I recognised immediately that Boris was going to be my most formidable opponent,' Livingstone told me. 'Because he makes people laugh and feel good about themselves. He therefore can get away with a lot.' From the other end of the political spectrum, Conrad Black, the proprietor of the *Telegraph* and *Spectator* who employed Johnson, summed up his appeal: 'Boris is a sly fox disguised as a teddy bear.'

When Johnson beat Livingstone in 2008, he regarded the mayoralty as a public audition for an even higher political stage. He became a zealous convert to the London 2012 Olympics, having initially been very sceptical. 'It was a very jammy trick to pull to be mayor during the Olympics,' he told me. The Games offered a matchless stage to project to the world his winning brand of feel-good optimism – that contrasted so sharply with what he called the 'drink your own urine' message of the coalition's austerity politicians.

'The Geiger-counter of Olympomania is going to go zonk off the scale,' he declaimed at the Hyde Park curtain-raiser. 'Our Team GB athletes are going to win more gold, silver and bronze medals than you'd need to bail out Greece and Spain together.'

'It was very bad for the ego,' Johnson said as we filmed him watching footage of the huge crowd chanting 'Boris! Boris!

Boris!' 'But you do understand', he continued, 'why Roman Emperors put on great Games. Suddenly you think: "Wow!"'

'Would you like to be a Roman Emperor?' I asked him.

'No,' he replied, 'because they invariably came to a sticky end.'

A sticky end was the *mot juste* for his celebrated zipwire trip to promote the Olympics, which we also filmed him watching. He became almost hysterical with laughter as he viewed himself dangling in mid-air when he got stuck on the wire. Wearing a harness, a city suit and a crash helmet and clutching two Union flags, he was shouting: 'Get me a ladder!'

'That was far more painful and frightening than you might think,' he said with tears of laughter in his eyes. 'It was jolly high up, and after you were stuck up there for a while, things started to chafe.'

'Where was it chafing?'

'I don't want to go into details, Michael,' he said.

'But,' I countered, 'in your book about the London Olympics, you said: "There was chafing in the groin area."'

'Did I? Oh, right.'

'That's what's so difficult about interviewing you, Boris,' I said. 'You can't even recognise your own words.'

'I can never remember what I've written – but if it's in my book, it must be true.'

I always thought that 'Chafing in the Groin Area' might be a good title for a biography of Boris Johnson.

'If any other politician anywhere in the world got stuck on a zipwire it would be disastrous,' said David Cameron, then Prime Minister. 'But with Boris it's an absolute triumph. He defies all forms of gravity.' Johnson saw it differently. 'How could anyone elect a prat who gets stuck in a zipwire?' he said.

Boris Johnson has always sought to play by his own rules. When he was at Eton, his housemaster reported: 'I think Boris honestly sees it as churlish of us not to regard him as an exception – one who should be free of the network of obligation that binds everyone else.'

'This is why Boris is dementing for other politicians,' says Rachel Johnson. 'Because they're all to an extent playing the part assigned to them by the party: you have to be loyal, you have to be a good Tory. Boris realised quite early on that he would go further if he broke all those rules – and people would love him even more – which is a genius piece of casting.'

Johnson had become the most popular politician in the country. But while some saw him as a future Prime Minister, others claimed he was a duplicitous, gaffe-prone joker who flew by the seat of his pants. And at No. 10, David Cameron was convinced that Johnson was always seeking to upstage him.

After our Johnson documentary went out, Cameron told me that he had never realised until watching it how much it had hurt Johnson to learn that Cameron had got a first-class degree at Oxford, while he had only got a 2:1. When I asked Johnson about it, he said disdainfully: 'Dave got a first in PPE, my degree was in classics, which is a real subject.' And Rachel Johnson told me: 'When Boris and Dave are together, it's rather sweet. Even though Dave is taller than my brother, he somehow looks up at Boris, as if he were still head boy at school; Cameron was two years younger, the young pup. And it gives Boris a continuing sense of superiority.'

Guto Harri, who was Mayor Johnson's press secretary for four years, told me: 'Often there's that pattern where Boris seems to want to upstage the PM. Nine times out of ten the row is about something of substance, not some sort of game being played between him and the Prime Minister.' And the tenth time? 'It goes back to school, and we all know what it's like with school friends. So even if one of you has ended up as Prime Minister and the other as Mayor of London, to a certain extent they are both still at Eton in their short shorts, sparring with each other.'

Johnson had always made a point of deflecting questions about his political ambitions. In our final interview I asked him whether he would like to be Prime Minister. 'I would *like* to be the lead singer of an international rock group. That was my aim. Or a good guitarist. I would love to have been a world-famous painter or a composer. There are many things that I would like to have been able to do.' But, I persisted, would you like to be Prime Minister? His response might have come straight from the playing fields of Eton: 'I think it's a very tough job being Prime Minister. Obviously, if the ball came loose from the back of a scrum – which it won't – it would be a great, great thing to have a crack at. But it's not going to happen.'

Our documentary was called *Boris Johnson: The Irresistible Rise*. Johnson wrote to me after it had been transmitted: 'So many people have said kind things about your biopic that I feel obliged to write and thank you for the tact and care with which you handled the whole project. And when people ask me why I collaborated, it's the same reason you pose for Rembrandt or Lucian Freud or some other top artist: partly vanity, partly 'cos it's a blooming honour!'

Talk about piling it on thick.

CHAPTER 30

THE BORIS AND DAVE SHOW

In 2016, as Boris Johnson was ending his second term as mayor and had once again become a Tory MP, the chances of the ball coming his way from the scrum increased significantly. David Cameron's long-promised Brexit referendum was to take place in June, and it could well put his premiership on the line. Having failed to win the support of Michael Gove for the Britain Stronger in Europe campaign, Cameron passionately wanted on his side the man he called his very good friend: Boris Johnson. The PM calculated that joining forces with the most popular politician in the country, who was also a brilliant campaigner, would more or less guarantee victory for the Remainers.

Private opinion polling told Cameron that if Johnson were on board Remain would lead by 8 per cent, but if he went for Leave the lead would fall to 1 per cent. The PM said privately: 'Without Johnson – the only leading politician whose favourability rating was higher than mine – the Leave campaign would lack credibility. With him on the Leave side, it would legitimise their cause and help detoxify the Brexit brand.'

Yet Cameron could see Johnson becoming ever more tempted

by the Leave cause, and the PM felt the determining factor for Johnson was deciding which option would do most to promote his lifelong ambition to reach No. 10. But the congenitally indecisive Johnson would not commit himself, and Cameron decided to work on him face to face. In early January 2016, he arranged for them to meet for a game of tennis at the US ambassador's court in London, where they could play and talk in private. Cameron beat his ultra-competitive opponent on the court, although when Craig Oliver, the No. 10 press secretary, asked Johnson the result, he replied: 'Dave needs to sink a few thousand pounds into his backhand.' Oliver added: 'I noted he'd skilfully had a go at the PM, without revealing he'd lost to him.'

Cameron had less success in getting a straight answer on the Brexit question. At the tennis court, he promised Johnson a 'top five' Cabinet job if he came out for Remain. 'I'm not going to be Prime Minister for ever,' Cameron told Johnson, 'and at the next leadership election, you've got every opportunity to win it. This will give you the best possible chance.'

But, according to Cameron, Johnson was most concerned that the senior Tory who took the lead on the Brexit side would become the darling of the party. And Johnson did not want to risk allowing someone else with a high profile – Michael Gove in particular – to win that crown. At the same time, Johnson said he was certain the Leave campaign would lose the referendum.

With their argument at deuce, the two men left the ambassador's residence promising to stay in touch with each other by text. The following month, as the PM prepared to fire the starting gun on the referendum campaign, he still did not have a definite answer from Johnson. But glass-half-full Cameron says he had not given up hope. He felt that in his heart Johnson wanted Britain to stay in Europe. That view was confirmed to me by Sir Nicholas Soames, the Old Etonian Tory MP who is Churchill's grandson: 'Boris is my friend and I like him. But he is not an outer – he's told me that. And he told lots of other people he wasn't an outer.'

Although Johnson had fanned the flames of Euroscepticism in his days as a Brussels correspondent for the *Telegraph* and had strongly supported campaigns for a referendum, he had always publicly insisted he was in favour of Britain staying in a reformed EU. Yet the Prime Minister could see the Leave option becoming increasingly enticing for Johnson: after all, said Cameron privately, the Brexit campaign would be 'loaded with images of patriotism, independence and romance'. And he knew Johnson enjoyed thumbing his nose at the liberal metropolitan elite, most of whom were what Brexiteers called 'Europhiliacs'. Along with my producer Jenny Parks, I made a film for *Newsnight* about the referendum campaign and the continuing Tory tragi-comedy starring Boris and Dave.

On Saturday 20 February, as Cameron prepared to announce the date and details of the referendum, the London mayor-cum-MP admitted to the press that he was 'veering all over the place like a wonky supermarket trolley' about which side he would support. Cameron said: 'I was texting him furiously, saying if you're not sure, don't take the course that you fundamentally think is wrong for the country.' At midday, just before the PM was due to make his statement on the steps of No. 10, Johnson pinged Cameron a text saying: 'I have been a tortured soul, but I have to go with my heart and support Leave.'

But two hours later a fresh text from Johnson appeared on Cameron's BlackBerry saying: 'Depression is setting in,' and that he was 'dithering' and might change his mind and back Remain after all. Then Boris Johnson went incommunicado.

He had driven to his Oxfordshire bolthole to make up his mind. He was due to deliver his well-rewarded weekly column for the following Monday's *Daily Telegraph*, for which he was paid £275,000 a year. I was the first journalist to learn that Johnson wrote two articles – one putting the case for the status quo; the other for Brexit. Johnson's sister, Rachel, who was with him in Oxfordshire, read both drafts. She told me when she returned to London that she thought his case for staying in was the more powerful and persuasive.

When I later put this to Johnson on the referendum campaign trail, without revealing the name of my informant, he huffed and puffed: 'Well... on the contrary... the one... I don't know... what your conceivable sources for that information may be... I can tell you seriously that I decided it was much better for our country to go... perhaps... what I can say is... I'll tell you what the second article said... what it said was... actually... erm... irrespective of my objections to the way the EU was going, in order to support my party and the Prime Minister it would be better to stay in... and I thought in the end that wasn't a good enough reason.'

Soon after Johnson had finished the interview, having surmised who my source might have been, he rang his sister, got her to confess and tore her off a strip.

On Sunday 21 February, just nine minutes before Johnson made his decision public, he texted the PM yet again. He said Brexit would be crushed in the referendum 'like the toad beneath the harrow' (a line from Kipling), but he could not look at himself in the mirror if he campaigned to remain. He emerged from his Islington house and told a clamorous pack of journalists, snappers and TV people: 'After a huge amount of heartache, I have made an agonisingly difficult decision. I will be advocating Vote Leave or whatever it's called – I understand there are a number of them – because I want a better deal for the people of this country.'

Asked about the charge that his decision was 'just a naked grab for power and the premiership', Johnson replied: 'On the contrary, really and truly it would be the best thing possible for people who are genuinely wondering in their minds which way to go.'

'I felt my brother had backed the wrong side, quite possibly not for entirely selfless reasons,' says Rachel Johnson. 'But his rat-like nose for power – and channelling the sublime instincts and soaring desires of the British people – could not ever be doubted.' Nicholas Soames told me at the time: 'Boris believes the next Tory leader will be an outer – which I don't think is necessarily true. But that contributed to Boris's Damascene conversion to the Leave cause.' For his part, the Prime Minister said publicly he was 'disappointed' by Johnson's decision. That was putting it mildly. The word I got from No. 10 was: 'The fury here is uncontrollable.' Craig Oliver noted in his diary: 'It will be a proper fight now; the two biggest Conservatives in the country locked in mortal combat.'

The stage was set for the latest chapter in the turbulent relationship between Boris and Dave, which went back forty years – to Eton, where both of them had said they wanted to be PM; to Oxford and the infamous Bullingdon photograph; and to the Commons, where both won nearby Oxfordshire seats in the same year. But only one of them thus far had gone on to reach the top of the greasy pole.

In Parliament, on the day after Boris Johnson had outed himself as an outer, the Prime Minister said pointedly in a statement on the referendum: 'I am not standing for re-election. I have no other agenda than what's best for the country.' And he mocked Johnson's statement that he might support a second referendum, saying: 'I have known a number of people who have begun divorce proceedings, but I don't know any who have begun divorce proceedings in order to renew their marriage vows.' To Johnson's indignation, it sounded like a jibe against the state of his marriage. He thought it was a prime ministerial blow beneath the belt.

When he launched the Leave campaign, Johnson did not respond in kind. But he made clear his target was the political Establishment, whose chief honcho was the Prime Minister. 'This is a David and Goliath fight. This is the struggle of the little platoons against the big battalions. And they have the CBI, Goldman Sachs and Peter Mandelson.'

As he launched the Tory Stronger In campaign, the Prime

Minister said: 'I have huge respect for Boris as a politician. He is a great friend of mine. He's a fantastic Mayor of London. I think he has got a lot to give to the Conservative Party and to the country. But on this issue I think he's reached the wrong conclusion. So we're going to have, I hope, a very reasonable, civilised argument.'

There was some quickly stifled mocking laughter from the audience.

In Cameron's view, the Remain side had 'very strong technical and economic arguments', while the Leave side had a 'very powerful emotional argument', plus there was the issue of immigration. With Labour under Jeremy Corbyn largely absent for the referendum campaign, it turned into what Cameron said he most wanted to avoid: a battle between the two wings of the Tory Party. The well-to-do Cameroon Remainers were up against the insurrectionist Leavers led by Johnson, Gove and their subversive strategist Dominic Cummings – whom Cameron had previously forced out as Gove's special adviser and labelled 'a career psychopath'.

On the basis of public and private opinion polls, Cameron was cautiously confident of victory. Citing his success in the 2015 general election and the Scottish referendum the year before that, he said: 'I am a winner.' Now, he wanted to avoid the campaign becoming so damaging that it would make the party unmanageable afterwards. So, he said there must be no 'blue-on-blue' battles – personal attacks by senior Remain Tories on Johnson and Gove and vice versa. 'I don't want this to become a Tory psychodrama between me and Boris,' he said.

For Johnson the referendum campaign turned into one elongated opportunity to display to the public his credentials for the top job. But he soon found it was no easy task. He learned that Cameron was planning to co-opt the most powerful man in the world into the Remain campaign. President Obama was about to make an official visit to Britain and was reportedly going to come out in favour of Britain staying in the EU. Johnson decided to make two pre-emptive personal attacks on the President.

First in his weekly *Daily Telegraph* column he wrote: 'Whether in code or *en clair*, the President will tell us all that UK membership of the EU is right for Britain, right for Europe, and right for America; and why? Because it is the only way we can have "influence" in the councils of the nations. It is wholly fallacious – and coming from Uncle Sam it is a piece of outrageous and exorbitant hypocrisy. There is no country in the world that defends its own sovereignty with such hysterical vigilance as the USA.'

Johnson followed up his first salvo with an article in *The Sun* the next day. He recounted a story of Obama having a bust of Churchill removed from the Oval Office and went on: 'Some said it was a snub to Britain. Some said it was a symbol of the part-Kenyan's ancestral dislike of the British Empire, of which Churchill had been such a fervent defender.' A row broke out, with Johnson accused of dog-whistle racism.

And Obama himself was less than delighted. At a press conference in the grand Locarno Suite in the Foreign Office, with David Cameron by his side, the President trained his six-shooter on Johnson. Obama confirmed he had moved the bust of Churchill from his Oval Office and replaced it with one of

Martin Luther King. 'I thought that was appropriate as the first African-American President – and I think most people in Britain might agree.' But Obama revealed he had another Churchill bust outside his private study in the White House residence: 'and I see it every day – including on weekends when I'm going into that office to watch a basketball game – the primary image I see is a bust of Winston Churchill. I love the guy.'

Churchill's grandson, Nicholas Soames, told me: 'Boris has really bogged it and showed himself up as an ocean-going clot.' At his Foreign Office press conference, President Obama also made a direct attack on Johnson's claim that the UK would be able to strike an immediate post-Brexit trade deal with the US. 'I figured', he said, 'that you might want to hear from the President of the USA what I think America is going to do.' He said his priority was the EU and if the UK left it they would be 'at the back of the queue' for any trade deal.

It was a would-be killer line that Cameron and the Chancellor George Osborne had worked out with the President in No. 10 the previous day – translating the Americanism 'back of the line' into 'back of the queue'. The Remainers were delighted that the President had done everything they wanted – and more. It seemed like a hammer blow against Boris Johnson and there was despondency in the Vote Leave camp. But to the disappointment of No. 10, there was no 'Obama bounce', with a number of the polls showing many voters objected to an American President coming and telling the Brits how they should vote. It was not to be the only time that the best-laid plans of Stronger In backfired.

David Cameron prepared a big speech using one of the arguments that had worked so effectively in the 1975 referendum – that after two world wars in the first part of the century only a unified Europe could prevent further wars. As one of the Keep Britain In campaign's posters at the time had put it: 'It's better to lose a little national sovereignty than to lose a son or daughter.'

We filmed in the impressive Establishment surroundings of the British Museum, where Cameron came up with his version of the 1975 line. He argued in a speech that the EU – with Britain in it – had helped bring together countries that had been 'at each other's throats for decades'. And he continued: 'Isolationism has never served this country well. Whenever we turn our back on Europe sooner or later we come to regret it. The serried rows of white headstones in lovingly tended Commonwealth war cemeteries stand as silent testament to the price this country has paid to help restore peace and order in Europe.'

The Prime Minister also referred to 'Britain's role in pivotal moments in European history: Blenheim, Trafalgar, Waterloo, our country's heroism in the Great War and, most of all, our lone stand in 1940'. And he recalled how 'Winston Churchill argued passionately for Western Europe to come together, so our continent would never again see such bloodshed. Can we be sure peace and stability on our continent are assured beyond any shadow of doubt? Is that a risk worth taking? I would never be so rash as to make that assumption.'

The Prime Minister's speech was immediately interpreted by much of the press as what the Leave campaign called 'Project Fear'. 'Vote Remain, says PM, Or it's World War Three' was the gist of the headlines. And Boris Johnson said: 'I think it is very, very curious that the Prime Minister is now warning us that World War Three is about to break out. I think all this talk of world war and bubonic plague is totally demented smear-mongering.'

A week later Johnson came up with his own contentious version of European war and peace. He said: 'European history has seen repeated attempts to rediscover the golden age of peace and prosperity under the Romans. Napoleon, Hitler, various people tried to unify Europe by force, and it ends tragically. The EU is an attempt to do this by different methods.' 'That was a bloody awful, stupid thing to say,' Nicholas Soames told me, and the media had another field day.

Doorstepped as he left his house, Johnson said: 'This discussion is bedevilled by all kinds of media twit storms and hysteria. In the last 2,000 years people have made repeated attempts to unite Europe by force; the EU is very different, but it is a profoundly anti-democratic institution. Fundamentally what is lacking is the eternal problem, which is that there is no underlying loyalty to the idea of Europe.'

The campaign was turning out to be anything but civil. Cameron admitted publicly that it was damaging his relationship with Johnson: 'We are still friends – just not such good friends.' And then, in the midst of all the war talk, there was a sudden, brief truce: a mini-version of the Christmas Day football game between British and German soldiers on the front line in 1914.

To mark the end of his eight years as mayor, the bus-loving Boris Johnson had a farewell to City Hall party at the London

Transport Museum near Covent Garden. Among the red buses, and early Tube train carriages were his staff and friends. He had also invited the Prime Minister. To general surprise, Cameron turned up. And he made a generous, funny speech, calling Johnson 'a great partner' and recounting his favourite story of their rivalry. He said that when he was first Prime Minister, Boris as mayor came to No. 10 to try to procure more money for London. Cameron had been given a Treasury brief about just how far to go if Johnson cut up rough. The PM was holding the document when the mayor said, 'Let me see that' and made a lunge for it. And the two grappled. Cameron told the crowd at the museum: 'That came as a great surprise to my PPS [parliamentary private secretary], who walked in to find two grown men wrestling on the floor.'

In the past both men had given the story different endings – with each claiming victory. In his speech the PM said, 'I'm not quite sure who got the piece of paper.' From the wings at the party, Johnson shouted out: 'I did,' which was consistent with his previous account where he had said: 'I won. I had Dave basically pulverised.'

In his own speech, Johnson joked that he was only Cameron's 'third choice' as candidate for mayor and acknowledged that he had not always been No. 10's flavour of the week. Many people left the museum thinking, if only the two Old Etonians had been on the same side, what a formidable double act they would have been and what a difference it could have made to the eventual result.

Instead, the truce was over, and the two sides were back to

daggers drawn. Cameron and Stronger In were becoming concerned at how well Johnson seemed to be coming over in his battle-bus tour of Britain. His celebrity status ensured him big crowds wherever he went, and he was turning out to be surprisingly popular in the north of England. But the Prime Minister's refusal to sanction personal attacks on Johnson and Gove was increasingly worrying some of the prominent figures in the multi-party Stronger In campaign. Labour's master of the dark arts, Peter Mandelson, said he thought the Leave leaders were building up too much visibility and authority – their personal flaws needed to be played up. Mandelson told George Osborne, Cameron's closest campaign ally: 'We feel like sometimes we are taking a spoon to a knife fight.'

The PM was refusing all TV requests to appear in a head-to-head debate, which Johnson was happy to have. Cameron said he feared such blue-on-blue confrontations would just 'make the campaign look like a Conservative spat'. But with polls starting to move against the Remainers, Cameron decided to authorise personal attacks on Johnson. He would not yet make one himself. Instead, in the manner of modern TV crime dramas, the Stronger In Europe campaign chose a woman to do the dirty deed. Their choice was the Energy Secretary and fervent Europhile Amber Rudd. She would represent the PM in a six-sided ITV debate – with Johnson and two female Leave MPs, Labour's Gisela Stuart and the Tories' Andrea Leadsom, up against Rudd, SNP leader Nicola Sturgeon and Labour's Angela Eagle.

Both sides were heavily coached and provided with sound bites by the spin doctors of their respective campaigns. Amber

Rudd was also given a pep talk before the show by Alastair Campbell, Tony Blair's controversial media maestro. 'This can be a really, really big moment for you,' Campbell told Rudd. 'Show that you have got fight. The TV debates in the general election made Nicola Sturgeon a national figure. The same thing can happen for you: show Boris Johnson he is in for a fight.'

Amber Rudd came onto the live programme well prepared. She attacked Johnson's 'misinformation' and poured scorn on the contentious claim, painted on his battle bus, that Britain handed £350 million a week to the EU. In another argument about figures, she said: 'I fear the only number that Boris is interested in is the one that says No. 10.' And she took up Michael Gove's claim that experts were not to be trusted, saying: 'If I want an expert on the economy, I'll ask an economist. If I want to build a bridge, I'll ask a bridge builder. If I want an expert on jokes, I'll ask Boris.'

Then Rudd delivered her carefully prepared zinger: 'Boris is the life and soul of the party, but he is not the man you want driving you home at the end of the evening.' It was a double whammy, referencing his rackety sex life and his unreliability. Johnson declined to rise to the bait. He put on a bewildered look and refused to engage in verbal fisticuffs, demonstrating a self-restraint few knew he possessed, which probably won him a few points.

Cameron praised Rudd's performance in a tweet and called her 'a star'. Alastair Campbell saw it differently. He felt her attack had moved from the political to the personal and was a gift for the Leave campaign. 'It allowed Boris to play the victim,' said Campbell. 'If, like Leave, you are doing an underdog campaign, then that's actually quite helpful.'

David Cameron and the Remain campaign were becoming panicky. They had based their campaign on the economy and how badly Brexit would affect people's standard of living. And they steered well clear of the immigration issue, which Vote Leave saw as their trump card. The Leavers were helped inadvertently almost every day of the campaign by the news bulletins on the BBC, ITV and Sky.

There were a record number of immigrants coming across the Mediterranean to Greece and Italy each day in dinghies and other even less seaworthy craft. Often these would sink, and the passengers had to be picked up by European coastguard vessels. The regular TV news images showing boatloads of African, Asian and Arab would-be immigrants apparently bound for Britain played directly into the narrative of the various Leave campaigns. From the slightly less strident Vote Leave headed by Johnson and Gove to the social media posts of the self-defined bad boys of Brexit led by Nigel Farage and Arron Banks, the message was the same: Keep Them Out. The TV news coverage was like daily party-political broadcasts for the Leavers.

Then, the latest annual immigration figures came out. They showed that 330,000 new immigrants, over half of them from the EU, had come to Britain in 2015. The numbers made a mockery of Cameron's oft-repeated pledge that he was going radically to reduce the numbers. Johnson and Gove decided to send a personal letter to Cameron. They wrote: 'Voters were promised repeatedly at elections that net immigration could be cut to the tens of thousands. This promise is plainly not achievable as long as the UK is a member of the EU and the failure to keep it is corrosive of public trust in politics.'

The letter was leaked to the *Sunday Times*, which splashed it under the headline: 'Boris and Gove lash Cameron on immigration'. And it quoted a senior source in Vote Leave, who said: 'You can read this as a direct challenge to Cameron's authority.' The PM hit back by publicly accusing the Leave campaign of 'resorting to total untruths to con people into taking a leap in the dark'. And he authorised a poster showing Johnson rolling the dice, Gove drinking whisky and Nigel Farage smoking cigars in a casino together with the slogan: 'Don't let them gamble with your future'.

The PM later said: 'The campaign turned into this terrible Tory psychodrama and I couldn't seem to get through to people. It was like one of those dreams where you're trying to shout but no sound is coming out.' He said that Johnson and Gove had 'behaved appallingly attacking their own government and the pair seemed to be different people by the end. Gove, the liberal-minded, carefully considered Conservative intellectual, had become a foam-flecked Faragist warning that the entire Turkish population was about to come to Britain.'

In the early morning of 24 June, David Cameron threw in the towel. The Leavers had won a shock referendum victory by 52 to 48 per cent. On the steps of No. 10, Cameron announced his resignation as Prime Minister, saying: 'The will of the British people is an instruction that must be delivered.' But he was not the man to do it. Johnson and Gove appeared at a press conference with their heads hanging low and their hands clasped in front of them. According to the Scottish Tory leader Ruth Davidson, they looked like a couple of teenage arsonists who couldn't quite believe what they had done. Or as Sarah Vine had put it to her husband in the small hours: 'You were only supposed to blow the bloody doors off.'

Johnson left it for a few hours after the resignation and then texted Cameron: 'Dave, I am so sorry to have been out of touch but I couldn't think of what to say and now I am absolutely miserable about your decision. You have been a superb PM and leader and your country owes you eternally.' And Rachel Johnson's eighteen-year-old son, Oliver, told his mother: 'Uncle Boris has just stolen our futures.' Suddenly Johnson had become the hot favourite in the race to become Prime Minister.

Cameron now says that not a day goes past without him feeling haunted – as he puts it – by the demons of Brexit that he unleashed. So, does he now wish he hadn't called a referendum?

'If you are asking me do I have regrets – yes. Am I sorry about the state the country has got into? Yes. Do I feel some responsibility for that? Yes. It was my referendum, my campaign, my decision to try and renegotiate with the EU. I accept all of those things and people will have to decide how much blame to put on me. I accept – and I can't put it more bluntly than this – that attempt failed.'

Privately, Cameron was less self-culpatory: 'Boris ruined my bloody career,' he told the by then former Europe Minister Sir Alan Duncan at a breakfast.

I watched Cameron at his final PMQs, in front of a packed

house. He produced a bravura last hurrah: self-assured, witty and sometimes poignant. 'I have done a bit of research, Mr Speaker,' said the departing Prime Minister. 'I have addressed 5,500 questions from this despatch box. I'll leave it to others to work out how many I have actually answered.' Riding the mixed cheers and jeers, Cameron said: 'I will miss the roar of the crowds – I will miss the barbs of the opposition. And the last thing I'd say is that you can achieve a lot of things in politics, you can get a lot of things done. Nothing is really impossible, if you put your mind to it. After all, as I once said: "I was the future once."'

As the soon to be ex-Prime Minister sat down, the MPs on the Tory benches all stood up to wave their order papers, to cheer and – against the conventions of the House – to clap. Nine years earlier, when Cameron's original role model, Tony Blair, left the Chamber for the last time to a standing ovation from Labour MPs, the then opposition leader Cameron had stood up clapping and gestured to his MPs to follow suit – which they did. But I noticed that this time the Labour leader, Jeremy Corbyn, remained resolutely seated – like virtually all his MPs.

As Cameron left the Chamber – he was at the age of forty-nine the youngest ex-Prime Minister since Victorian times – he told one of his ministers: 'There are only three people who can do my job: George Osborne, Boris Johnson and Theresa May.'

CHAPTER 31

MAY DAY! MAY DAY!

Being Prime Minister is always a lonely job, but few were lonelier at the top than Theresa May. Yet it had all started so well. When David Cameron resigned after his calamitous Brexit referendum, the then Home Secretary was first off the mark to try to put her kitten heels into Cameron's shoes. The hot favourite when the leadership election began was the leader of the Leavers, Boris Johnson. Theresa May, who had been a low-profile Remainer, was an outsider.

I went to her leadership launch. Mrs May was determined to differentiate herself from the Bullingdon Club posh boys, Boris, Dave and George. Like John Major, she played up her humble origins: 'I grew up the daughter of a local vicar and the granddaughter of a regimental sergeant major. Public service has been a part of who I am for as long as I can remember.'

In contrast to the omnishambles of the Brexit campaign, she was seen as a cool head in a crisis: not flash, just Theresa – the only adult in the room. 'I don't tour the TV studios. I don't gossip over lunch,' she said. 'I don't drink in Parliament's bars.

I don't wear my heart on my sleeve. I just get on with the job in front of me. My pitch is very simple: I'm Theresa May and I'm the best person to be Prime Minister.'

She felt certain that her main opponent in the leadership election would be Boris Johnson, with whom she'd had an abrasive relationship during her six years as Home Secretary, while he was London mayor. She presented herself as a reliable candidate who had the negotiating experience to do the job 'from day one'. And she couldn't resist having a dig at Johnson, saying: 'Boris negotiated in Europe. I seem to remember the last time he did a deal with the Germans he came back with three nearly new water cannons.' The London mayor had spent £300,000 on them only to have Mrs May as Home Secretary ban their use.

Johnson was due to launch his own leadership campaign straight after Mrs May. The pitch was that he and his campaign manager, Michael Gove, were the 'dream team'. But then, in a ploy not customarily recommended in the campaign manager's playbook, Gove stabbed his candidate in the back. Despite having been a friend and admirer of Johnson since Oxford and having spent months campaigning together for the referendum, Gove said that he had become convinced in the previous week that Johnson was not up to the job of being PM. But he had suddenly realised he himself was – despite having always categorically ruled himself out as totally unqualified. One of Johnson's campaign team, Jake Berry MP, tweeted: 'As a traitor, Gove leaves Judas Iscariot standing.'

With previously pledged MPs fast defecting from him, Johnson pulled out of the leadership race. He looked as far away as ever from the job he had always craved. And Mrs May sent him a message saying: 'I am very sorry it has ended up like this for you. You have been treated very badly.' The whole episode was a clear omen of blood-soaked troubles ahead.

Mrs May won the leadership without a final vote, as one after another her opponents crashed out of the contest. One of her first problems as Prime Minister was what to do about Johnson. He was very pessimistic about his chances of getting a job from her. It is always said that a Prime Minister needs to be a good butcher in putting together the Cabinet, and Mrs May the vicar's daughter quickly proved herself adept with a meat cleaver. She sacked George Osborne, who had been Chancellor for six years, saying to him: 'I hope you understand if I give you some advice as "an elder sister": you need to go away and get to know the party better.' A bitter Osborne later told a number of people: 'I won't rest until I have her chopped up in bags in my freezer.'

Next for the chop from the Cabinet was Michael Gove, whom she relegated to the back benches, saying he needed to learn about loyalty. In all, Mrs May showed seven ministers the door, and almost all the rest were moved to other departments, with only four remaining *en poste*.

To Boris Johnson, the new Prime Minister said: 'I've decided to give you a really big job. I want you to be Foreign Secretary.'

'This is a great honour,' replied Johnson, saying how much he wanted the job. 'I feel having played a part in making Brexit happen, I have a real responsibility in making sure it works out.'

The PM responded: 'You and I have a patchy history. But I know there are two Borises: a deadly serious, intellectual, capable and very effective person; and a playing-around person. I want this to be your opportunity to show you can be the former.'

Later, as Johnson went to the Foreign Office, our cameras caught him saying to the chief mandarin, Sir Simon McDonald, about his appointment: 'I was very, very surprised. You could have knocked me down with a feather.'

'Yes,' responded McDonald, 'the office was very, very surprised, too.'

At the end of his first day, Johnson appeared in the Foreign Office courtyard with a progress report. One journalist said to him: 'Diplomacy is about relationships. Today, the French Foreign Secretary said you told a lot of lies in the referendum campaign. The German Foreign Secretary said some of the stuff you have done is outrageous and irresponsible. How are you going to get on with them?' An unfazed Johnson came back: 'Well, after a vote like the referendum of 23 June it is inevitable that there's going to be a certain amount of plaster coming off the ceiling in the chancelleries of Europe, because it wasn't the result they were expecting. And clearly they are making their views known in a frank and fair way. In fact, I have to say the French Foreign Minister sent me a charming letter just a couple of hours ago.'

A key reason for Johnson's appointment was to give the Remain voter Mrs May credibility with Brexiteers in Parliament and the country. She appointed her old Oxford friend and contemporary Alan Duncan to be Johnson's No. 2 as Minister for Europe. Duncan told me: 'For Theresa, winning the leadership was a turbocharged hospital pass. It was the worst possible set of circumstances to inherit on coming into No. 10.'

The job in front of her was the most daunting challenge up to that time in Britain's peacetime history: to unravel more than forty years of integration with Europe. It would require supreme levels of decisiveness, cunning and persuasive charm. It was not altogether evident to me – from having talked to and filmed her over the years – that these were Theresa May's strongest suits. Instead, diligence, caution and duty seemed to be her watchwords.

But in her first speech outside No. 10, the new Prime Minister confounded expectations with a radical promise to the people: 'The government I lead will be driven not by the interests of the privileged few, but by yours. That means fighting against the burning injustice that, if you're born poor, you will die on average nine years earlier than others. If you're black, you are treated more harshly by the criminal justice system than if you're white. If you're from an ordinary working-class family, life is much harder than many people in Westminster realise. We won't entrench the advantages of the fortunate few. We will do everything we can to help anybody, whatever your background, to go as far as your talents will take you.'

It was a dramatically egalitarian speech for a new Tory Prime Minister to make. And it went down well. For her first months in office, it seemed Theresa May could walk on water. She was heralded as the new Iron Lady – and she said the person in history she most identified with was Queen Elizabeth I. She was also extremely rude to parts of the media, accusing them of being obsessed with trivia, personalities and scandal – although not to the *Daily Mail*.

Like many Prime Ministers, Mrs May determined to do things very differently from her immediate predecessor. There was to be no more Cameron-style chumocracy and chillaxing. She threw out the comfortable sofas from what he had called 'the den' where he worked and replaced them with hard-back chairs and a glass-topped round table for meetings. It was honour enough to be working inside No. 10, Mrs May told her staff, and they shouldn't expect a gong at the end of it. 'She said, if you are lucky you'll get a Jaffa Cake,' one insider revealed.

But the PM did bring with her a couple of fiercely loyal special advisers, who had worked with her at the Home Office and were soon to become hugely controversial. They were Fiona Hill, a sparky Scot, and Nick Timothy, who sported a bushy black beard à la Rasputin. Hill was a media and presentation specialist and Timothy a policy wonk and speechwriter. They were each given the title chief of staff and became known in No. 10 and Whitehall as 'The Chiefs'. From the first, they zealously guarded access to the PM. And they made themselves highly unpopular with Cabinet ministers, senior mandarins and Tory MPs alike. They were repeatedly to brief against and sideline ministers who themselves had a different name for The Chiefs: 'The gruesome twosome'.

I had known Fiona Hill for some years and went to see her in No. 10 about the possibility of documentary-filming with Mrs May. Contrary to her media reputation of being high-handed and breathtakingly rude, on this occasion Ms Hill was charm itself. She proudly showed me a framed copy of the PM's 'burning injustices' speech, saying that she'd had a number of other framed copies made and placed prominently in all the offices in No. 10 and the adjoining Cabinet Office. 'I did that to show the civil servants who work here that we are deadly serious about what we want to do,' Hill told me. I asked her if I might be able to get access to film with the Prime Minister behind the scenes in Downing Street. She replied: 'I have been thinking about all the historic things that we are doing in No. 10 as a government and that they should be chronicled. And I think you are just the person to do it.'

'Flattery will get you anywhere,' I replied, adding that it was something I would very much like to do.

She said: 'Good. I'll put it to the Prime Minister. I haven't mentioned it to her yet. And I'll make sure when I do speak to her, it will be before lunch.'

I was surprised. 'You mean she drinks too much at lunch?'

'Oh no,' she replied. 'She's not a drinker. It's just that I have found working with her over the years that she is much more receptive to my proposals before rather than after lunch.' It was only sometime later that I realised it may have been Fiona Hill's persuasive skills that were less effective after she herself had had a jolly lunch. She asked me to put a proposal on paper and arranged a date for us to meet again soon after that.

In her 'burning injustices' speech, Mrs May had barely mentioned Brexit at all. She wanted to make ground-breaking changes to transform Britain into a fairer society, and she did not want to be defined as the Brexit Prime Minister. Yet she knew that her overriding task was to take Britain out of the EU, and she needed somehow to keep Remainers and Leavers alike happy. She decided to start by talking tough. Her former Cabinet colleague Ken Clarke had been picked up by the microphones describing her as 'a bloody difficult woman'. At first Mrs May objected to the language, but Hill and Timothy advised that it could work to her advantage, so she took to drinking from a mug printed with the words. And she said in an interview: 'I was described by one of my colleagues as a bloody difficult woman and I said the next person to find that out would be Jean-Claude Juncker.'

The President of the European Commission was less than impressed by Mrs May's approach to Brexit negotiations. Beyond helpfully declaring 'Brexit means Brexit', or 'no deal is better than a bad deal', the PM was making little or no progress with the people she needed to convince on either side of the Channel.

The Chiefs Hill and Timothy suggested she call a snap general election to increase her majority and strengthen her negotiating hand with the EU. Mrs May was unconvinced. On one hand, she feared that she might lose the thing she had wished for since childhood: the premiership. Against that was a deep desire to win a majority off her own bat. She hated being reminded that she was only in power due to David Cameron's general election victory. Hill said later: 'Theresa May always felt a degree of imposter syndrome, feeling she wasn't elected by the public. It really meant something to her.'

Eventually, and egged on by both the Brexit Secretary David Davis and her Chancellor Philip Hammond, the Prime Minister made an uncharacteristically bold decision. She called a snap general election. Nearly twenty points ahead in the opinion polls, Mrs May was up against Labour's Jeremy Corbyn, the aged Marxist widely seen as useless. To run the campaign Mrs May employed Lynton Crosby, the Australian known as the Wizard of Oz for his success running previous Tory election campaigns. She agreed to pay his firm £4 million for his services.

Crosby had a hard-nosed approach to campaigning: stick to powerful, simple messages – and keep repeating them. Don't let your opponents define the agenda on any day. His plan, backed by private polling, was to make full use of May's popularity in the country. The campaign would be relentlessly focused on the PM and the slogan would be 'Strong and stable leadership – in the national interest'.

Other Cabinet ministers would play little or no part in the campaign. Conservative central office would run the logistics, while the controversial Hill and Timothy would stay out of the limelight. But there was a fundamental flaw in Crosby's approach – and that was the Prime Minister herself. She had never before played a prominent role in a general election campaign, let alone been the leading lady and star of the show.

The plan was for her to tour the country in a big blue battle bus displaying the words 'Theresa May: For Britain' along with her signature. She would make speeches on the stump and at rallies and do walkabouts and photo opportunities.

But as the campaign swung into action there was trouble. Each day vividly displayed the shortcomings as a campaigner of the secretive and enigmatic Prime Minister. With no Hill and Timothy choreographing her every move – as they had done for her first ten months in office – she came over as wooden and uncomfortable faced with the probing of the journalists and the cameras.

The PM was not helped in the campaign by a Tory manifesto written in conditions of strict secrecy by Nick Timothy. It aimed to attract working-class Labour voters at the expense of well-to-do Tories. One section which Mrs May was very keen on dealt with the perennially postponed problem of funding social care. The manifesto proposal significantly raised costs for richer elderly people receiving care at home. Fiona Hill was convinced the plan would be savaged in the campaign. She and Timothy, who normally marched in lockstep, had a ferocious argument in front of the PM at a meeting in No. 10.

According to May's biographer, Anthony Seldon: 'The Prime Minister banged her fists on her desk, had tears in her eyes and was distraught at finding her two closest advisers on opposite sides of such a major argument.' Mrs May told Hill: 'I want to be honest about all the things that are wrong with this country. And I want to show that I am the person who can fix them. If I don't have the social care plan in the manifesto – it will become an empty manifesto.'

'That would be good,' responded Hill.

But Mrs May insisted: 'We are going to do this.'

'Fine,' said Hill, 'but you'll have to phone every major newspaper editor. It's going to be bumpy and nasty.'

Hill was not wrong. Labour immediately dubbed the plan a 'dementia tax'. The section was hurriedly rewritten, but Mrs May made things worse by repeating in interviews: 'Nothing has changed, nothing has changed.' And the campaign went from bad to worse as she turned out to be no match on the stump for Corbyn, who had honed his open-air campaigning skills in a political career that had been one long protest march, demonstration and rally speech.

Mrs May came increasingly to resent life on the campaign trail, saying: 'I am the leader of the Conservative Party. I am not an American presidential candidate. I don't want it to be about me.' Yet that was what she had bought into when Lynton Crosby had first revealed his plan to make her the cynosure of all eyes in the campaign. As the PM became ever more withdrawn and hesitant, Crosby felt she was 'in a cocoon'.

Fiona Hill decided to travel in the campaign bus with the Prime Minister and was shocked at what she found: 'The journalists didn't like her. She was surly and not particularly pleasant. She was very quiet and seemed unhappy. I asked her: "Have you been down to talk to the journalists at the front of the bus?" She replied: "Why should I?" I said: "Because we're campaigning and you have to tell them the story."'

I asked Mrs May's director of strategy, Chris Wilkins, why things had all gone belly-up for the Prime Minister in the campaign. He said: 'We ended up in the ridiculous situation where a politician who had founded her career on unflashy, quiet competence was suddenly travelling around the country in a bus with her name on it. I remember one moment midway through the campaign, I was in a meeting where the PM said: "I just hate this campaign. It's not the campaign I wanted. I'm being told where to stand, what to say. I'm even being told what to wear, and I am not allowed to be me."'

Mrs May had left it a little late to say that.

Her old friend Alan Duncan told me: 'Theresa's biggest mistake was to think you can have a cult of personality when you don't really have much of a personality. Remember during the election she was asked by Julie Etchingham on ITV: "What is the naughtiest thing you've ever done?" And Theresa said: "I ran through fields of wheat." If only she had added the word "naked" how different it all might have been.'

When the election results came through, Mrs May was the biggest loser: ten government ministers lost their seats and the Tories became the largest party in a hung parliament, with Corbyn's Labour gaining thirty seats.

Under pressure from her depleted party and from many ministers who had suffered at the hands of Fiona Hill and Nick Timothy, Mrs May forced The Chiefs to make a ritual self-sacrifice and resign. 'We called an early election and it didn't work,' said Timothy. 'We ran a bad campaign. One of the mistakes was the manifesto, which I wrote. There is no point in pretending I didn't have my hands in the blood.' He and his co-chief fell on their swords. And Fiona Hill's departure meant that any chance of my making the access film inside No. 10 that she had been so keen on went with her. But I did make a film about Mrs May's premiership with producer Warwick Harrington for *Newsnight*, which was transmitted on the day she left office.

The PM decided to stay on after the election and succeeded in cobbling together a shaky deal with the Ulster Democratic Unionist Party. She had lost her majority, her authority, her two best political friends – and her voice. Jan Ravens, the Theresa

May impressionist for the Radio 4 programme *Dead Ringers*, told me: 'Her voice is her worst enemy. It's always giving up on her and I think that's because she's got this voice that's diplophonic. It's two voices at the same time – one high, one very low. And if, as an impressionist, you try to do that voice you are straining your throat the whole time.'

Losing her larynx was just one of her problems. As she returned to Brussels to continue her Brexit negotiations, she was ritually dismembered by the EU. The PM insisted, like the Black Knight in Monty Python, it was just a flesh wound. But among her own supporters, who used to claim that loyalty was the Conservative Party's secret weapon, disloyalty was now the default setting.

As Foreign Secretary, Boris Johnson at first saw it differently. 'We are a government working together,' he said. 'We are a nest of singing birds.' But the occupants of the nest turned out to be birds of prey, and with Johnson among them, the birds flocked to dive-bomb the PM. Having at first endorsed her painstakingly negotiated Chequers proposal for a Brexit deal, Johnson resigned as Foreign Secretary, saying privately: 'You can't polish a turd.'

Dubbed the Maybot for her robotic style and persistent indecision, Mrs May made innumerable attempts to persuade the Commons to pass a Withdrawal from Europe Bill. All of them failed – one by the largest margin in parliamentary history – and she reluctantly resigned as Prime Minister. Her former Home Secretary, Amber Rudd, said: 'The reason she went is because nobody trusted her any more. It wasn't that she lied but she just didn't deliver for anyone. She implied to everyone they would get what they wanted.' At her final PMQs, Mrs May struck a rare humorous note, saying to Jeremy Corbyn: 'As a party leader who has accepted when her time is up, may I just suggest that perhaps the time is now for him to do the same thing.' Cheers and laughter from the Tory benches.

The PM ended her farewell address from the lectern outside No. 10 with the words: 'I will shortly leave the job that it has been the honour of my life to hold – the second female Prime Minister but certainly not the last. I do so with no ill will, but with enormous and enduring gratitude to have had the opportunity to serve the country I love.'

Her voice cracked on the last sentence, and she was in tears as she turned to walk back into No. 10. Waiting in the hall were her closest advisers and officials. 'I'm sorry for crying,' she said to her chief of staff, Gavin Barwell, who responded: 'Don't apologise. You have nothing to apologise for.'

Barwell was subsequently rewarded in Mrs May's resignation honours list – not with the Jaffa Cake she had promised her staff if they were lucky, but with a peerage. And the two chief scapegoats, Fiona Hill and Nick Timothy (who had shaved off his beard), were each given a CBE.

Theresa May was the first modern Prime Minister who had not been either Leader of the Opposition or Chancellor of the Exchequer – both jobs which require skills as a performer and familiarity with the whole political scene. Her people tried to project her as strong and stable, when in reality she was weak and wobbly.

During her time at No. 10, the vicar's daughter faced sexism and misogyny. But in the end, she fell short as Prime Minister not because she was a woman but because of the woman she was. And she became the fourth Tory Prime Minister in a row for whom the vexatious issue of Europe proved fatal.

CHAPTER 32

WORLD KING TAKES
THE THRONE

As Theresa May left No. 10 for the last time, Boris Johnson's former boss Conrad Black, the disgraced ex-*Telegraph* proprietor, declared: 'The time for Boris has come. He is in some ways a scoundrel and a charlatan, of course; but so have many great leaders been – including Disraeli and Lloyd George.'

While he was still Mayor of London and the most popular politician in the country, I asked Johnson: 'Do you have any doubts about your ability to fulfil the role of Prime Minister?'

He replied: 'I think people who don't have doubts or anxieties about their ability to do things probably have something slightly terrifyingly awry. You know, we all have worries and insecurities … But I think I've done a pretty good job so far in City Hall – and that's what I want to continue to do.'

Of all the would-be premiers I had asked the question, Johnson was the most apparently candid about his doubts.

Five years later, on 24 July 2019, I was in Downing Street as Johnson returned from Buckingham Palace to the prime ministerial lectern outside No. 10. Watched by his girlfriend, Carrie

Symonds, and his new Svengali, Dominic Cummings, he had beaten nine other contenders and won the Tory leadership election by a landslide. Aged fifty-five, he had become Britain's fifty-fifth Prime Minister and the Queen's fourteenth, starting with Johnson's hero, Winston Churchill.

'Although the Queen has just honoured me with this extraordinary office of state, my job is to serve you, the people, because the people are our bosses,' said the new PM. 'We are going to restore trust in our democracy. And the doubters, the gloomsters and the doomsters who bet against Britain are going to lose their shirts.'

Johnson's old friend and fellow Etonian, Churchill's grandson Nicholas Soames told me he had texted Johnson shortly before he had gone to kiss hands on appointment. Soames said: 'In the text I wrote that on the day my grandfather became Prime Minister, he opened a bottle of champagne with the family. And he proposed a toast: "Here's to not buggering it up." And I said to Boris in the text: "I can't vote for you. But I pray for all our sakes that you don't bugger it up." And that is my hope for Boris.'

'And what is your fear?' I asked.

'My fear is that he could bugger it up.'

It was a fear shared by many. Peter Hennessy, a constitutional historian, told me: 'There is a spectrum of opinion about Boris Johnson. One is that he will be the most unsafe pair of hands ever to open a prime ministerial red box. And at the other end, people think here is a man of brilliance and flair. I veer to the anxiety end of the spectrum – because you cannot busk being Prime Minister.'

And Rory Stewart, who served as a Foreign Office Minister under Johnson, said: 'Johnson is the most accomplished liar in public life – perhaps the best liar ever to serve as Prime Minister.'

His premiership so far has been like no other I've filmed over the years – and you probably have to go back all the way to Britain's first Prime Minister, Robert Walpole, to find a comparably larger than life, unpredictable and often outrageous figure. It has been like a Netflix series penned by a scriptwriter on speed, blending Shakespeare, Monty Python and *The Sopranos*.

The new PM wasted no time in stamping his authority. In an unprecedentedly brutal reshuffle, Johnson sacked eleven Cabinet ministers who had not voted for him in the leadership election or were not sufficiently Brexit-y or had crossed him in other ways. A further six pre-emptively resigned. He was living out what he said was his favourite movie scene: 'The multiple retribution killings at the end of *The Godfather*.'

Johnson's own consigliere, Dominic Cummings, believed in creative destruction. He had worked for previous Tory leaders, and it had always ended in tears. But the PM credited Cummings with a magic touch. While running the Leave campaign in the Brexit referendum, Cummings had told his staff: 'We do all our best work in the gutter.'

Johnson had decided to live dangerously. In just over six months after winning the Tory leadership, he had been condemned by the Supreme Court for proroguing Parliament; kicked twenty-one anti-Brexit Tory MPs out of the party; and inveigled the Labour leader Jeremy Corbyn to support a general election, partly by taunting him in the Commons as a 'big girl's blouse'. And then he had won that election by a landslide. By the end of January 2020, he had delivered in a fashion on Brexit, long seen as the most intractable political problem since the Second World War. Then, almost at once, a far more deadly challenge came along in the form of Covid-19.

Initially, the Prime Minister totally underestimated the scale of what he jokingly referred to as 'the Kung Flu'. He said it was 'just a scare story – it's the new swine flu'. And, according to Dominic Cummings, Johnson told ministers he was prepared to have the government's chief medical adviser Chris Whitty 'inject me with the virus on live television, so that everyone realises it is nothing to be frightened of'. Then, as the infection rate rose, the PM said that 'Brexit Britain' would 'send the virus packing' within a few weeks. The country, he said, was 'ready to take off its Clark Kent spectacles and leap into the phone booth and emerge with its cloak flowing as the supercharged champion'. And he joked in a meeting with ventilator manufacturers that their task should be code-named 'Operation Last Gasp'.

Partly Johnson's levity came from his conviction that he was invulnerable. As I had seen for myself on both the tennis court and the cricket pitch, he's the most fiercely competitive of men: his alpha-male image had helped make him PM. He didn't believe in illness and scoffed at people who took time off from work, saying that being sick was for wimps.

But suddenly things became deadly serious. The scientists advising the government said there would be hundreds of thousands of deaths if the country did not take drastic action and go into immediate lockdown. Such a prospect went against

WORLD KING TAKES THE THRONE

all Johnson's strongly held libertarian and anti-nanny state instincts – and he hesitated. It took nine days before he acted. In
a direct-to-camera broadcast, the PM said: 'From this evening
I must give the British people a very simple instruction: you
must stay at home.' And he introduced the most draconian set
of restrictions on people's lives, work and play since the Second
World War.

Just four days later, with his unerring knack for inserting
himself into the story – or as his sister puts it: 'He likes his limelight neat' – the Prime Minister tested positive for Covid-19.
Johnson went into self-isolation in his Downing Street flat,
with his papers and meals being left outside the door. His advisers sought to convey that it was business as usual, claiming he
was doing well. But, speaking anonymously, another aide who'd
watched him at a Zoom meeting said: 'The PM was coughing
and spluttering all over the place. He looked as if he had been
hit by a sledgehammer.'

Johnson resisted the idea of going into hospital, as he didn't
want it to appear that he was receiving preferential treatment.
'I was in denial … I was really feeling pretty groggy,' he later
said. 'The doctors got anxious and I was told I had to go into
St Thomas's' – the country's leading hospital for respiratory
diseases, which is just half a mile from No. 10. After a quick
assessment, he was fitted with a tube beneath his nose – what he
called 'a little nose jobbie' – and pumped with oxygen. He was
also given antibiotics, antivirals and pills to prevent blood clots.

The official No. 10 line at the time was that the PM had been
admitted 'for tests as a precautionary measure, on the advice of

his doctors'. And the spokesman quoted the PM as saying: 'I'm in good spirits and keeping in touch with my team.' The following day, Downing Street released the shock news that the Prime Minister had been moved into intensive care. 'The doctors gave me a full face mask and I was going through litres and litres of oxygen for a long time,' said Johnson later in a candid interview with David Wooding of the *Sun on Sunday*. 'It was hard to believe that in just a few days my health had deteriorated to this extent. I was just incredibly frustrated, because the bloody indicators kept going in the wrong direction and I thought, "There's no medicine for this kind of thing and there's no cure." That was the stage when I was thinking, "How am I going to get out of this?"'

Johnson admitted he was coming to terms – perhaps for the first time – with his own mortality: 'It got a bit scary. I was fully conscious and all too aware of what was going on. The bad moment came when it was 50:50 whether they were going to have to put a tube down my windpipe.' The doctors were deciding whether to put the PM on a ventilator, which meant that as an overweight, at-risk patient he would have had only a one in three chance of surviving.

Back in Downing Street, the Cabinet was informed that Johnson's life was in danger. 'Most of us were too shocked to say anything,' said one Cabinet minister. 'I remember going for a walk and thinking: fucking hell – what if he dies? It was a moment of shock and panic and grief.'

The Johnson family were told just how ill the Prime Minister really was. 'I was frightened,' says Stanley Johnson, the PM's father. 'We thought it was curtains.' Johnson himself said later: 'It would be wrong to say that I thought, "Oh my goodness, this is it." Some terrible buoyancy within me kept convincing me that everything would almost certainly be all right in the end. And after three nights, thanks to the miraculous work of the medical team, I was returned to the general ward without the need of ventilation.'

The PM was discharged from St Thomas's and went to convalesce at Chequers on 12 April, saying: 'I'm a very lucky man. Things could have gone either way. The NHS has saved my life, no question.' It was Easter Sunday, and his father Stanley rejoiced with the words: 'He is risen.' His son later joked: 'I was at my most popular with the British people when they thought I was about to die.'

By the end of May, the country was still in lockdown, with one of the highest death tolls in the world and the economy taking one of the biggest hits. At the same time, Johnson's relationship with Dominic Cummings was steadily worsening. The PM had not forgiven his chief adviser for breaching lockdown rules with his farcical excursion to Barnard Castle 'to test his eyes', though he publicly rejected Tory MPs' calls to sack Cummings.

At a meeting in No. 10, Cummings told Johnson that he had decided to leave the government by the end of December at the latest: 'The PM asked why and I said because this whole system is chaos, this building is chaos. You are more frightened of me having the power to stop the chaos than you are of the chaos, and this is a completely unsustainable position for us both to be in. The PM laughed and said, "You're right. Chaos isn't that bad, chaos means that everyone has to look to me to see who's in charge.'"

The two men were at odds about where to go next in dealing with the Covid pandemic. In early July 2020, Johnson had decided to lift the lockdown after four months. He was determined to get the economy up and running again, even if it meant a second wave. 'I thought that perspective was completely mad,' said Cummings later.

For his part, Johnson sought relentlessly to keep people's spirits up, saying it will all be over by Christmas – just as the politicians had done in 1914. His fierce aversion to bearing bad news fuelled his customary indecision. According to texts between staff at Tory HQ, the PM said that the summary of what was in the media he received each morning had become too negative; the PM wanted more positive material – and less gloom and doom.

But in September there was a series of government gaffes: among them the plan to break international law over a treaty the PM himself signed, the shambles following the decision to drop a controversial algorithm to forecast A-level results, and the continuing debacle of the 'world-beating' Test and Trace system. Johnson came under attack from an unexpected quarter. Fraser Nelson, editor of *The Spectator* whom Johnson had always seen as a reliable media 'friend', accused the PM of presiding over 'disorder, debacle, rebellion, U-turn and confusion'. And *The Times* carried a scathing piece quoting a senior Conservative who met the Prime Minister regularly: 'This is all weighing very heavily on him. You can see the misery etched on his face. He doesn't seem to be enjoying being at the helm in rough seas.' Another insider said: 'Boris is pin-sharp one day and then he will say, "Why haven't you briefed me on that?" and he'll be told, "You were told that yesterday."'

Johnson eventually ordered a second lockdown for November, having waited five weeks longer than he was advised by most of the scientists and Cummings. For Johnson, who saw himself as the ebullient representative of Merrie England, it was a bitterly painful decision. Meanwhile, inside No. 10 civil war was breaking out. Cummings had become convinced that Johnson's fiancée, Carrie Symonds, was scheming to get rid of him. As a former head of communications at Tory Party HQ, she was a consummate media operator and described Cummings as a 'Mad Mullah who spreads fear in Mafiaspeak'.

After a complex who-does-what battle in No. 10, Cummings walked out of the building into the November twilight famously carrying a cardboard box of secrets. He later told a Commons Select Committee: 'My resignation was definitely connected to the fact the Prime Minister's girlfriend [as he put it] was trying to change a whole load of appointments in No. 10 and appoint her friends to particular jobs. But that wasn't the heart of the problem, which was that fundamentally I regarded Boris Johnson as unfit for the job.'

After Cummings's departure, a new team was appointed to advise the PM, who were all FOC – Friends of Carrie. Both within No. 10 and in the outside world, she was becoming a highly divisive figure. A senior editor at *The Economist*, Anne McElvoy, quoted a friend of the Prime Minister saying:

'No. 10 has become something akin to a Tudor court, with Carrie Symonds driving knowledgeable staff wild by throwing her weight around.' Johnson, the friend continued, 'is absolutely knackered. It was never supposed to end up like this. The relationship was a thing on the side. I think he is a bit surprised as to where it has ended up.'

The country was still in lockdown, but the PM pledged that restrictions would be lifted for a few days to allow people to celebrate Christmas. In the Commons, he mocked the Labour leader Keir Starmer for wanting to 'cancel Christmas', saying it would be 'inhuman'. But just days afterwards, he changed his story.

At a No. 10 press conference on 21 December, Johnson said infection rates were spiralling due to the new mutant Kent or Alpha variant. With a haunted look on his face and shaking his head as if he couldn't quite believe his own words, he went on: 'It is with a very heavy heart that I must tell you we cannot continue with Christmas as planned.' Tim Shipman of the *Sunday Times* commented: 'The most bullish and ebullient politician I know has been transformed from buccaneering Cavalier into a Cromwellian Roundhead.'

Yet, three days later, on Christmas Eve 2020, Johnson managed to bounce back in one of the most surreal performances for the camera I have ever seen from a Prime Minister. Flanked by a Christmas tree, he appeared in a video on Twitter. 'At the end of this extraordinary year I want to say something about the meaning of Christmas,' the PM began, 'because I've never known a Christmas like it – not in my lifetime, and I bet not in yours either. In most years it's a moment for togetherness and celebration in which the generations are jumbled together in the same household for days on end, pulling crackers, snogging under the mistletoe, you name it. And yet this year, that is the one type of Christmas we simply cannot afford to have.

'And therefore, to all those who may be feeling momentarily cast down or a bit exhausted or frankly in need of any kind of cheering, I want to talk about what for me is the deeper meaning of Christmas: it's not about presents or turkey or brandy butter – much though I like all that kind of stuff – it's about hope, it's about a basic idea of rebirth and renewal.'

He continued that there really was a star in the sky that was growing brighter and brighter because of wise men and women who had created the Covid vaccine. And that in turn meant there would be people we love who would still be alive next Christmas – precisely because we made the sacrifice and didn't celebrate as normal this year.

'And by the way, tonight, for Christmas,' Johnson went on, 'I have a small present for anyone who may be looking for something to read in that sleepy post-Christmas lunch moment. And here it is.' The PM then stepped out of shot to pick up a 500-page print-out of the new Brexit trade deal that had only just been agreed with Brussels and not yet released in full. 'Here it is,' said the PM. 'Glad tidings of great joy, because this is a deal … which I believe will be the basis of a happy, successful and stable partnership with our friends in the EU for years to come.' And his fist punched the air in triumph: 'So that's it. That's the good news from Brussels. Now for the sprouts. And a happy Christmas to you all.'

It was vintage Johnson at his most Panglossian, as the deal would ultimately cause endless complications and rows with 'our friends in the EU'. But on the coronavirus question he had genuine grounds for hope.

Back in the summer of 2020, the PM had turned down the opportunity to join the EU's vaccine-procurement programme. Instead, he had taken what turned out to be an inspired decision to appoint venture capitalist Kate Bingham to head the government's vaccine task force. Partly through her contacts and partly by demanding meetings with CEOs until they gave in, Bingham and her team managed to secure more than 350 million doses of seven different vaccines – nearly half of them from Pfizer and Oxford/AstraZeneca.

Johnson appeared on a private Zoom call to the 1922 Committee of Tory backbenchers. 'The reason we have the vaccine success is because of capitalism, because of greed, my friends,' said the PM. 'Johnson realised he had messed up as soon as he had said it,' one MP told me later. 'He asked us all to forget he used the word "greed" and remove it from our collective memory.' Johnson knew, though, that what has been said cannot be unsaid – especially because Oxford is a publicly funded university and AstraZeneca had decided not to make a profit from its vaccine.

At this stage, Dominic Cummings re-emerged promising to spill the beans about what really went on behind the closed doors of No. 10. He planned to give evidence to a Commons Select Committee investigating the government's handling of the pandemic. A few days before the committee met, the

Prime Minister personally telephoned three newspaper editors, attempting to get his retaliation in first. Johnson accused Cummings of trying to rewrite history: 'He's going round saying, "If only competent people were in charge." This was a guy with unrivalled authority. He's trying to reframe the narrative. He wants to be seen as the guy who's pro-restrictions – not the rule breaker. He's a rank hypocrite.'

Johnson's briefing was seen as a somewhat rash move. As one source put it: 'You don't start a fire-fight with an arsonist.' At the committee hearing, Cummings characterised Johnson as 'a thousand times too obsessed with the media. The Prime Minister changes his mind ten times a day, and then calls up the media and contradicts his own policy, day after day, after day. He is like a shopping trolley smashing from one side of the aisle to another.' This was exactly the simile Johnson himself had used about his dithering on whether or not to back Brexit in the referendum campaign.

Cummings went on to say that if the previous September the Prime Minister had followed his advice and locked down early, 'tens of thousands of people would now still be alive'. And he confirmed that Johnson said he would have preferred to 'let the bodies pile high in the street' than have another lockdown. In the Commons, Johnson denied having said it, but he declined to comment further.

With a full set of nationwide elections looming, there were questions as to how far all this was cutting through to the public. On election day, the PM showed he had learned a bit about media manipulation from Cummings. The newspaper front pages carried photos of two British Navy patrol boats sporting cannons and machine guns beneath headlines like: 'Boris sends in the gunboats'. They had been despatched to see off a convoy of French fishing vessels that were blockading Jersey, the Channel Islands main port, over fishing rights: just the thing to stir patriots' blood as they set off to the polling booths.

When the results came through, Johnson had once again defied the laws of political gravity. Mid-term governments invariably lose elections. This time, the Tories gained seats across England and for good measure won the Hartlepool by-election held the same day. It was Peter Mandelson's old seat, and it had never before voted Tory. Despite Labour's attempts to paint the PM with the brush of incompetence and sleaze that Tony Blair had wielded so effectively against John Major, Johnson seemed indomitable.

In part it was because many voters had priced in his shortcomings and misdemeanours. In part he was a brilliant campaigner on the platform and on the stump. In part it was because the economy was bouncing back. But most of all it was because of the success of the vaccine programme. People had begun to stop feeling scared of the virus.

Yet within a month – as so often happens with Johnson in the fickle world of Westminster politics – everything had changed. In a by-election in the true-blue seat of Chesham & Amersham in Buckinghamshire, the Tories managed to lose one of their safest seats in the country, with a 25 per cent swing against the party. None of Johnson's quasi-magical powers had worked. But what most worried the PM and his MPs was that, having smashed Labour's Red Wall in the north, the Tories' southern Blue Wall might itself be crumbling.

As Boris Johnson marked his second anniversary in power, I asked some of those who'd appeared in my film when he became Prime Minister how they now rated him. At that time Nicholas Soames, using his grandfather Winston Churchill's language, said he hoped that Johnson would not bugger it up, but he feared that Johnson could. What does he think now? 'Well, Boris has and he hasn't buggered it up,' replied Soames. 'Remember, he faced the most extraordinary threat to security and health that ever confronted a new Prime Minister in peacetime – and there was no playbook for how to deal with it. But nobody who had their wits about them would have brought Dominic Cummings into No. 10 – and Boris is still suffering from it. And some of his Cabinet I wouldn't put in charge of a mouse house. But domestically he has been making real progress in the north. And he's got better in the Commons. Although the British like to have big characters with aplomb as their Prime Ministers, I think the jury is still out on Boris.'

Professor Peter Hennessy told me he had not resiled from his initial fear that Johnson would be the most unsafe pair of hands ever to open a prime ministerial red box. He added: 'You cannot expect Mr Toad to obey the highway codes. The particular skills he brought to the job of winning elections were of no use in facing a pandemic. But he did have a fresh chance after he came back from intensive care, knowing at first hand just how awful the virus was. It could have been his shining hour – to move from being a party leader to a national leader. But he hasn't done so. The problem is that it's a totally performative premiership: it's all about him creating the building blocks for his own legacy.'

Of all the PMs I have filmed over the years, Boris Johnson is the most difficult to categorise. Partly because he is a swirling mass of contradictions. He describes himself as a Brexit-y Hezza, meaning he is a Leaver but, like Michael Heseltine, an economic interventionist. Hezza himself says: 'Boris Johnson is a man who waits to see which way the crowd is running, then dashes in front and says: "Follow me."' Johnson claims to be a One Nation Tory who wants to keep the whole kingdom together, but he is a very English Prime Minister who doesn't play well in Scotland, Wales and Northern Ireland. Despite being an Etonian, he manages to appeal to Labour's traditional voters in the north and the Midlands. And like Tony Blair, he presents himself as an anti-politician – while he is political to his fingertips.

Always mentioned on the charge sheet against Johnson is that he doesn't do detail and is indecisive and flippant – even when the situation is deadly serious. Dominic Cummings produced a vivid description of Johnson's way of chairing meetings: 'telling rambling stories and jokes, and as soon as things get a bit embarrassing he does the whole "let's take it offline" shtick before shouting "forward to victory", giving a thumbs-up and pegging it out of the room before anybody can disagree'. No. 10 said it did not recognise that characterisation.

Others claimed that the Prime Minister's approach to decision-making is actually more subtle. Robert Colvile, one of the authors of Johnson's winning 2019 general election manifesto, said:

'Part of the PM's style is to throw out wild ideas, seek alternative views and often to deliberately provoke and amuse.' And James Forsyth of *The Spectator*, whose wife Allegra Stratton was appointed Johnson's press secretary, said: 'There is no doubt that the PM cultivates uncertainty about which side of an argument he is going to come down on. Sometimes it's not the other side in a negotiation that's kept guessing but his own Cabinet. He can adopt all sides of any argument, trying them on for size, to work out what he actually thinks – it's part of his decision-making method.'

In his two years at No. 10, Johnson has become the most televised Prime Minister in history – by a distance. There has been an endless round of coronavirus press conferences in No. 10 – with a strict limit on reporters' questions – as well as broadcasts to camera, statements in the House, PMQs and Twitter videos. Also, most days he is filmed in a school, a factory, a lab or a hospital, wearing the appropriate garb. And he always offers a carefully prepared sound bite that is pooled for the TV cameras to share. With unprecedented spending on private opinion polling, it has been like a permanent general election campaign.

But, although the public has seen images galore of the Prime Minister's public face, glimpses of what he is really like are rare. A former senior mandarin who didn't want to be named told me: 'In order to understand Boris Johnson, you need to observe his face in repose, when he is off stage. The humour and bonhomie evaporate in an instant and all you see is the cold calculus of reason as he weighs which prank, witticism or jibe will best serve his interests. It is surely revealing that when he is off guard and lets slip, he easily resorts to words of the "bodies piling high" genre.'

When filming with Johnson over many years, I have always noticed how swiftly he shrinks from any self-analysis, which he dismisses as 'psychobabble'. The nearest he has been to it recently was when he told the journalist Tom McTague that one of his heroes is the inscrutable George Smiley in John le Carré's *Tinker, Tailor, Soldier, Spy*. Apparently a cynic, Smiley turned out to be a romantic at heart. So, which of the two is Johnson? The PM replied: 'All romantics need the mortar of cynicism to hold themselves up.' And then he said no more.

Dominic Cummings maintains that Johnson is a much deeper and more complex character than the media generally portrays. 'Behind each mask lies another mask,' says Cummings. 'But there's no masterplan behind all the masks, just the age-old "will to power". He is happy to hide behind the mask of a clown, mostly unbothered by ridicule, while calculations remain largely hidden, including from parts of his own mind.'

The Prime Minister has a clear-eyed sense of what his own political fate will be. As he once wrote: 'Politics is the constant recognition, in cycles of varying length, of one of the oldest myths in human culture: of how we make kings for our societies and how after a while we kill them to achieve a kind of rebirth.'

But as the boy who wanted to be World King enters his third year in No. 10, the evidence of his first biennium suggests we are in for another white-knuckle ride as the least predictable PM in our history struggles to succeed in the country's most undoable job.

ACKNOWLEDGEMENTS

This book has been a long time in coming, and I am most grateful to all of those who kept the faith and chivvied me to write it. Among them my literary agent, Andrew Gordon (those oysters did not die in vain), and the prolific professor the Lord Peter Hennessy, who was just a humble hack when I first met him forty years ago. Dr Mark Stuart, former head of politics at Nottingham University, read the first draft of the book and was encouraging and perceptive in his response. My former boss at the BBC political documentaries unit, Anne Tyerman, also gave me a characteristically shrewd and frank assessment of the manuscript.

I owe a great debt to the many wonderful editors and producers who have over the years enabled me to acquire the raw material that forms the bedrock of the book. Among them are the big cheese *Panorama* editors Peter Pagnamenta, Chris Capron, Roger Bolton, George Carey and Peter Ibbotson. And in the post-*Panorama* world, Paul Watson, Clive Edwards, Jane Root, Peter Bazalgette, Anne Reevell, Ian Katz and Esmé Wren.

Many thanks also to fellow toilers I have been lucky enough to work with in the media vineyard, producers, presenters and directors: Sally Doganis, Bill Cran, Clive Syddall, John Peny-cate, David Mills, James Hogan, Alex Gerlis, Fred Emery, David Dimbleby, Philip Campbell, Adam Grimley, Matthew Barrett, Diana Martin, Bill Treharne Jones, Alison Cahn, Charles Miller, James Giles, Simon Finch, Clara Glynn, Tony Lee, Mark Dowd, Simon Coates, Habie Schwarz, Richard Heller, Simon Lloyd, Alicia Queiro, Jenny Parks, Warwick Harrington, Tom Mangold and the late and much missed Richard Lindley.

I want to thank my very supportive publisher James Stephens at Biteback and my unflappable editor Olivia Beattie, the eagle-eyed copy-editor Lucy Stewardson and publicity director Suzanne Sangster.

Also my family, who have been generous with suggestions and help. My daughter Rachel, who is writing a book of her own, took time off to go through my manuscript and punctiliously correct my punctuation and polish my prose – as did her sister, Alice. And the book has greatly benefited from the skilful eye of my beloved wife, Anna Lloyd.

In the book I have drawn on a contribution I made to Iain Dale's *Memories of Margaret Thatcher* as well as on pieces I wrote for *The Guardian* about Denis Healey, Ted Heath and the Cameron–Johnson relationship.

Finally, I want to express my gratitude to the numerous Prime Ministers and other top politicians who (mostly uncomplainingly) have consented to let me film and interview them over the years. They are constantly in the line of fire and theirs is an often thankless task – but without them this book wouldn't have happened.

Any surviving errors in the book are mine alone.

INDEX